# PRIDE & prejudice

**PRIDE & PREJUDICE.** Contains material originally published in magazine form as PRIDE & PREJUDICE #1-5. First printing 2009. ISBN# 978-0-7851-3915-7. Published by MARVEL PUBLISHING, INC., a subsidiary of MARVEL ENTERTAINMENT, INC. OFFICE OF PUBLICATION: 417 5th Avenue, New York, NY 10016. Copyright © 2009 Marvel Characters, Inc. All rights reserved. $19.99 per copy in the U.S. (GST #R127032852); Canadian Agreement #40668537. All characters featured in this issue and the distinctive names and likenesses thereof, and all related indicia are trademarks of Marvel Characters, Inc. No similarity between any of the names, characters, persons, and/or institutions in this magazine with those of any living or dead person or institution is intended, and any such similarity which may exist is purely coincidental. **Printed in the U.S.A.** ALAN FINE, EVP - Office Of The Chief Executive Marvel Entertainment, Inc. & CMO Marvel Characters B.V.; DAN BUCKLEY, Chief Executive Officer and Publisher - Print, Animation & Digital Media; JIM SOKOLOWSKI, Chief Operating Officer; DAVID GABRIEL, SVP of Publishing Sales & Circulation; DAVID BOGART, SVP of Business Affairs & Talent Management; MICHAEL PASCIULLO, VP Merchandising & Communications; JIM O'KEEFE, VP of Operations & Logistics; DAN CARR, Executive Director of Publishing Technology; JUSTIN F. GABRIE, Director of Publishing & Editorial Operations; SUSAN CRESPI, Editorial Operations Manager; ALEX MORALES, Publishing Operations Manager; STAN LEE, Chairman Emeritus. For information regarding advertising in Marvel Comics or on Marvel.com, please contact Mitch Dane, Advertising Director, at mdane@marvel.com. For Marvel subscription inquiries, please call 800-217-9158. **Manufactured between 8/31/09 and 9/30/09 by R. R. DONNELLEY, SALEM, VA, USA.**

10 9 8 7 6 5 4 3 2 1

# PRIDE & prejudice

ADAPTED FROM THE NOVEL
BY JANE AUSTEN

Writer: NANCY BUTLER
Artist: HUGO PETRUS
Colorist: ALEJANDRO TORRES
Letterer: DAVE SHARPE

Cover Artists: SONNY LIEW & DENNIS CALERO
Associate Editor: NATE COSBY
Senior Editor: RALPH MACCHIO

Collection Editor: MARK D. BEAZLEY
Assistant Editors: JOHN DENNING & ALEX STARBUCK
Editor, Special Projects: JENNIFER GRÜNWALD
Senior Editor, Special Projects: JEFF YOUNGQUIST
Senior Vice President of Sales: DAVID GABRIEL
Production: JERRY KALINOWSKI
Book Design: SPRING HOTELING

Editor in Chief: JOE QUESADA
Publisher: DAN BUCKLEY
Executive Producer: ALAN FINE

# PRIDE & prejudice

## INTRODUCTION

I've been a fan of comic books since I was a kid sneaking off during family parties to read Superman with my cousin David—who always brought the latest issues with him. Once I was older, working as a graphic designer and writer, comics appealed to me because they were the only publications that still included art and prose. Sadly, by then, the heyday of illustrated magazines geared for adults was long past. So comic books were the last examples of a long, honored tradition.

As an adult I occasionally wandered into a comics store, usually to be greeted by many familiar faces—the stalwart DC heroes, the angsty Marvel heroes, and the noirish newbies from Dark Horse and other independents. It was all business as usual. But then suddenly things started heating up. I noticed a lot of kids were buying multiple copies of the X-Men comics. "One to read, and one to save," they all said, "because they'll be worth something in the future." The idea of kids saving comics as investments intrigued me. These youngsters were hip to something—that comics were not just pulp fiction, but an actual art form . . . something of value.

You can imagine my delight when I met Marvel editor Ralph Macchio through a mutual friend. We often discussed the X-Men phenomenon; it wasn't just the comics that were flying out of the stores, but also trading cards and action figures. The time was ripe for a bold move—and Marvel made it. They turned the X-Men craze into a hugely successful movie franchise. And thus X-Men begat Spider-Man and Hulk and Iron Man and their various sequels.

Ah, but what does all this have to do with a 19th century novel written by a parson's daughter? I'll tell you. Whenever Ralph and I chatted, I would always bring up something I'd noticed at the comics stores—girls stayed outside. There didn't seem to be anything to lure them inside and a lot of posters of impossibly buxom she-heroes to keep them outside. This was just wrong. Preteen and teenage girls have as much disposable income as their male peers, possibly more when you factor in babysitting money. Was Marvel missing out on a whole segment of the buying public?

So when Marvel started up their Marvel Illustrated line, adapting classic books to a graphic novel format, I asked Ralph when they were going to do something female friendly. I mean *Treasure Island* and *Man in the Iron Mask* are great books, but they are *boy* books. He asked me to suggest some titles that might appeal to girls and women. As the author of 12 Signet Regency romances (which were set in Jane Austen's time period), I immediately thought of *Pride and Prejudice*. I assured him that any book that had lasted two centuries, that was still studied in high school and college, and that had given rise to numerous movies and TV productions and countless websites had to have a huge fan base. He was convinced.

Here's the kicker . . . Marvel asked *me* to write the adaptation. Reader, I was overwhelmed. Gobsmacked. Thrilled. Scared to death. I had been living in the Regency romance universe for more than a decade (since the publication of my first Signet Regency), attending conferences, giving workshops, posting on Regency loops, reading Regency blogs, and the one thing I knew was "You Don't Mess with the Jane." I could already feel the bull's-eye forming on my back.

The first thing I did was go back to the canon; I reread *Pride and Prejudice* for the umpteenth time, but with new eyes. I needed to take this paragon of parlor talk, this ode to witty banter and insightful prose, and reduce it to captions and dialogue balloons. Without losing the flavor or texture. At first I tried modernizing the language and softening the social commentary, but in the end, it was Austen's own words and sharp-eyed observations that won the day. You don't update a classic; you give it free rein.

One thing that greatly aided my efforts was working with Spanish illustrator Hugo Petrus. He had already done the two Dumas books for Marvel Illustrated and had a nice feel for historical eras. With each issue, he would take my rough plot outlines and dash off loose gesture drawings before he sat down to do the pencil art. That way I could vet the artwork and make sure there was enough room in each panel for the oh-so-necessary Austen dialogue. It worked like a charm—in spite of that constant nagging need to add more hats to the art! Sorry, Hugo, someday we'll do a book together where everyone is bareheaded.

As each new issue appeared, I began to feel a sense of relief. The elements were coming together, slowly forming a cohesive whole. The Austen magic was happening. And when the fifth and final issue was released, I felt such pride (and not a lick of prejudice). Young readers would now get a chance to meet the Bennets, the Bingleys, and Mr. Darcy—and maybe be tempted to investigate the actual book. Adult readers who knew the book would get to revisit their favorite characters in a graphic format.

I've already received several emails from parents who read the five issues and passed them to their kids. One woman told me her son and daughter were arguing over who got to read issue five first. What a concept! It is what I'd hoped for all those years ago when Ralph and I first discussed Marvel bringing in more female readers—a story that appeals to readers of *both* sexes and of any age. Thank you, Miss Austen. My work here is done.


Nancy Butler


*Nancy Butler is the author of 12 Signet Regencies and three Signet Christmas novellas. She was twice awarded the RITA by the Romance Writers of America, won two Reviewer's Choice Awards from* Romantic Times Magazine, *and was retired to the Hall of Fame by the New Jersey Romance Writers after winning four Golden Leaf awards. Under her own name, Nancy Hajeski, she is also the author of young adult nonfiction, including the Hammond Book of Presidents, Hammond Undercover Princesses and Hammond Undercover Rocks and Minerals.*

It is a truth universally acknowledged, that a single man in possession of a good fortune must be in want of a wife.

However little known the feelings or views of such a man may be on his first entering a neighbourhood, this truth is so well fixed in the minds of the surrounding families, that he is considered as the rightful property of some one or other of their daughters.

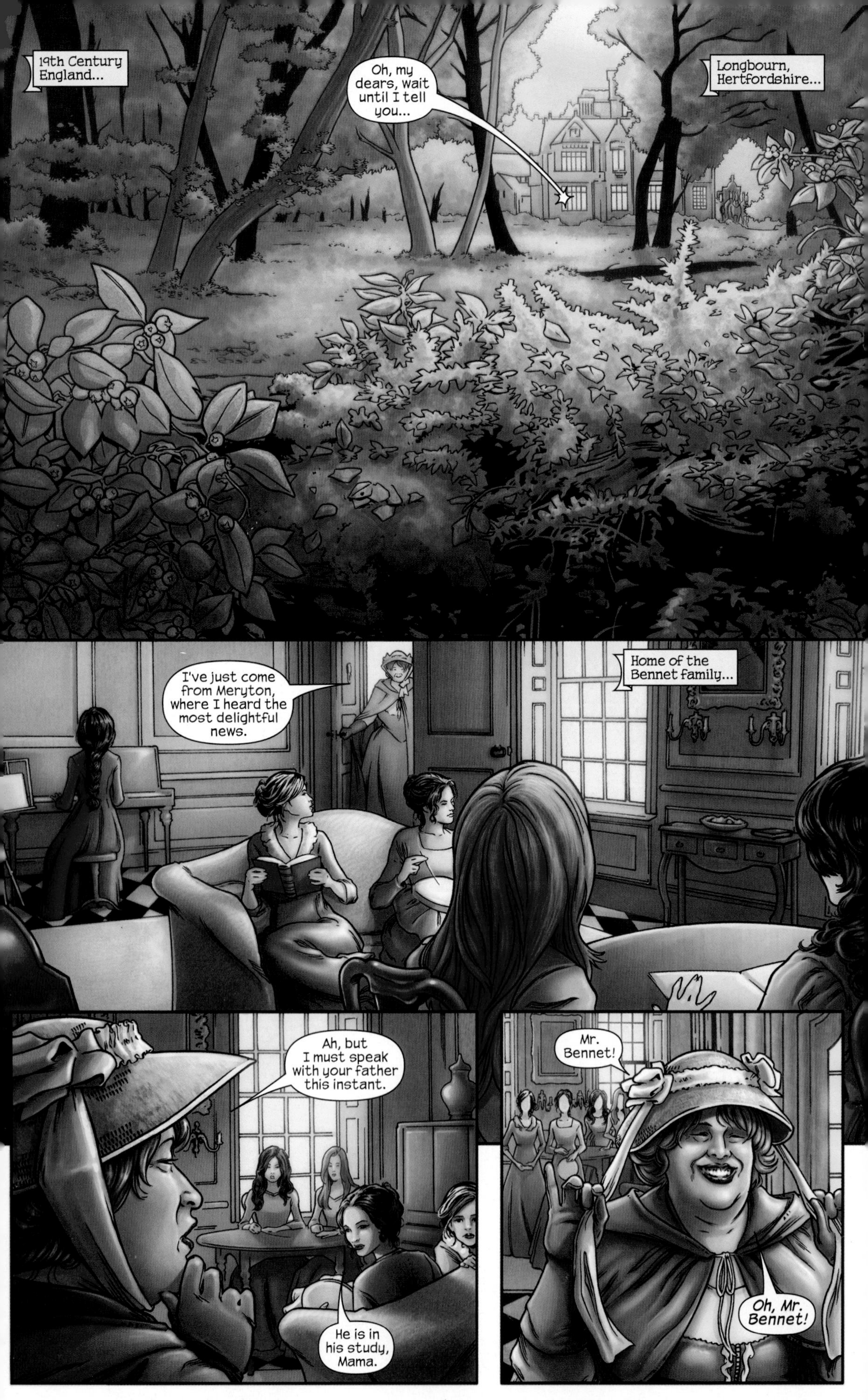
19th Century England...
Oh, my dears, wait until I tell you...
Longbourn, Hertfordshire...
I've just come from Meryton, where I heard the most delightful news.
Home of the Bennet family...
Ah, but I must speak with your father this instant.
He is in his study, Mama.
Mr. Bennet!
Oh, Mr. Bennet!

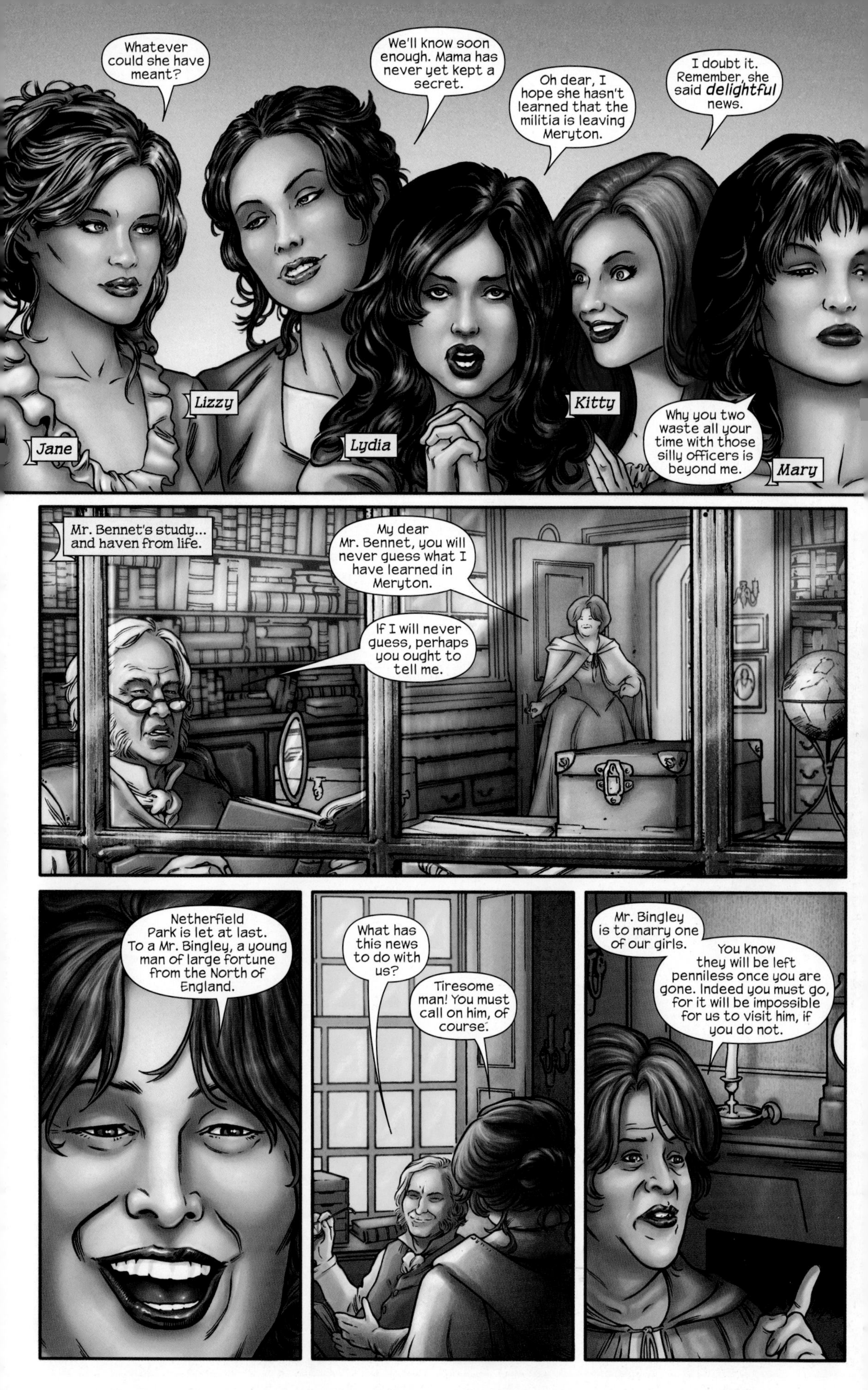
Whatever could she have meant?
We'll know soon enough. Mama has never yet kept a secret.
Oh dear, I hope she hasn't learned that the militia is leaving Meryton.
I doubt it. Remember, she said *delightful* news.
Jane
Lizzy
Lydia
Kitty
Why you two waste all your time with those silly officers is beyond me.
Mary
Mr. Bennet's study... and haven from life.
My dear Mr. Bennet, you will never guess what I have learned in Meryton.
If I will never guess, perhaps you ought to tell me.
Netherfield Park is let at last. To a Mr. Bingley, a young man of large fortune from the North of England.
What has this news to do with us?
Tiresome man! You must call on him, of course.
Mr. Bingley is to marry one of our girls.
You know they will be left penniless once you are gone. Indeed you must go, for it will be impossible for us to visit him, if you do not.

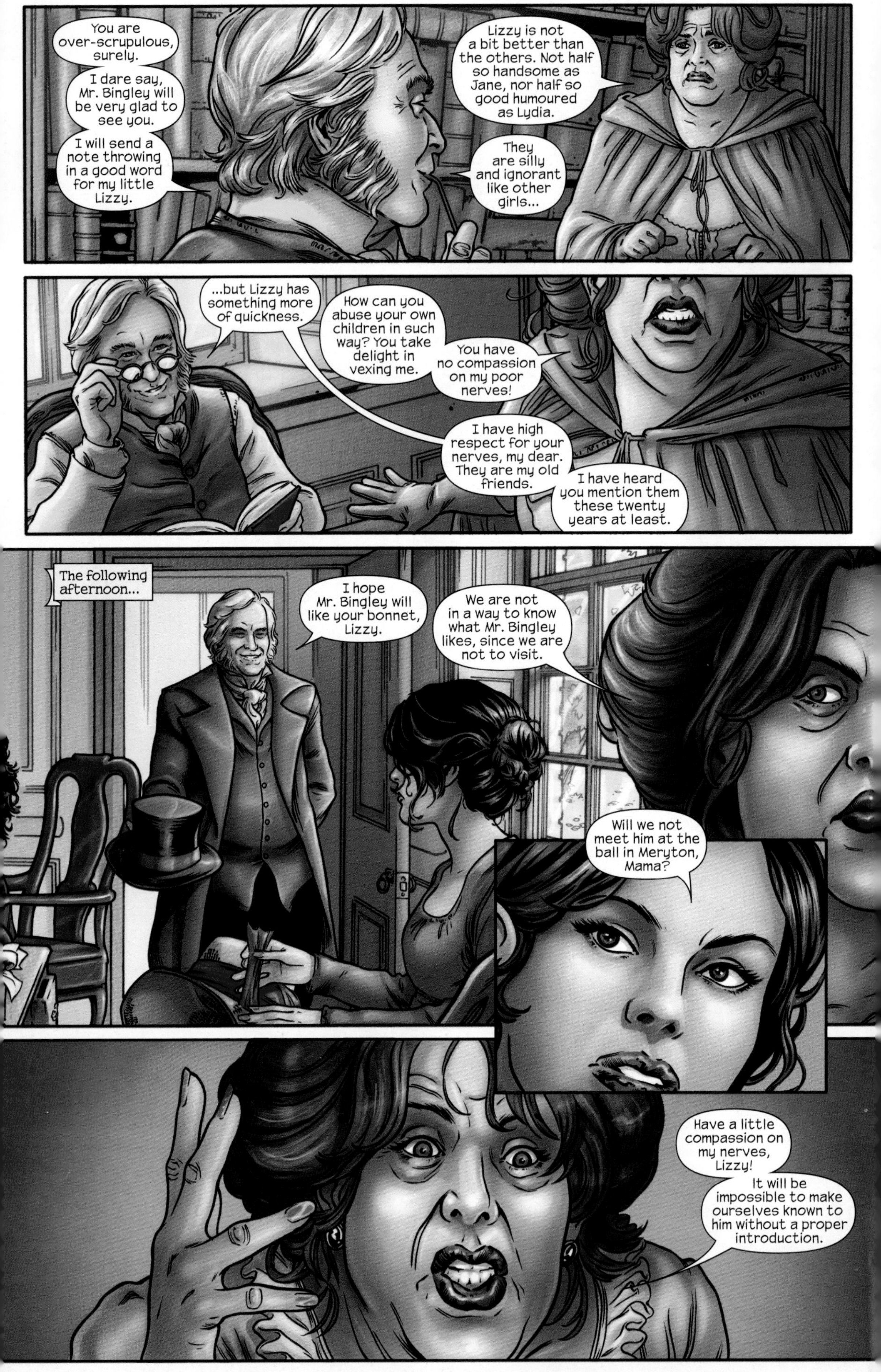
You are over-scrupulous, surely.
I dare say, Mr. Bingley will be very glad to see you.
I will send a note throwing in a good word for my little Lizzy.
Lizzy is not a bit better than the others. Not half so handsome as Jane, nor half so good humoured as Lydia.
They are silly and ignorant like other girls...
...but Lizzy has something more of quickness.
How can you abuse your own children in such way? You take delight in vexing me.
You have no compassion on my poor nerves!
I have high respect for your nerves, my dear. They are my old friends.
I have heard you mention them these twenty years at least.
The following afternoon...
I hope Mr. Bingley will like your bonnet, Lizzy.
We are not in a way to know what Mr. Bingley likes, since we are not to visit.
Will we not meet him at the ball in Meryton, Mama?
Have a little compassion on my nerves, Lizzy!
It will be impossible to make ourselves known to him without a proper introduction.

My dear, you may have the advantage of introducing your friends to Mr. Bingley.

I am sick of Mr. Bingley.

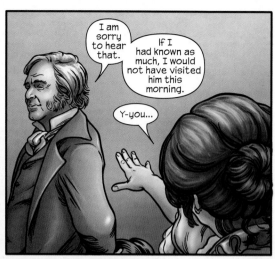

I am sorry to hear that.

If I had known as much, I would not have visited him this morning.

Y-you...

How good it was of you, my dear Mr. Bennet!

But I knew I would persuade you.

What an excellent father you have, girls!

The rest of the evening was spent determining when they should invite Mr. Bingley to their home.

A few days later...

It is Mr. Bingley!

Let me see!

What is he wearing?

He doesn't appear very tall.

I think he might have a pleasant face.

I hope he reads, or he and Papa will have nothing to discuss.

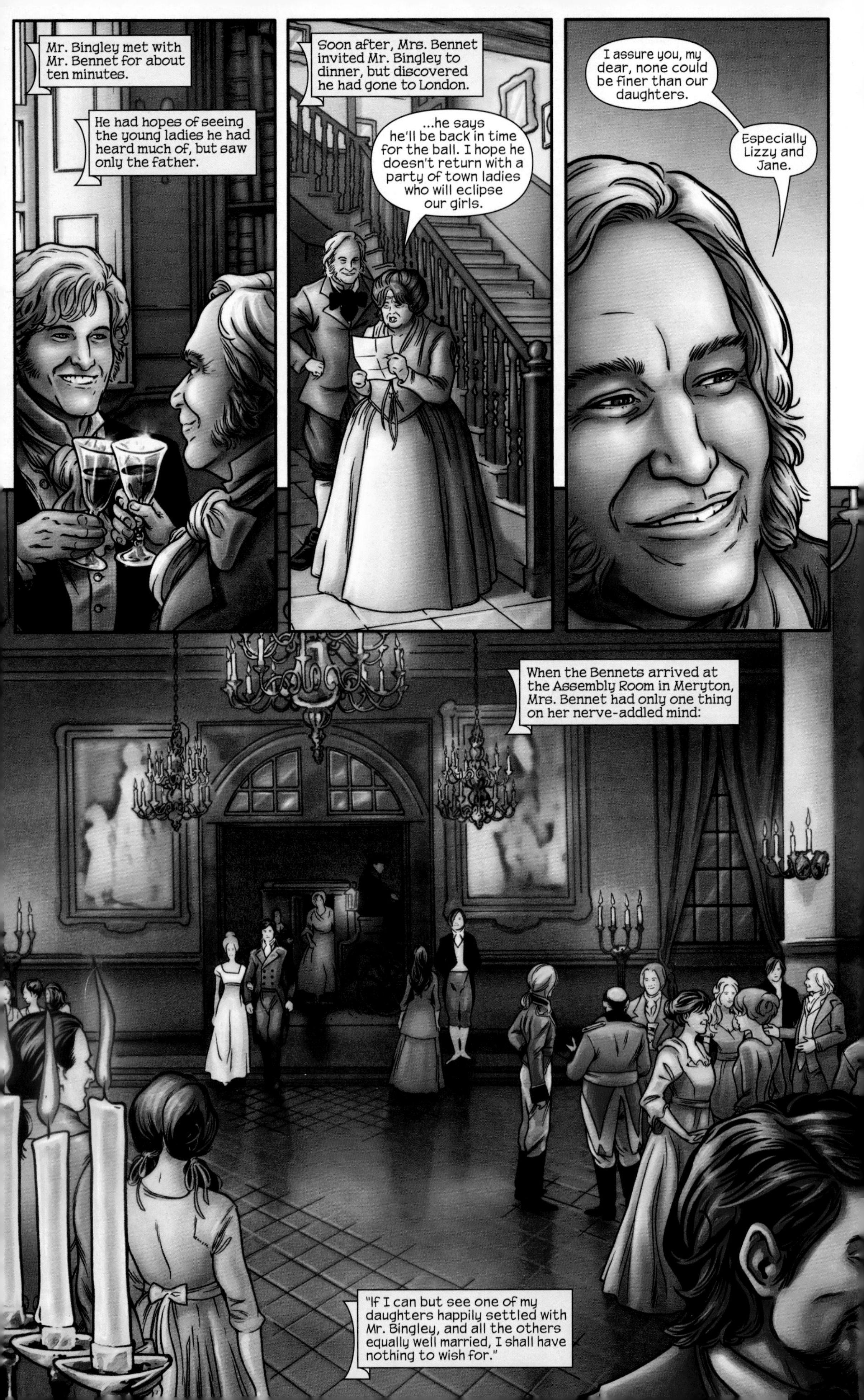
Mr. Bingley met with Mr. Bennet for about ten minutes.
He had hopes of seeing the young ladies he had heard much of, but saw only the father.
Soon after, Mrs. Bennet invited Mr. Bingley to dinner, but discovered he had gone to London.
...he says he'll be back in time for the ball. I hope he doesn't return with a party of town ladies who will eclipse our girls.
I assure you, my dear, none could be finer than our daughters.
Especially Lizzy and Jane.
When the Bennets arrived at the Assembly Room in Meryton, Mrs. Bennet had only one thing on her nerve-addled mind:
"If I can but see one of my daughters happily settled with Mr. Bingley, and all the others equally well married, I shall have nothing to wish for."

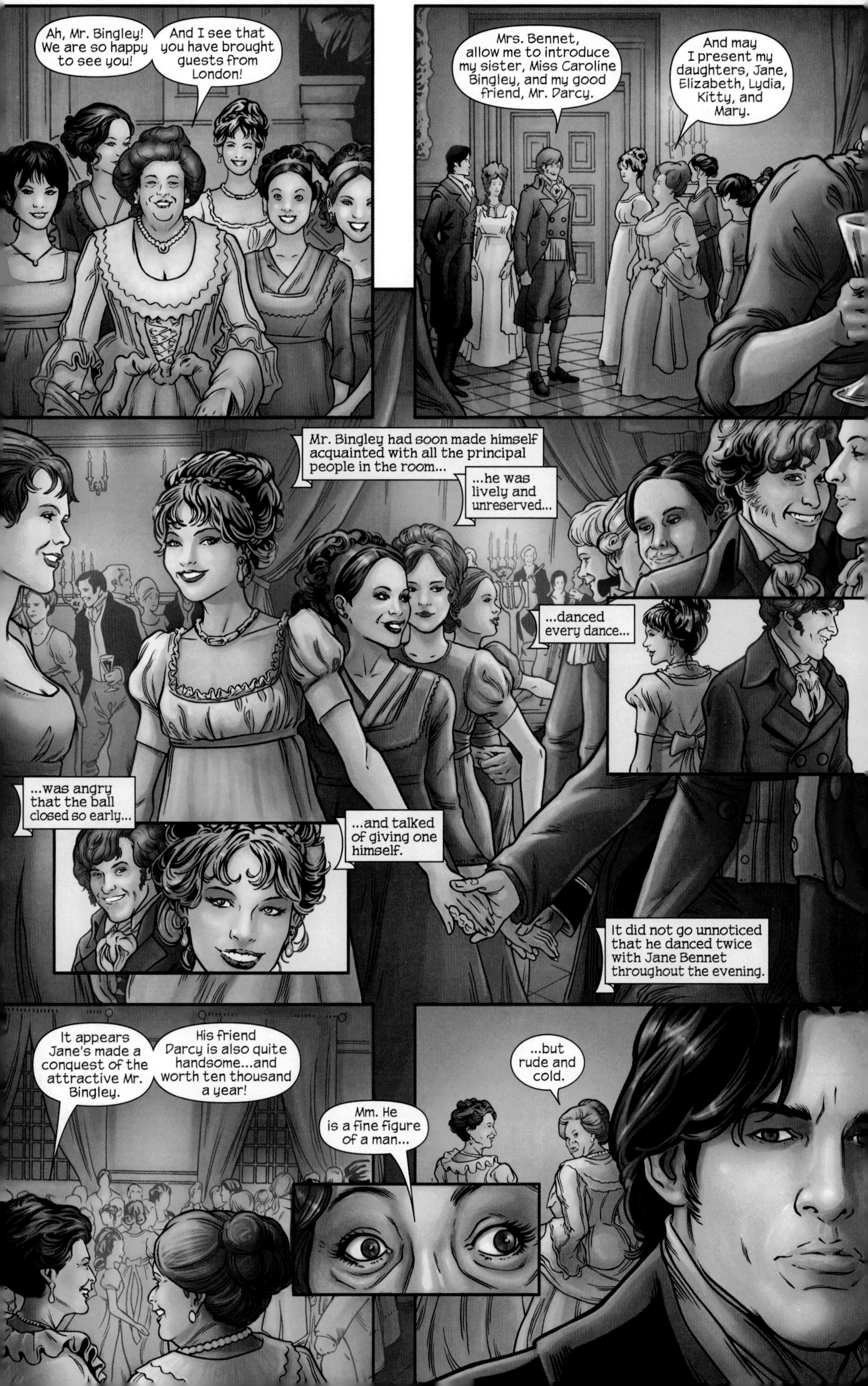
Ah, Mr. Bingley! We are so happy to see you!
And I see that you have brought guests from London!
Mrs. Bennet, allow me to introduce my sister, Miss Caroline Bingley, and my good friend, Mr. Darcy.
And may I present my daughters, Jane, Elizabeth, Lydia, Kitty, and Mary.
Mr. Bingley had soon made himself acquainted with all the principal people in the room...
...he was lively and unreserved...
...danced every dance...
...was angry that the ball closed so early...
...and talked of giving one himself.
It did not go unnoticed that he danced twice with Jane Bennet throughout the evening.
It appears Jane's made a conquest of the attractive Mr. Bingley.
His friend Darcy is also quite handsome...and worth ten thousand a year!
Mm. He is a fine figure of a man...
...but rude and cold.

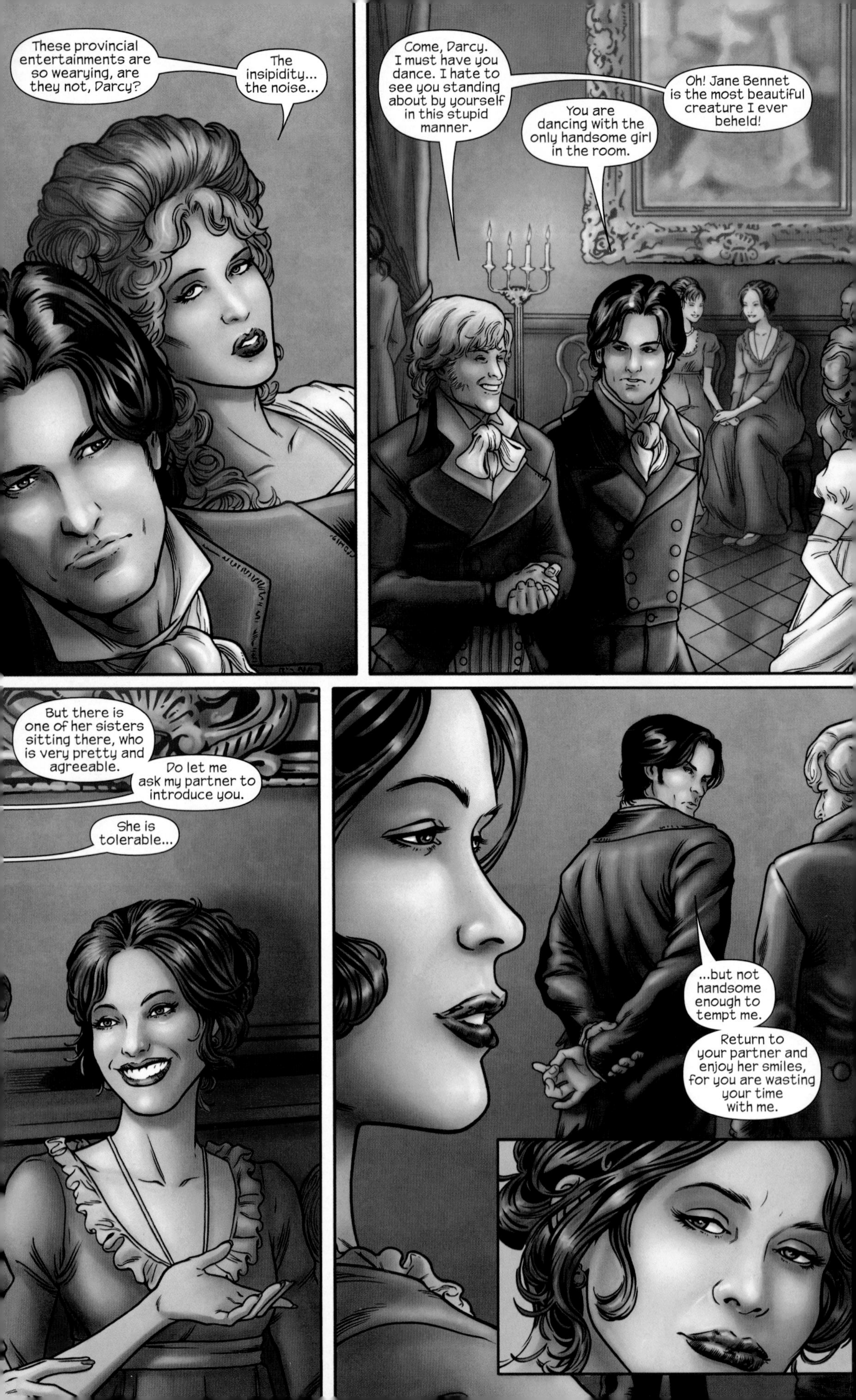
These provincial entertainments are so wearying, are they not, Darcy?
The insipidity... the noise...
Come, Darcy. I must have you dance. I hate to see you standing about by yourself in this stupid manner.
You are dancing with the only handsome girl in the room.
Oh! Jane Bennet is the most beautiful creature I ever beheld!
But there is one of her sisters sitting there, who is very pretty and agreeable.
Do let me ask my partner to introduce you.
She is tolerable...
...but not handsome enough to tempt me.
Return to your partner and enjoy her smiles, for you are wasting your time with me.

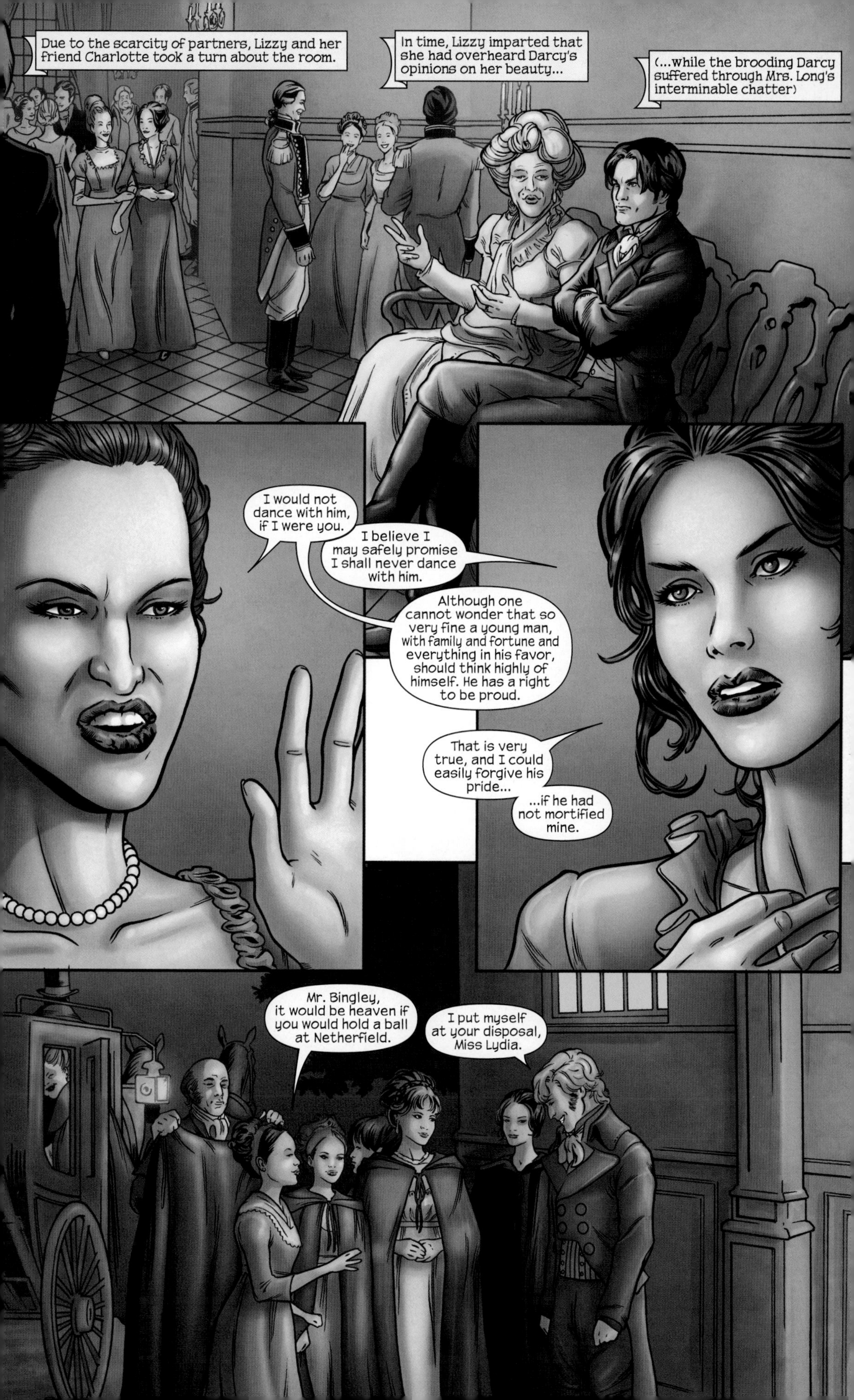
Due to the scarcity of partners, Lizzy and her friend Charlotte took a turn about the room.
In time, Lizzy imparted that she had overheard Darcy's opinions on her beauty...
(...while the brooding Darcy suffered through Mrs. Long's interminable chatter)
I would not dance with him, if I were you.
I believe I may safely promise I shall never dance with him.
Although one cannot wonder that so very fine a young man, with family and fortune and everything in his favor, should think highly of himself. He has a right to be proud.
That is very true, and I could easily forgive his pride...
...if he had not mortified mine.
Mr. Bingley, it would be heaven if you would hold a ball at Netherfield.
I put myself at your disposal, Miss Lydia.

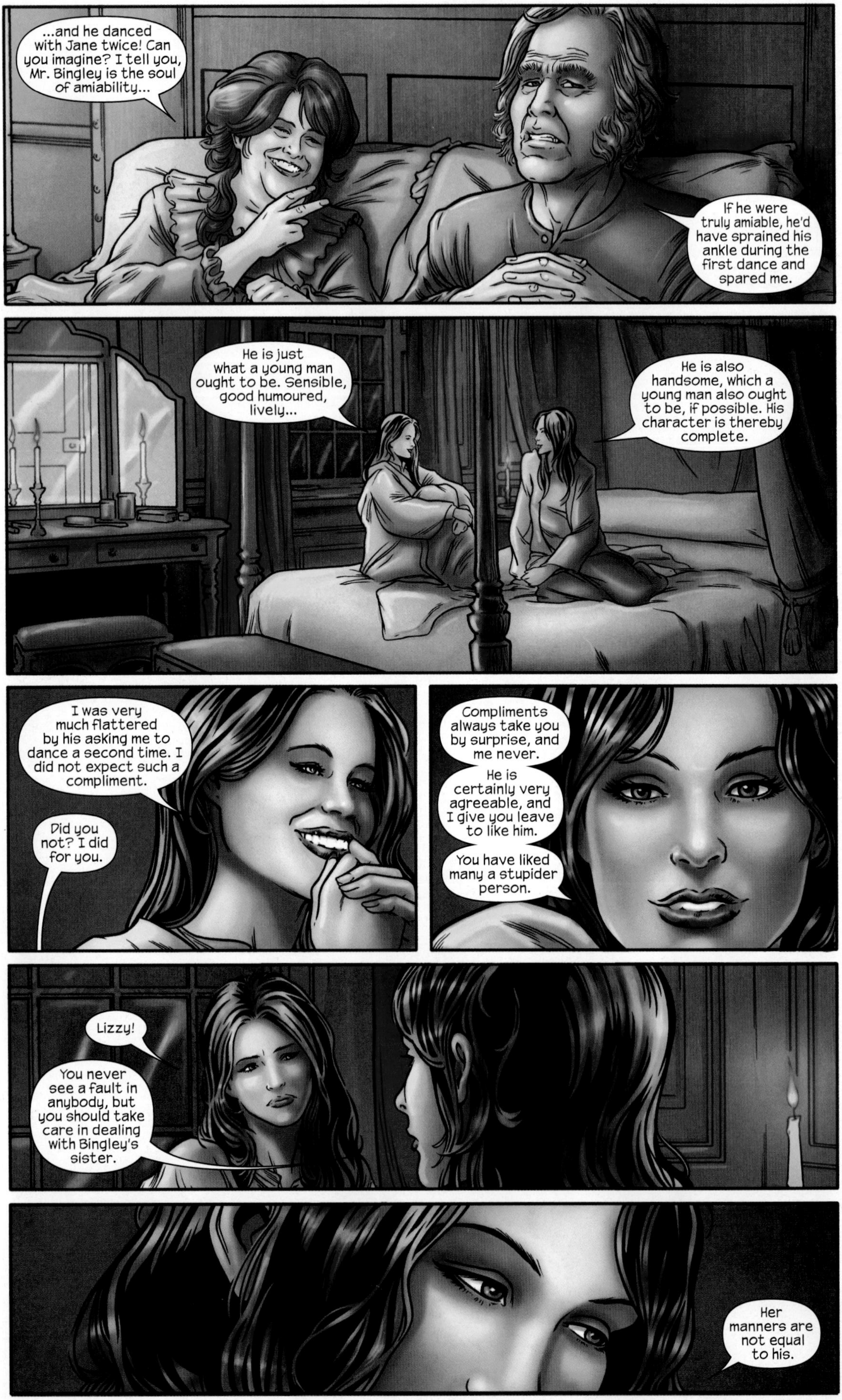
...and he danced with Jane twice! Can you imagine? I tell you, Mr. Bingley is the soul of amiability...
If he were truly amiable, he'd have sprained his ankle during the first dance and spared me.
He is just what a young man ought to be. Sensible, good humoured, lively...
He is also handsome, which a young man also ought to be, if possible. His character is thereby complete.
I was very much flattered by his asking me to dance a second time. I did not expect such a compliment.
Did you not? I did for you.
Compliments always take you by surprise, and me never.
He is certainly very agreeable, and I give you leave to like him.
You have liked many a stupider person.
Lizzy!
You never see a fault in anybody, but you should take care in dealing with Bingley's sister.
Her manners are not equal to his.

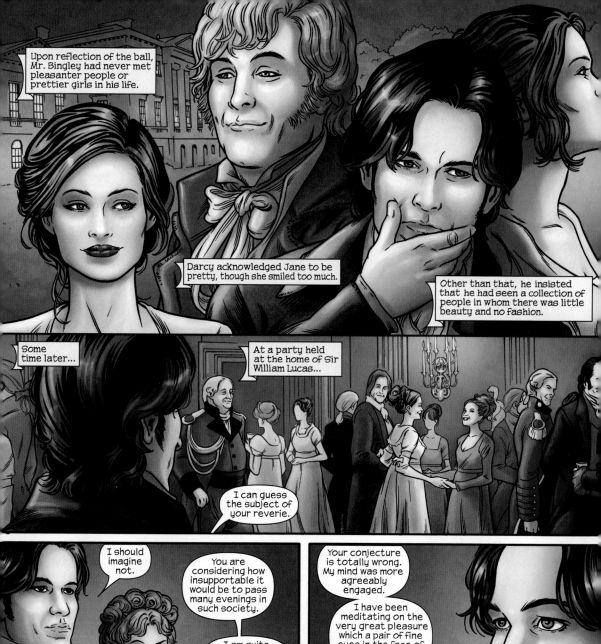

Upon reflection of the ball, Mr. Bingley had never met pleasanter people or prettier girls in his life.

Darcy acknowledged Jane to be pretty, though she smiled too much.

Other than that, he insisted that he had seen a collection of people in whom there was little beauty and no fashion.

Some time later...

At a party held at the home of Sir William Lucas...

I can guess the subject of your reverie.

I should imagine not.

You are considering how insupportable it would be to pass many evenings in such society.

I am quite of your opinion. I was never more annoyed!

Your conjecture is totally wrong. My mind was more agreeably engaged.

I have been meditating on the very great pleasure which a pair of fine eyes in the face of a pretty woman can bestow...

Miss Elizabeth Bennet.

I am all astonishment. When am I to wish you joy?

That is exactly the question I expected you to ask.

A lady's imagination jumps from admiration to love, from love to matrimony.

I wish you all the joy in the world.

You will have a charming mother-in-law, indeed, and of course she will be always at Pemberley with you.

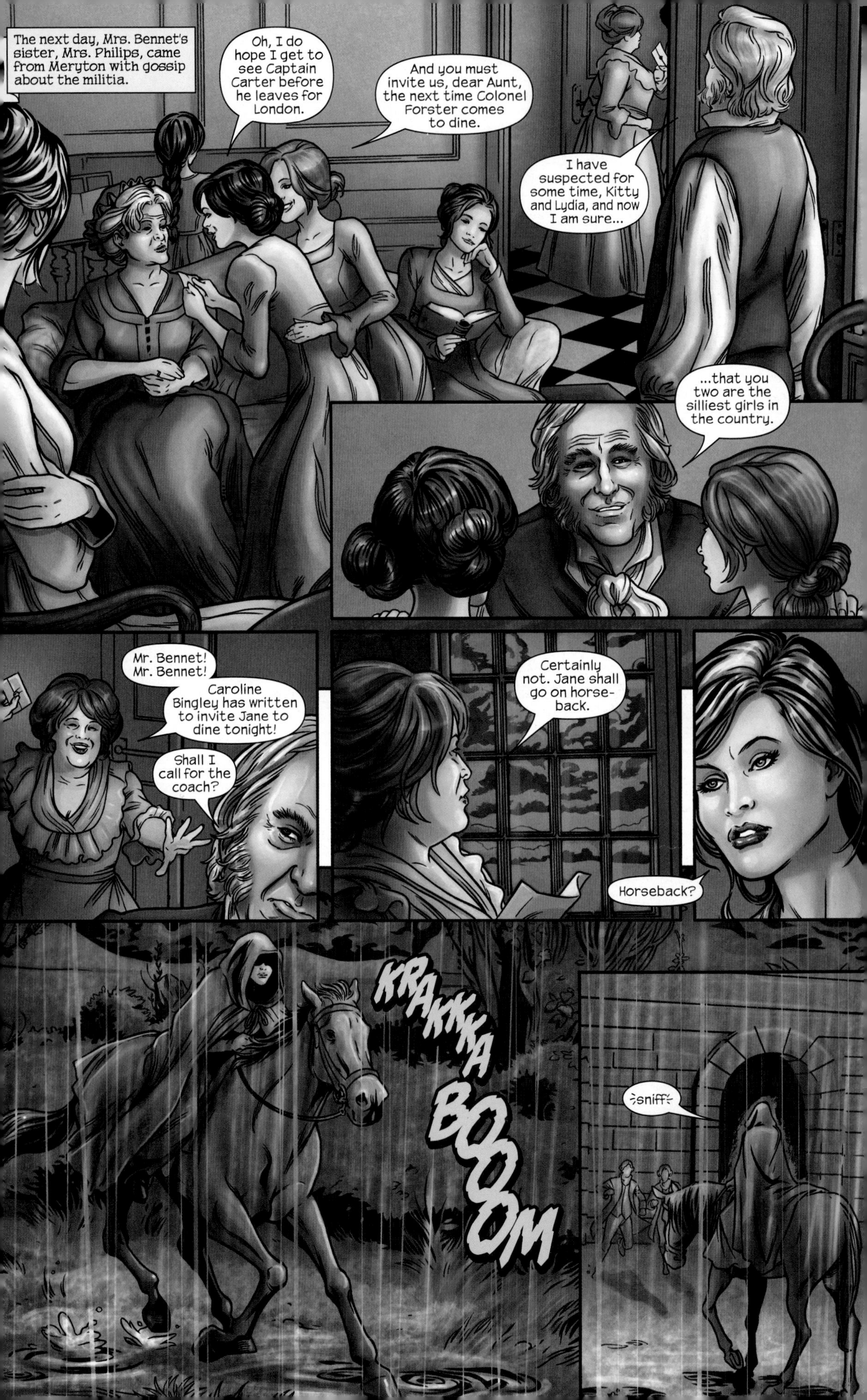
The next day, Mrs. Bennet's sister, Mrs. Philips, came from Meryton with gossip about the militia.
Oh, I do hope I get to see Captain Carter before he leaves for London.
And you must invite us, dear Aunt, the next time Colonel Forster comes to dine.
I have suspected for some time, Kitty and Lydia, and now I am sure...
...that you two are the silliest girls in the country.
Mr. Bennet! Mr. Bennet!
Caroline Bingley has written to invite Jane to dine tonight!
Shall I call for the coach?
Certainly not. Jane shall go on horse-back.
Horseback?
KRAKKKA BOOOM
sniff

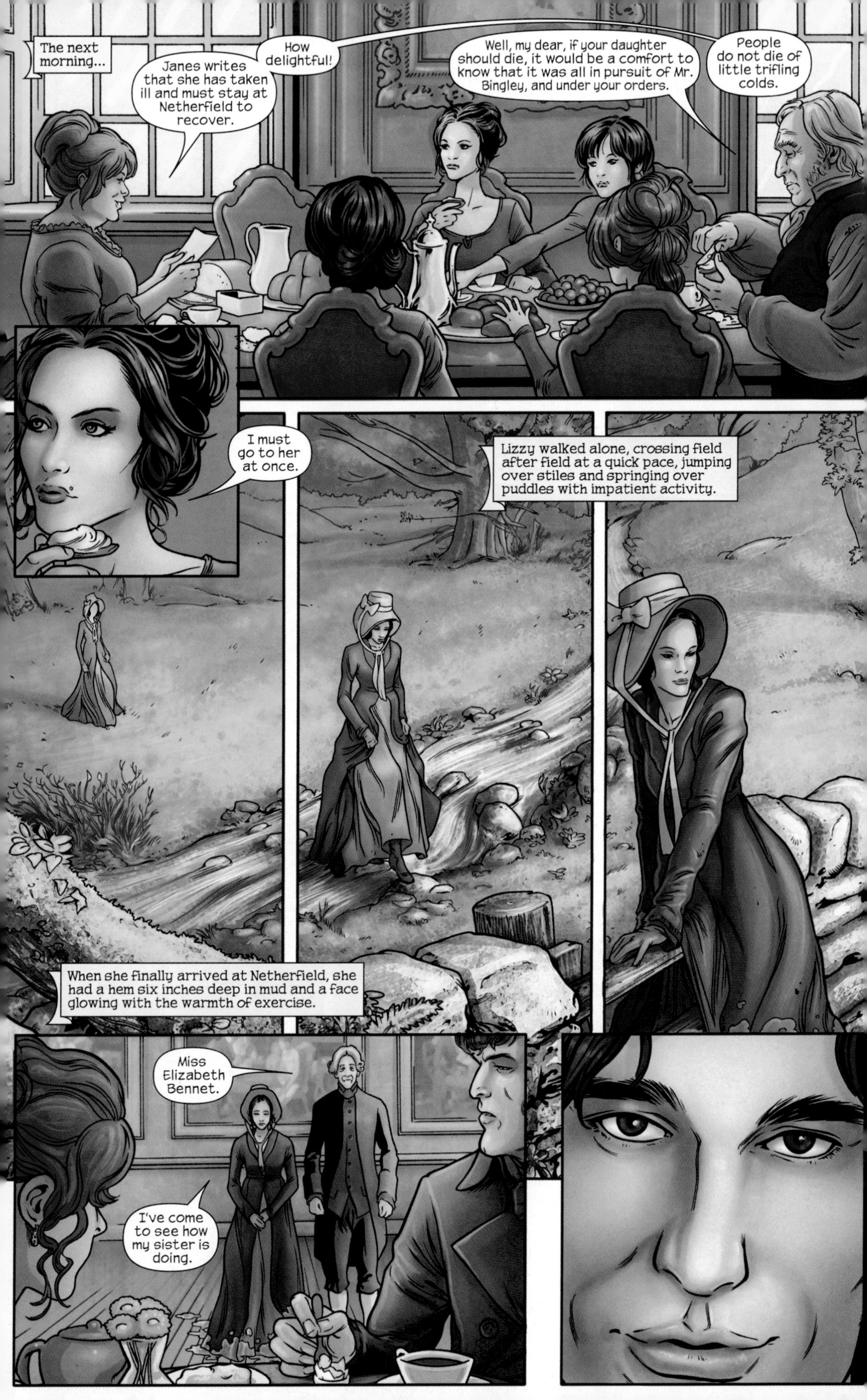
The next morning...
Janes writes that she has taken ill and must stay at Netherfield to recover.
How delightful!
Well, my dear, if your daughter should die, it would be a comfort to know that it was all in pursuit of Mr. Bingley, and under your orders.
People do not die of little trifling colds.
I must go to her at once.
Lizzy walked alone, crossing field after field at a quick pace, jumping over stiles and springing over puddles with impatient activity.
When she finally arrived at Netherfield, she had a hem six inches deep in mud and a face glowing with the warmth of exercise.
Miss Elizabeth Bennet.
I've come to see how my sister is doing.

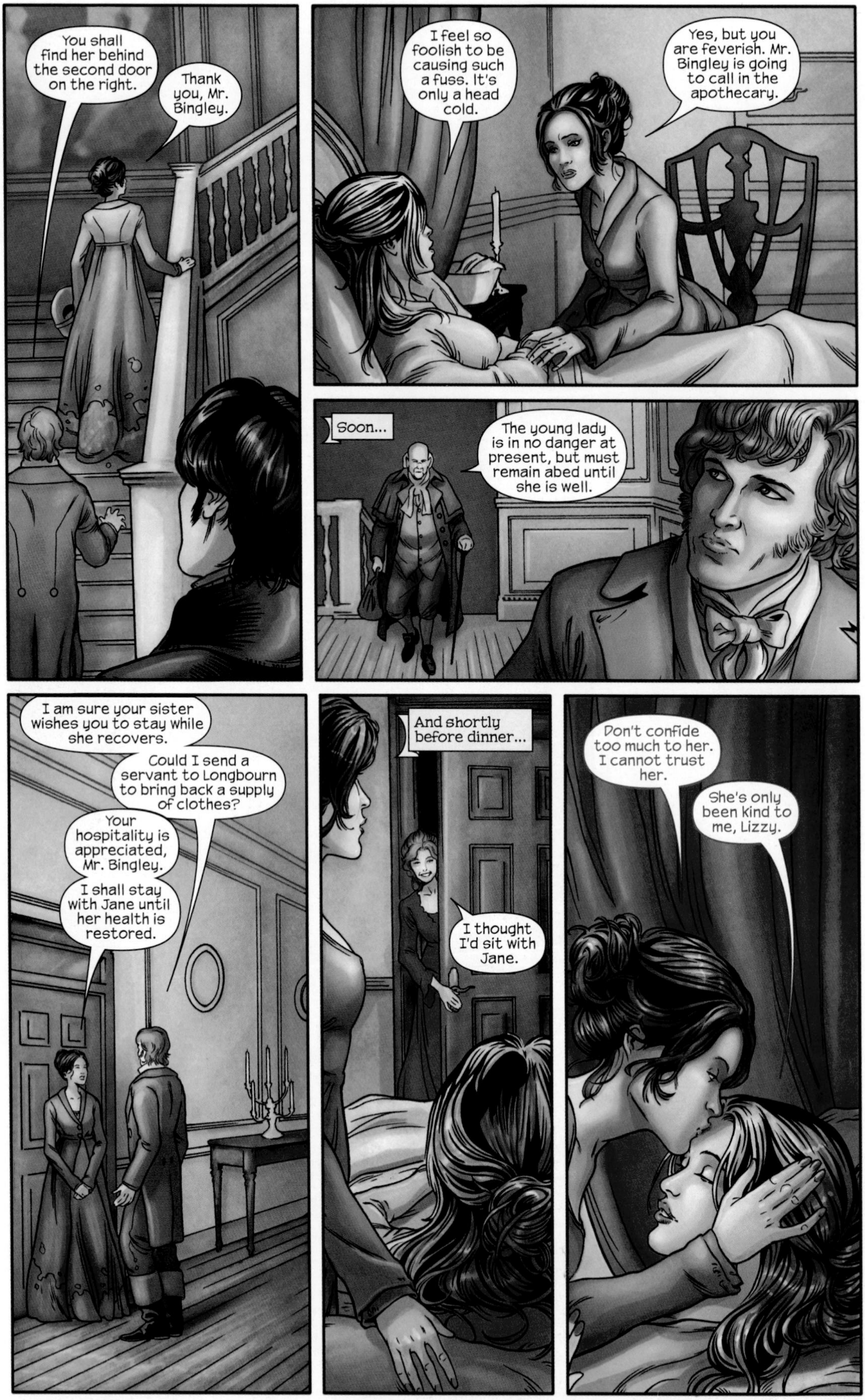
You shall find her behind the second door on the right.
Thank you, Mr. Bingley.
I feel so foolish to be causing such a fuss. It's only a head cold.
Yes, but you are feverish. Mr. Bingley is going to call in the apothecary.
Soon...
The young lady is in no danger at present, but must remain abed until she is well.
I am sure your sister wishes you to stay while she recovers.
Could I send a servant to Longbourn to bring back a supply of clothes?
Your hospitality is appreciated, Mr. Bingley.
I shall stay with Jane until her health is restored.
And shortly before dinner...
I thought I'd sit with Jane.
Don't confide too much to her. I cannot trust her.
She's only been kind to me, Lizzy.

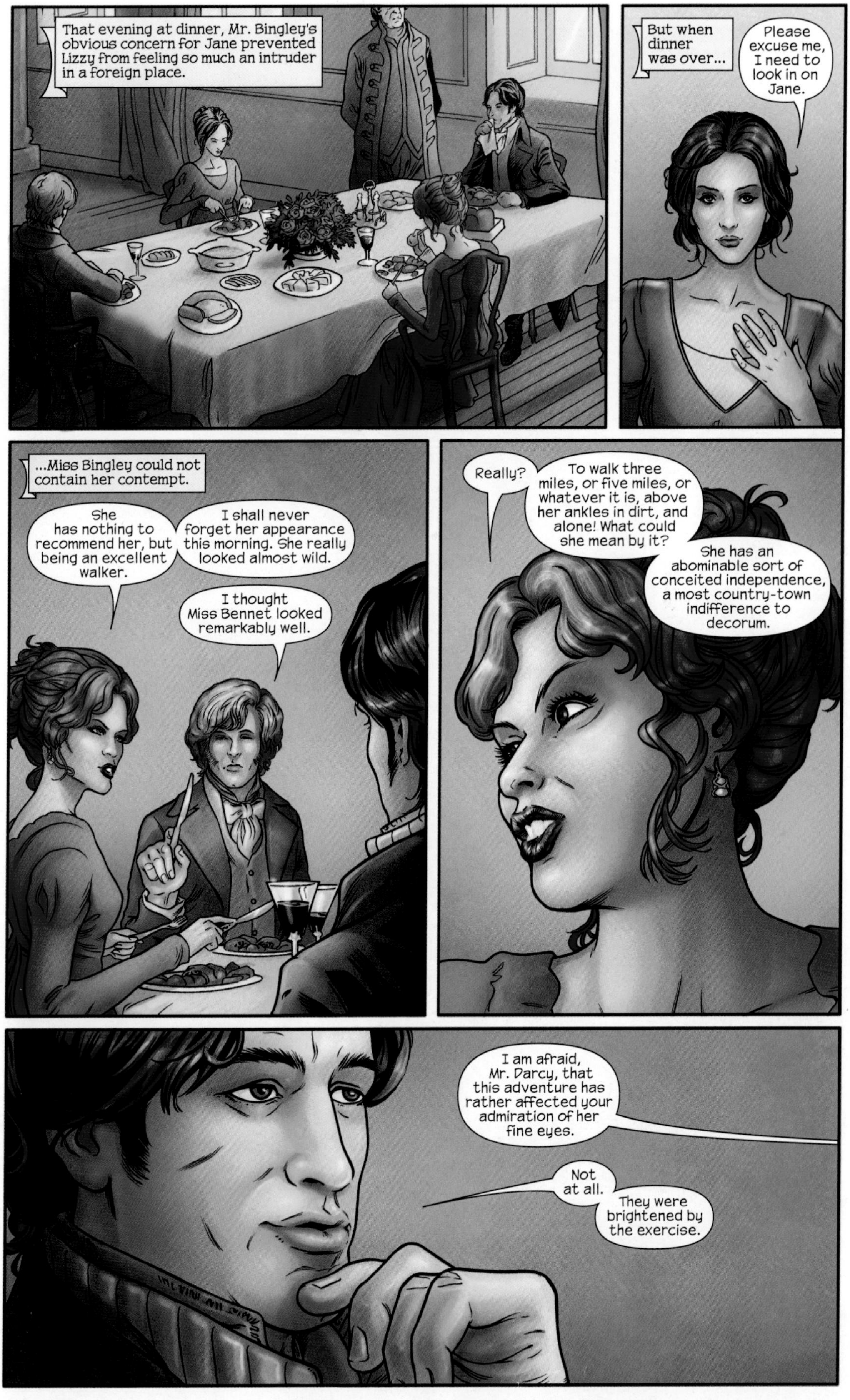
That evening at dinner, Mr. Bingley's obvious concern for Jane prevented Lizzy from feeling so much an intruder in a foreign place.
But when dinner was over...
Please excuse me, I need to look in on Jane.
...Miss Bingley could not contain her contempt.
She has nothing to recommend her, but being an excellent walker.
I shall never forget her appearance this morning. She really looked almost wild.
I thought Miss Bennet looked remarkably well.
Really?
To walk three miles, or five miles, or whatever it is, above her ankles in dirt, and alone! What could she mean by it?
She has an abominable sort of conceited independence, a most country-town indifference to decorum.
I am afraid, Mr. Darcy, that this adventure has rather affected your admiration of her fine eyes.
Not at all.
They were brightened by the exercise.

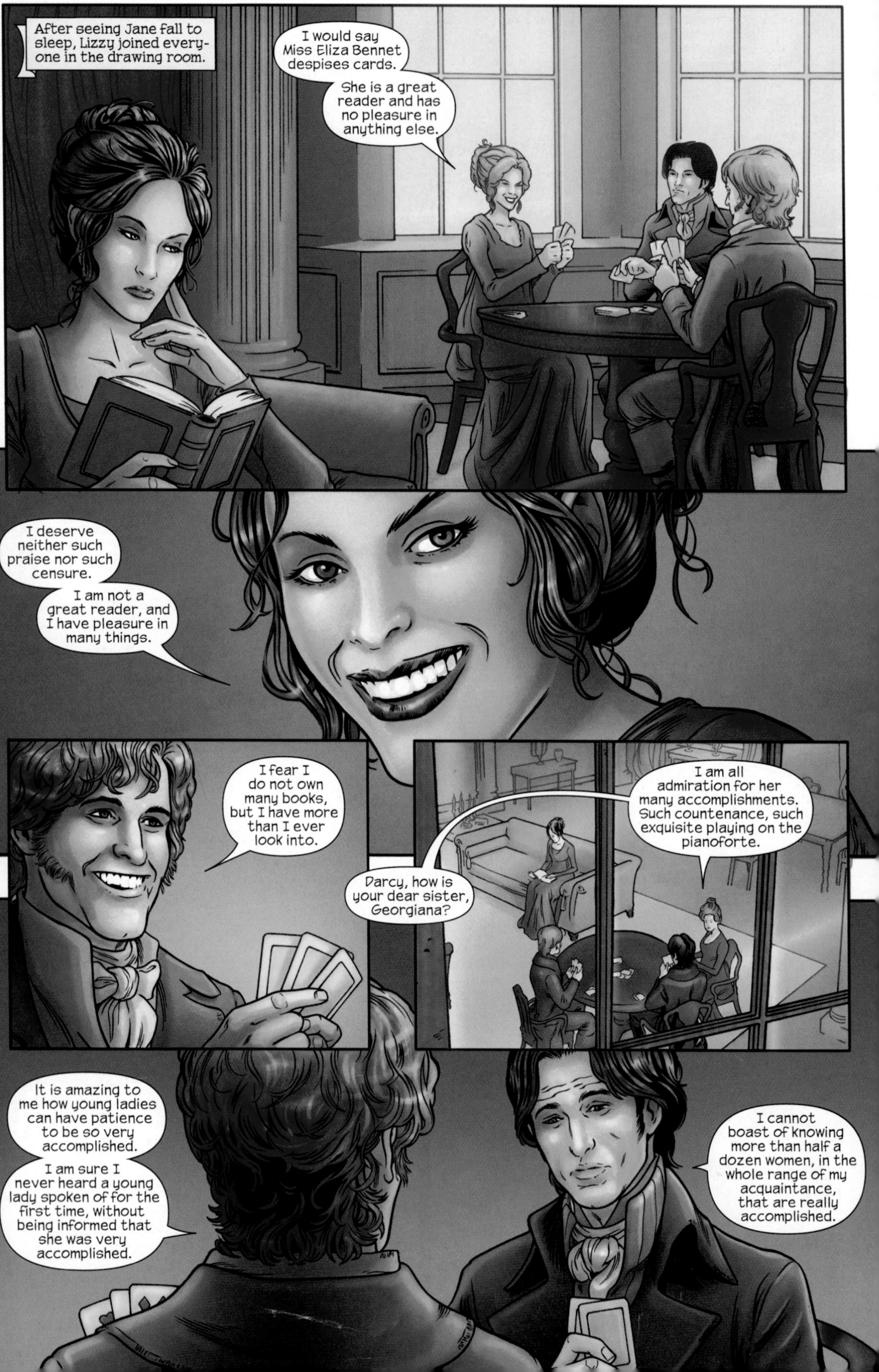
After seeing Jane fall to sleep, Lizzy joined everyone in the drawing room.
I would say Miss Eliza Bennet despises cards.
She is a great reader and has no pleasure in anything else.
I deserve neither such praise nor such censure.
I am not a great reader, and I have pleasure in many things.
I fear I do not own many books, but I have more than I ever look into.
Darcy, how is your dear sister, Georgiana?
I am all admiration for her many accomplishments. Such countenance, such exquisite playing on the pianoforte.
It is amazing to me how young ladies can have patience to be so very accomplished.
I am sure I never heard a young lady spoken of for the first time, without being informed that she was very accomplished.
I cannot boast of knowing more than half a dozen women, in the whole range of my acquaintance, that are really accomplished.

Then you must comprehend a great deal in your idea of an accomplished woman.

I do comprehend a great deal in it.

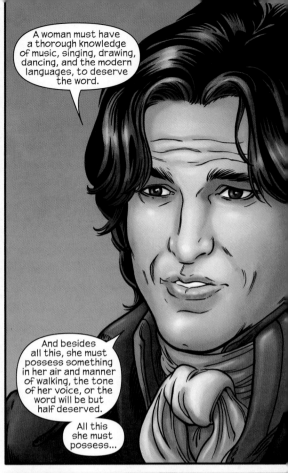

A woman must have a thorough knowledge of music, singing, drawing, dancing, and the modern languages, to deserve the word.

And besides all this, she must possess something in her air and manner of walking, the tone of her voice, or the word will be but half deserved.

All this she must possess...

...and to all this she must yet add something more substantial, in the improvement of her mind by extensive reading.

Oh, certainly, no one can be really esteemed accomplished, who does not greatly surpass what is usually met with.

I am no longer surprised at your knowing only six accomplished women. I rather wonder now at your knowing any.

Are you so severe upon your own sex, as to doubt the possibility of all this?

I never saw such a woman, I never saw such capacity, and taste, and application, and elegance, as you describe, united.

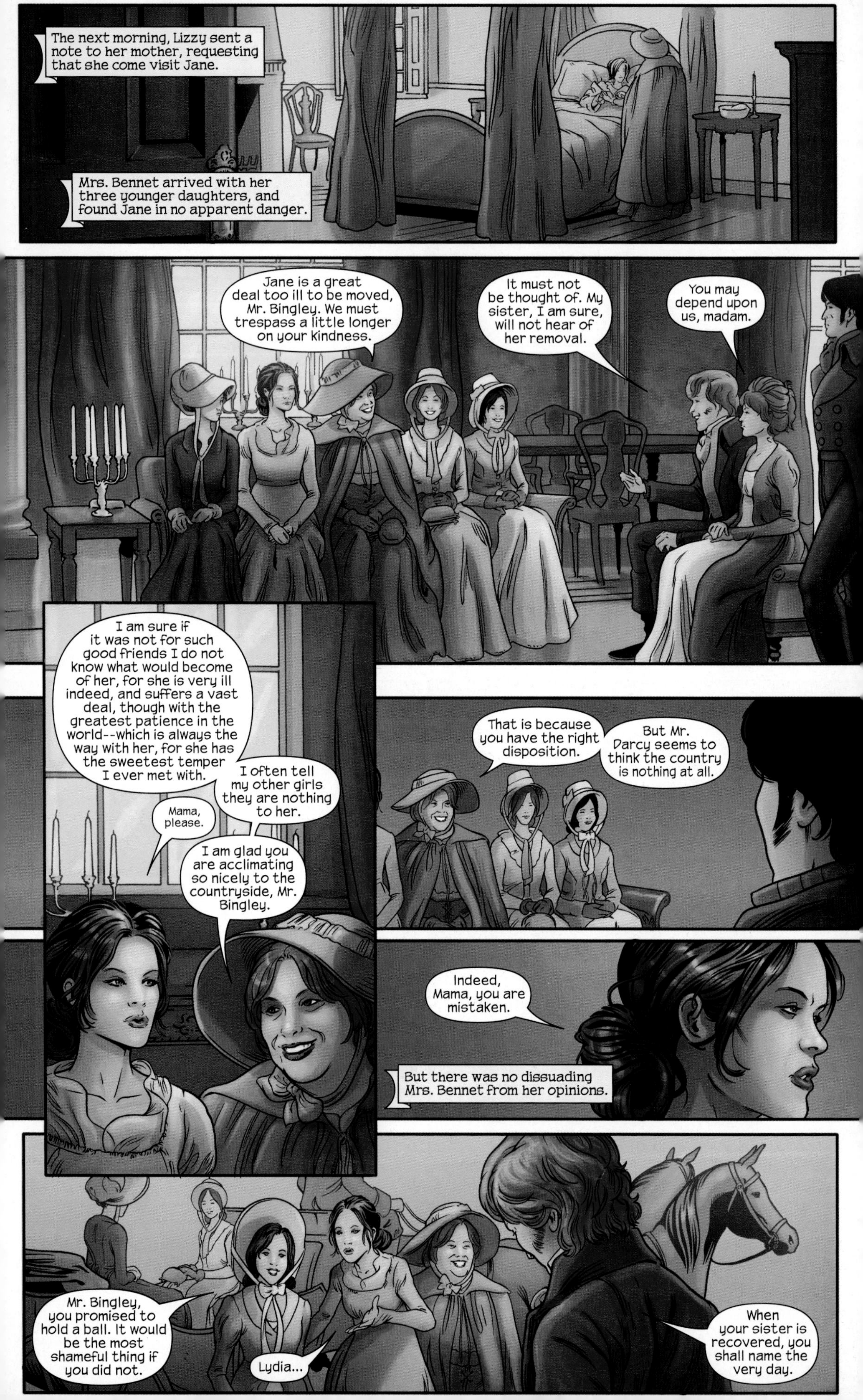

The next morning, Lizzy sent a note to her mother, requesting that she come visit Jane.
Mrs. Bennet arrived with her three younger daughters, and found Jane in no apparent danger.
Jane is a great deal too ill to be moved, Mr. Bingley. We must trespass a little longer on your kindness.
It must not be thought of. My sister, I am sure, will not hear of her removal.
You may depend upon us, madam.
I am sure if it was not for such good friends I do not know what would become of her, for she is very ill indeed, and suffers a vast deal, though with the greatest patience in the world--which is always the way with her, for she has the sweetest temper I ever met with.
I often tell my other girls they are nothing to her.
Mama, please.
I am glad you are acclimating so nicely to the countryside, Mr. Bingley.
That is because you have the right disposition.
But Mr. Darcy seems to think the country is nothing at all.
Indeed, Mama, you are mistaken.
But there was no dissuading Mrs. Bennet from her opinions.
Mr. Bingley, you promised to hold a ball. It would be the most shameful thing if you did not.
Lydia...
When your sister is recovered, you shall name the very day.

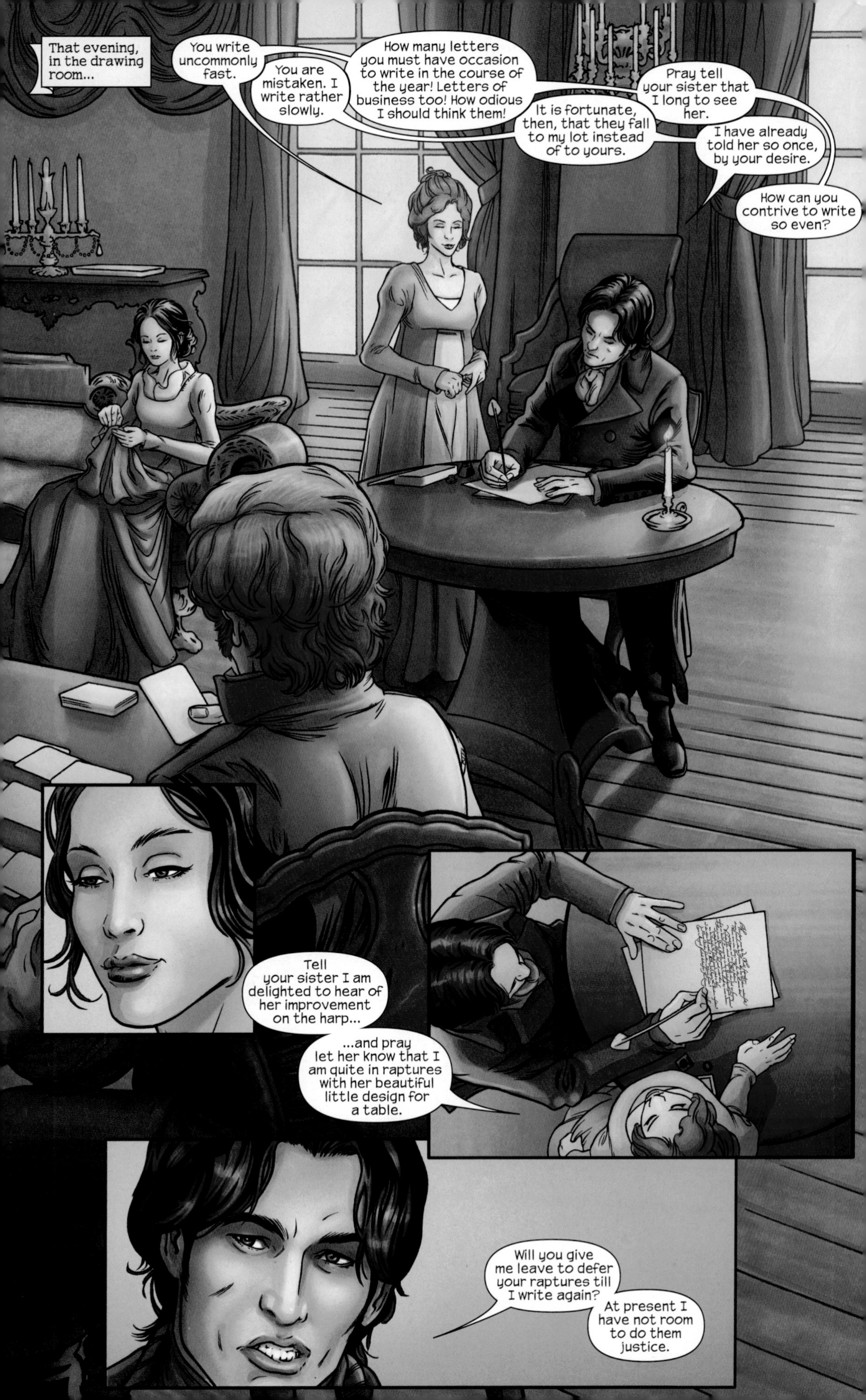
That evening, in the drawing room...
You write uncommonly fast.
You are mistaken. I write rather slowly.
How many letters you must have occasion to write in the course of the year! Letters of business too! How odious I should think them!
It is fortunate, then, that they fall to my lot instead of to yours.
Pray tell your sister that I long to see her.
I have already told her so once, by your desire.
How can you contrive to write so even?
Tell your sister I am delighted to hear of her improvement on the harp...
...and pray let her know that I am quite in raptures with her beautiful little design for a table.
Will you give me leave to defer your raptures till I write again?
At present I have not room to do them justice.

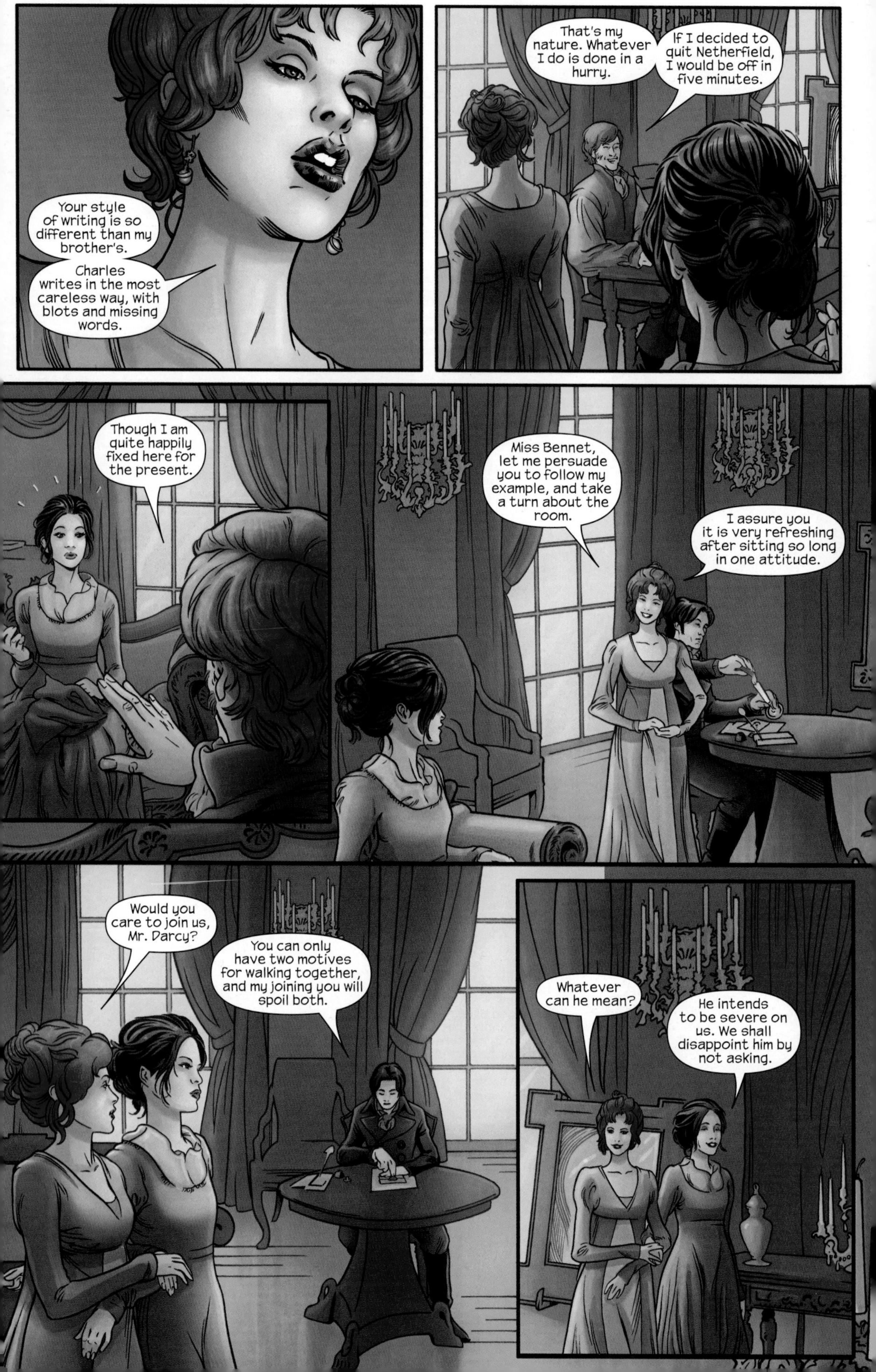
Your style of writing is so different than my brother's.
Charles writes in the most careless way, with blots and missing words.
That's my nature. Whatever I do is done in a hurry.
If I decided to quit Netherfield, I would be off in five minutes.
Though I am quite happily fixed here for the present.
Miss Bennet, let me persuade you to follow my example, and take a turn about the room.
I assure you it is very refreshing after sitting so long in one attitude.
Would you care to join us, Mr. Darcy?
You can only have two motives for walking together, and my joining you will spoil both.
Whatever can he mean?
He intends to be severe on us. We shall disappoint him by not asking.

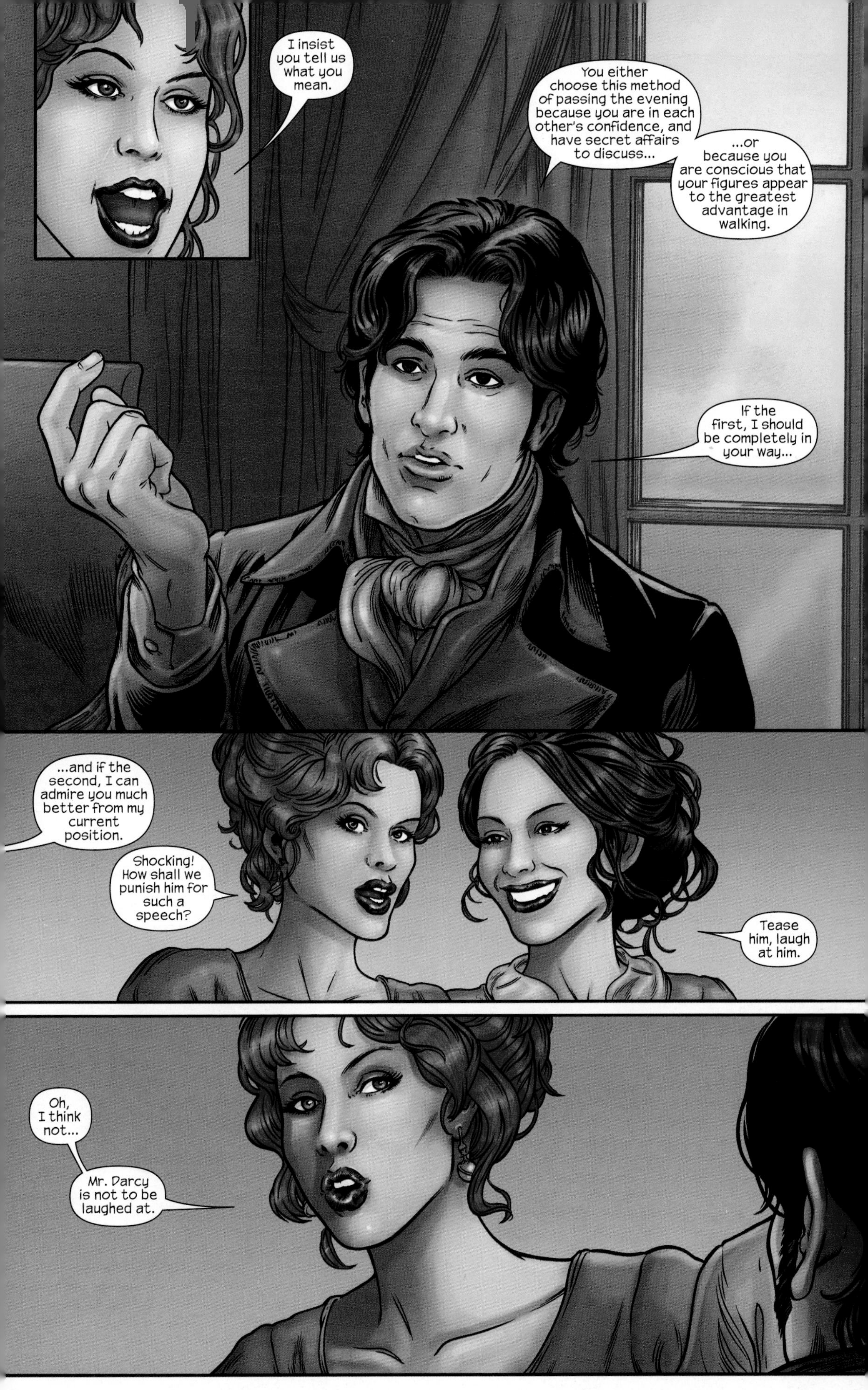

I insist you tell us what you mean.
You either choose this method of passing the evening because you are in each other's confidence, and have secret affairs to discuss...
...or because you are conscious that your figures appear to the greatest advantage in walking.
If the first, I should be completely in your way...
...and if the second, I can admire you much better from my current position.
Shocking! How shall we punish him for such a speech?
Tease him, laugh at him.
Oh, I think not...
Mr. Darcy is not to be laughed at.

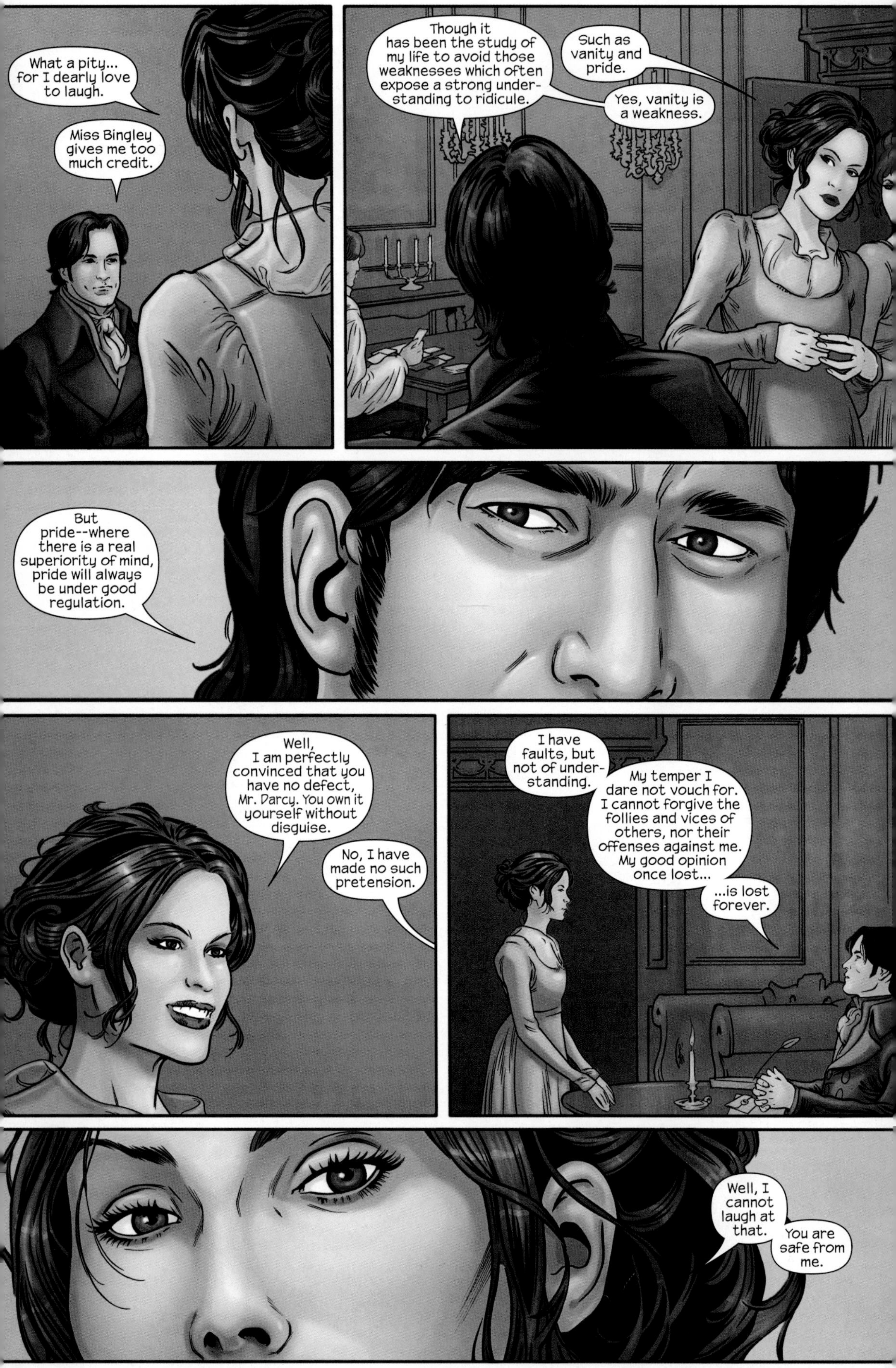
What a pity... for I dearly love to laugh.
Miss Bingley gives me too much credit.
Though it has been the study of my life to avoid those weaknesses which often expose a strong under-standing to ridicule.
Such as vanity and pride.
Yes, vanity is a weakness.
But pride--where there is a real superiority of mind, pride will always be under good regulation.
Well, I am perfectly convinced that you have no defect, Mr. Darcy. You own it yourself without disguise.
No, I have made no such pretension.
I have faults, but not of under-standing.
My temper I dare not vouch for. I cannot forgive the follies and vices of others, nor their offenses against me. My good opinion once lost...
...is lost forever.
Well, I cannot laugh at that.
You are safe from me.

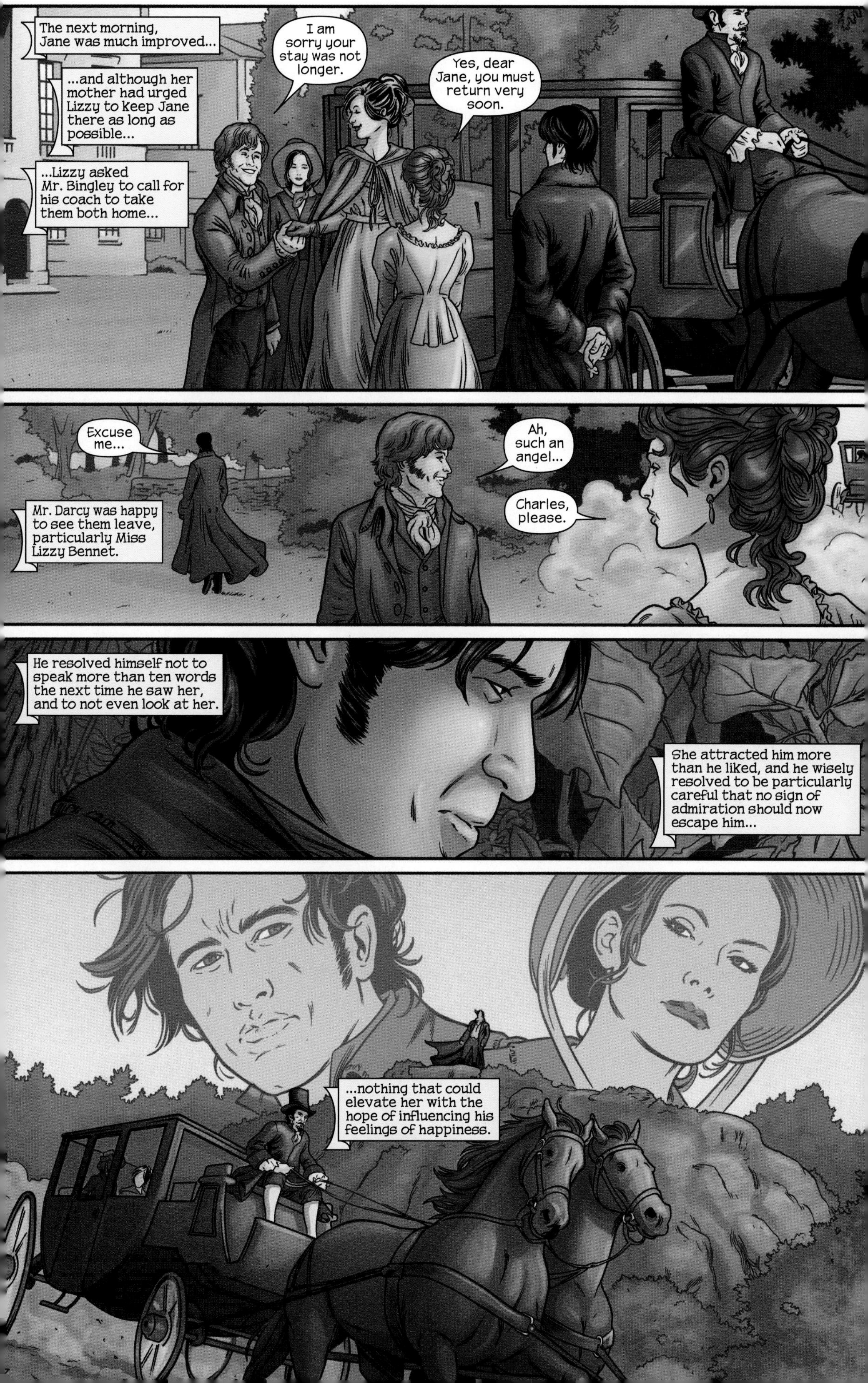
The next morning, Jane was much improved...
...and although her mother had urged Lizzy to keep Jane there as long as possible...
...Lizzy asked Mr. Bingley to call for his coach to take them both home...
I am sorry your stay was not longer.
Yes, dear Jane, you must return very soon.
Excuse me...
Mr. Darcy was happy to see them leave, particularly Miss Lizzy Bennet.
Ah, such an angel...
Charles, please.
He resolved himself not to speak more than ten words the next time he saw her, and to not even look at her.
She attracted him more than he liked, and he wisely resolved to be particularly careful that no sign of admiration should now escape him...
...nothing that could elevate her with the hope of influencing his feelings of happiness.

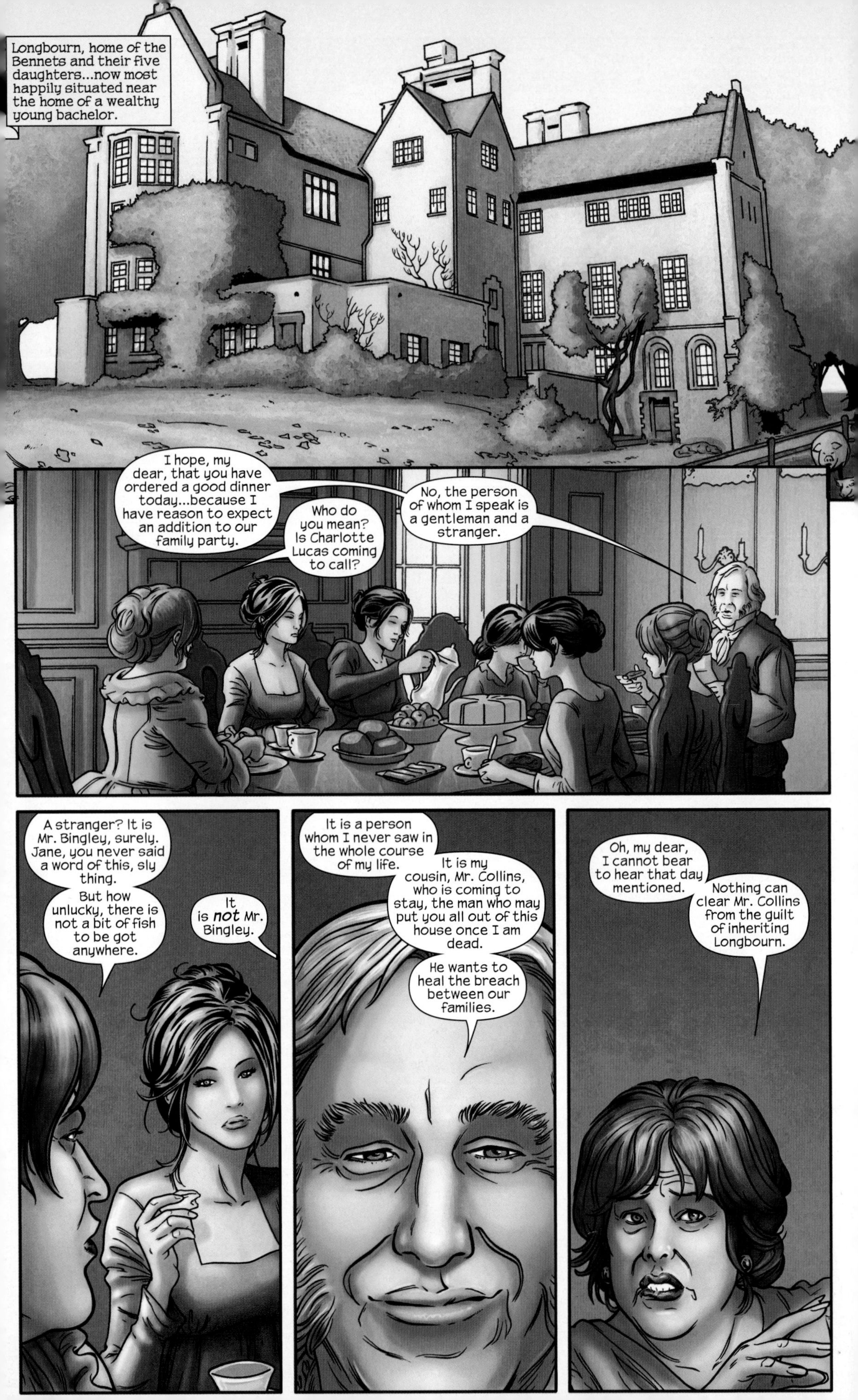
Longbourn, home of the Bennets and their five daughters...now most happily situated near the home of a wealthy young bachelor.
I hope, my dear, that you have ordered a good dinner today...because I have reason to expect an addition to our family party.
Who do you mean? Is Charlotte Lucas coming to call?
No, the person of whom I speak is a gentleman and a stranger.
A stranger? It is Mr. Bingley, surely. Jane, you never said a word of this, sly thing.
But how unlucky, there is not a bit of fish to be got anywhere.
It is *not* Mr. Bingley.
It is a person whom I never saw in the whole course of my life.
It is my cousin, Mr. Collins, who is coming to stay, the man who may put you all out of this house once I am dead.
He wants to heal the breach between our families.
Oh, my dear, I cannot bear to hear that day mentioned.
Nothing can clear Mr. Collins from the guilt of inheriting Longbourn.

Mr. Collins, a young clergyman of five and twenty, arrived punctually at 4 o'clock...

...and was entertained by the whole family.

Allow me to compliment you, ma'am, on your daughters. I have heard much of their beauty. They will no doubt marry well.

I wish it may prove so, for else they will be destitute enough.

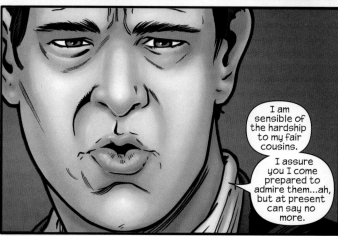

I am sensible of the hardship to my fair cousins.

I assure you I come prepared to admire them...ah, but at present can say no more.

I am full of admiration for this charming dining room and for this most marvelous repast. I beg to know to which of my fair cousins the excellence of its cookery is owing?

We are very well able to keep a good cook, Mr. Collins. My daughters do not toil in the kitchen.

Beg pardon, ma'am. Please allow me to offer my most sincere apologies.

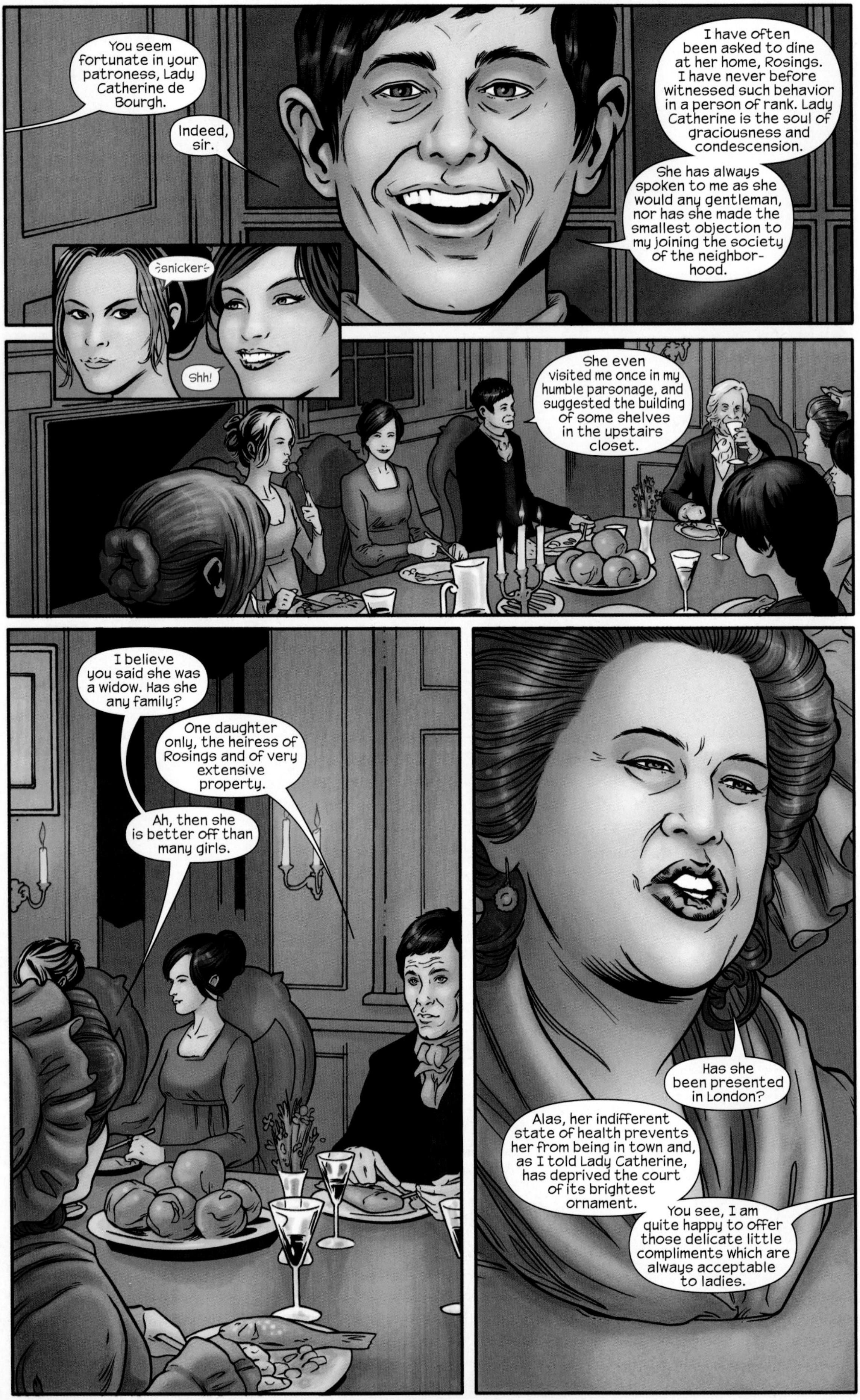

You seem fortunate in your patroness, Lady Catherine de Bourgh.
Indeed, sir.
I have often been asked to dine at her home, Rosings. I have never before witnessed such behavior in a person of rank. Lady Catherine is the soul of graciousness and condescension.
She has always spoken to me as she would any gentleman, nor has she made the smallest objection to my joining the society of the neighbor-hood.
snicker
Shh!
She even visited me once in my humble parsonage, and suggested the building of some shelves in the upstairs closet.
I believe you said she was a widow. Has she any family?
One daughter only, the heiress of Rosings and of very extensive property.
Ah, then she is better off than many girls.
Has she been presented in London?
Alas, her indifferent state of health prevents her from being in town and, as I told Lady Catherine, has deprived the court of its brightest ornament.
You see, I am quite happy to offer those delicate little compliments which are always acceptable to ladies.

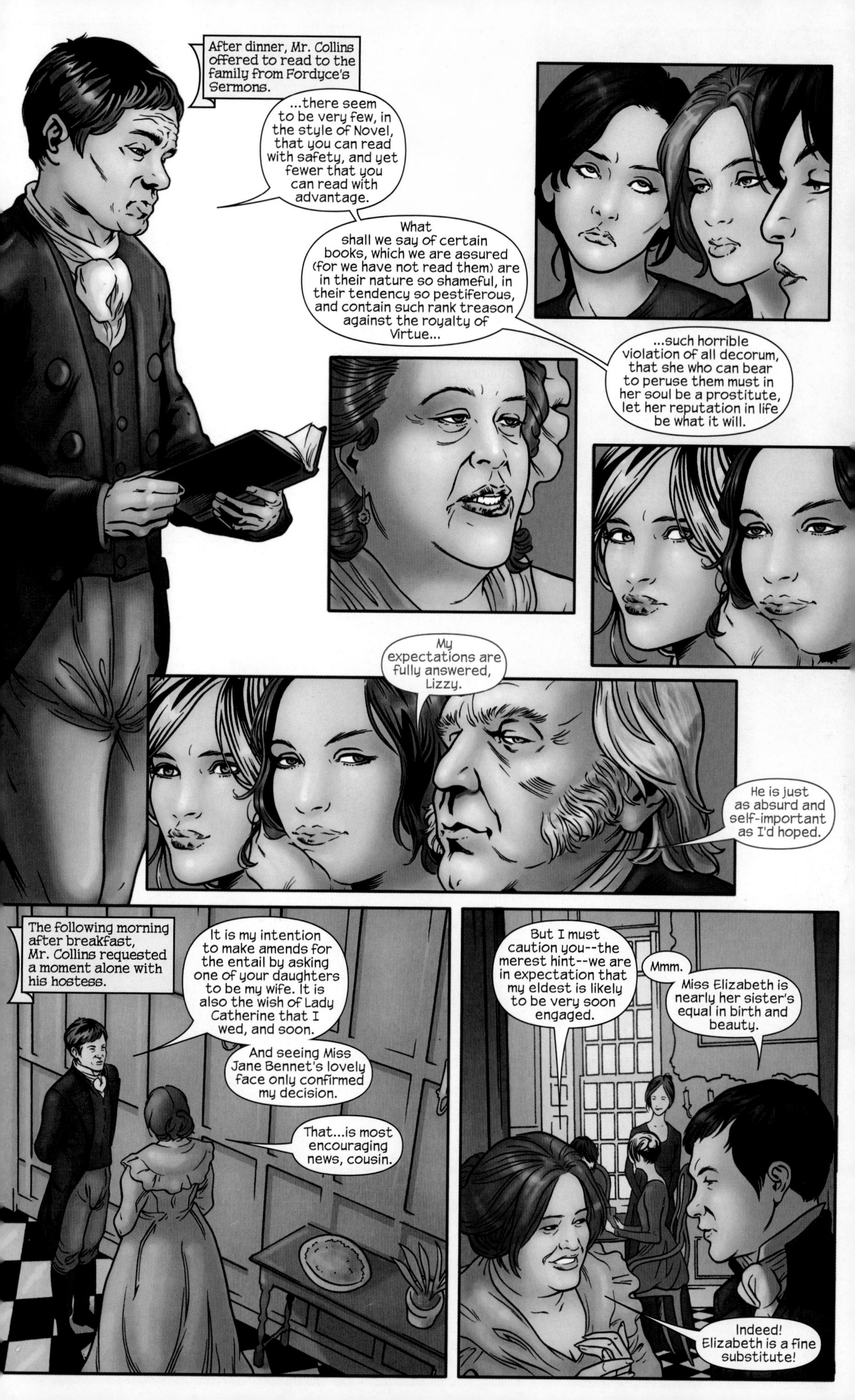
After dinner, Mr. Collins offered to read to the family from Fordyce's Sermons.
...there seem to be very few, in the style of Novel, that you can read with safety, and yet fewer that you can read with advantage.
What shall we say of certain books, which we are assured (for we have not read them) are in their nature so shameful, in their tendency so pestiferous, and contain such rank treason against the royalty of Virtue...
...such horrible violation of all decorum, that she who can bear to peruse them must in her soul be a prostitute, let her reputation in life be what it will.
My expectations are fully answered, Lizzy.
He is just as absurd and self-important as I'd hoped.
The following morning after breakfast, Mr. Collins requested a moment alone with his hostess.
It is my intention to make amends for the entail by asking one of your daughters to be my wife. It is also the wish of Lady Catherine that I wed, and soon.
And seeing Miss Jane Bennet's lovely face only confirmed my decision.
That...is most encouraging news, cousin.
But I must caution you--the merest hint--we are in expectation that my eldest is likely to be very soon engaged.
Mmm.
Miss Elizabeth is nearly her sister's equal in birth and beauty.
Indeed! Elizabeth is a fine substitute!

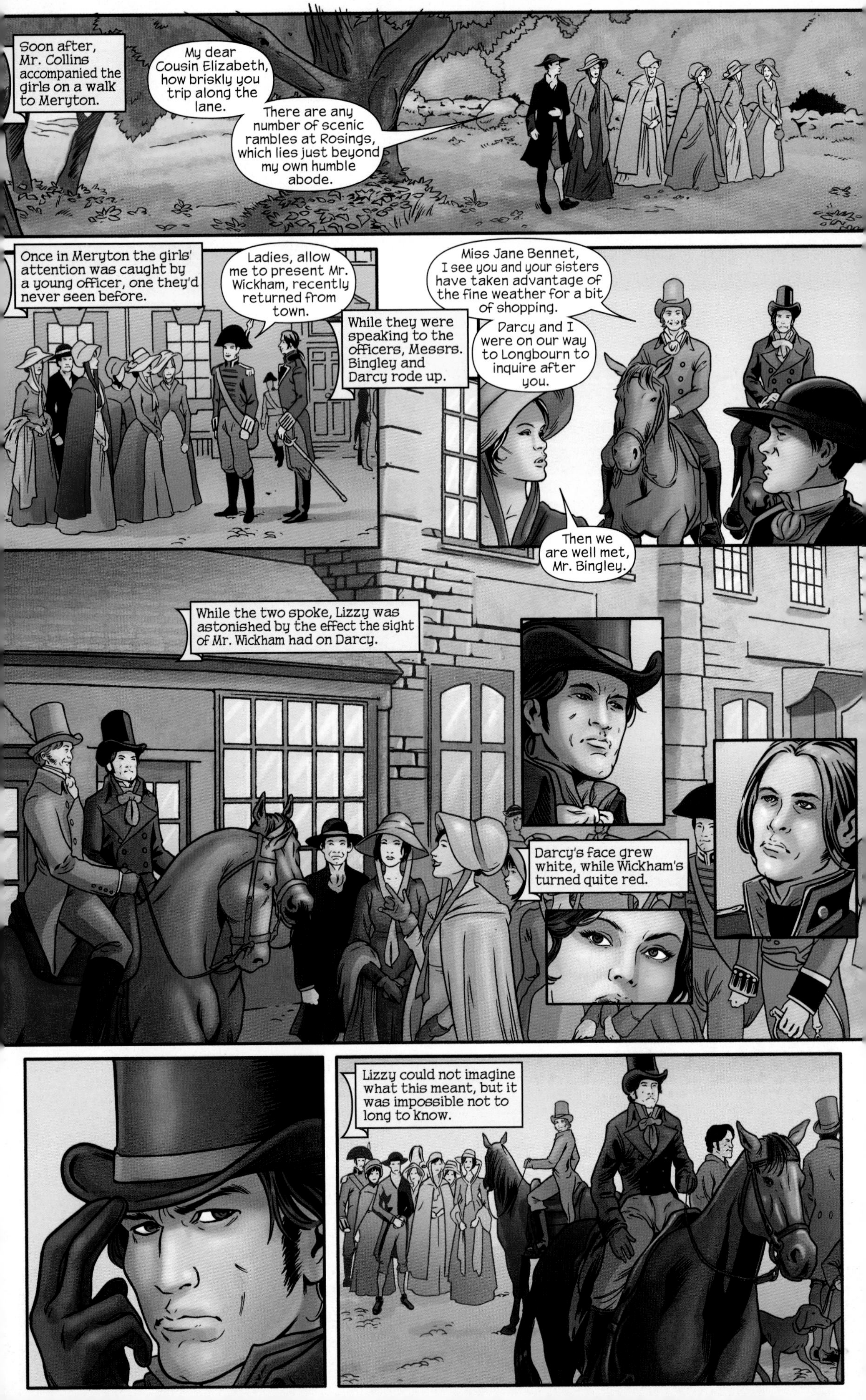
Soon after, Mr. Collins accompanied the girls on a walk to Meryton.
My dear Cousin Elizabeth, how briskly you trip along the lane.
There are any number of scenic rambles at Rosings, which lies just beyond my own humble abode.
Once in Meryton the girls' attention was caught by a young officer, one they'd never seen before.
Ladies, allow me to present Mr. Wickham, recently returned from town.
While they were speaking to the officers, Messrs. Bingley and Darcy rode up.
Miss Jane Bennet, I see you and your sisters have taken advantage of the fine weather for a bit of shopping.
Darcy and I were on our way to Longbourn to inquire after you.
Then we are well met, Mr. Bingley.
While the two spoke, Lizzy was astonished by the effect the sight of Mr. Wickham had on Darcy.
Darcy's face grew white, while Wickham's turned quite red.
Lizzy could not imagine what this meant, but it was impossible not to long to know.

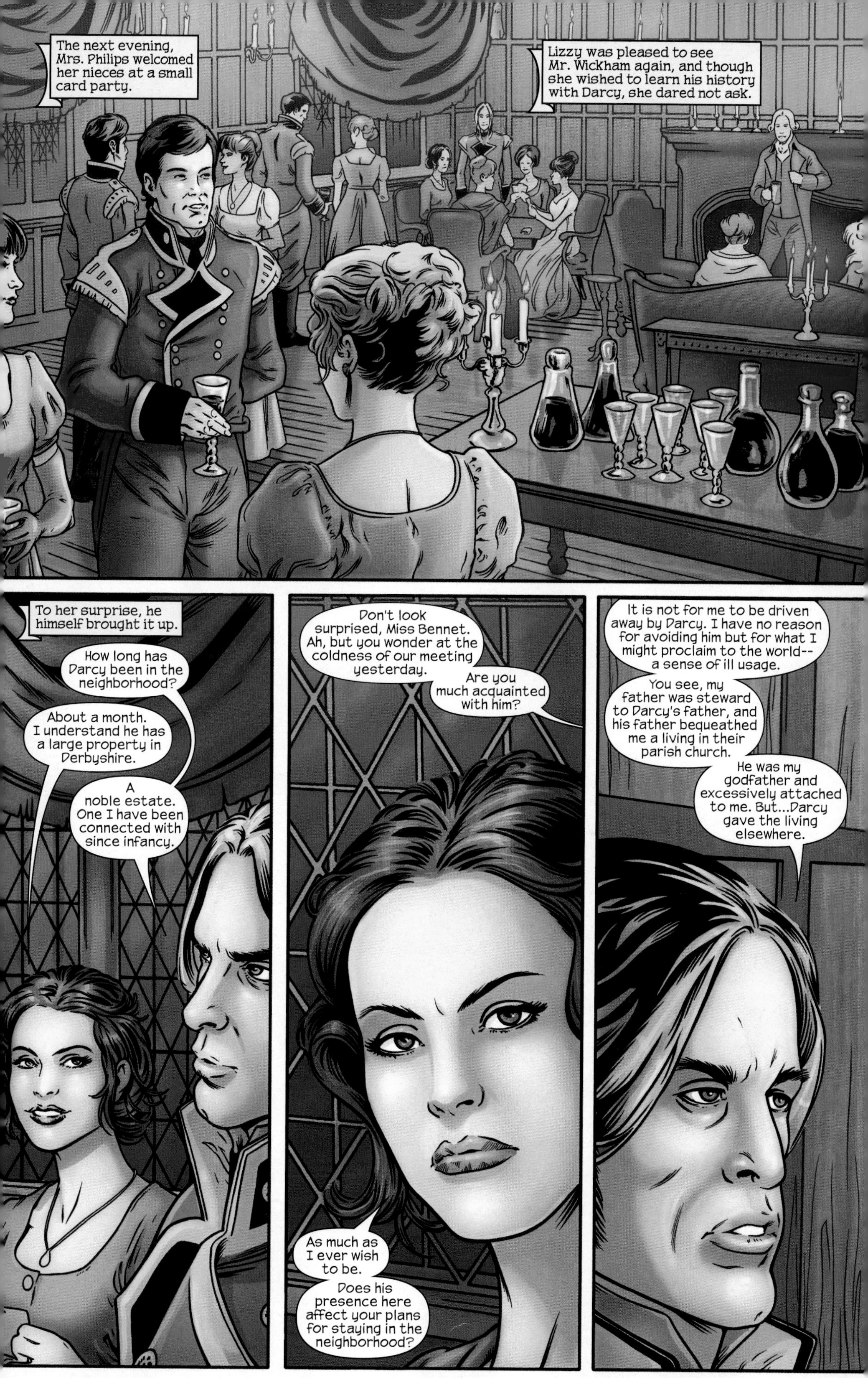
The next evening, Mrs. Philips welcomed her nieces at a small card party.
Lizzy was pleased to see Mr. Wickham again, and though she wished to learn his history with Darcy, she dared not ask.
To her surprise, he himself brought it up.
How long has Darcy been in the neighborhood?
About a month. I understand he has a large property in Derbyshire.
A noble estate. One I have been connected with since infancy.
Don't look surprised, Miss Bennet. Ah, but you wonder at the coldness of our meeting yesterday.
Are you much acquainted with him?
As much as I ever wish to be.
Does his presence here affect your plans for staying in the neighborhood?
It is not for me to be driven away by Darcy. I have no reason for avoiding him but for what I might proclaim to the world-- a sense of ill usage.
You see, my father was steward to Darcy's father, and his father bequeathed me a living in their parish church.
He was my godfather and excessively attached to me. But...Darcy gave the living elsewhere.

This is shocking! He ought to be publicly disgraced.

Sometime or other he will be.

But not by me, for the sake of his father's memory.

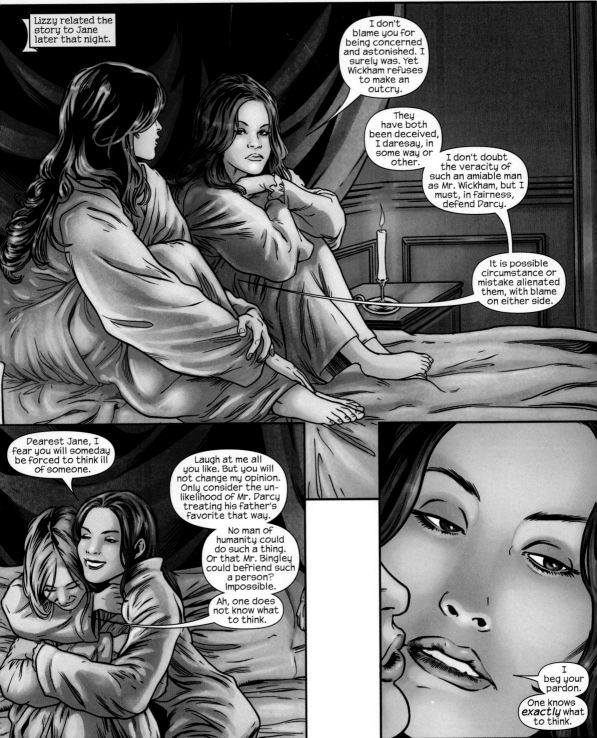

Lizzy related the story to Jane later that night.

I don't blame you for being concerned and astonished. I surely was. Yet Wickham refuses to make an outcry.

They have both been deceived, I daresay, in some way or other.

I don't doubt the veracity of such an amiable man as Mr. Wickham, but I must, in fairness, defend Darcy.

It is possible circumstance or mistake alienated them, with blame on either side.

Dearest Jane, I fear you will someday be forced to think ill of someone.

Laugh at me all you like. But you will not change my opinion. Only consider the unlikelihood of Mr. Darcy treating his father's favorite that way.

No man of humanity could do such a thing. Or that Mr. Bingley could befriend such a person? Impossible.

Ah, one does not know what to think.

I beg your pardon.

One knows *exactly* what to think.

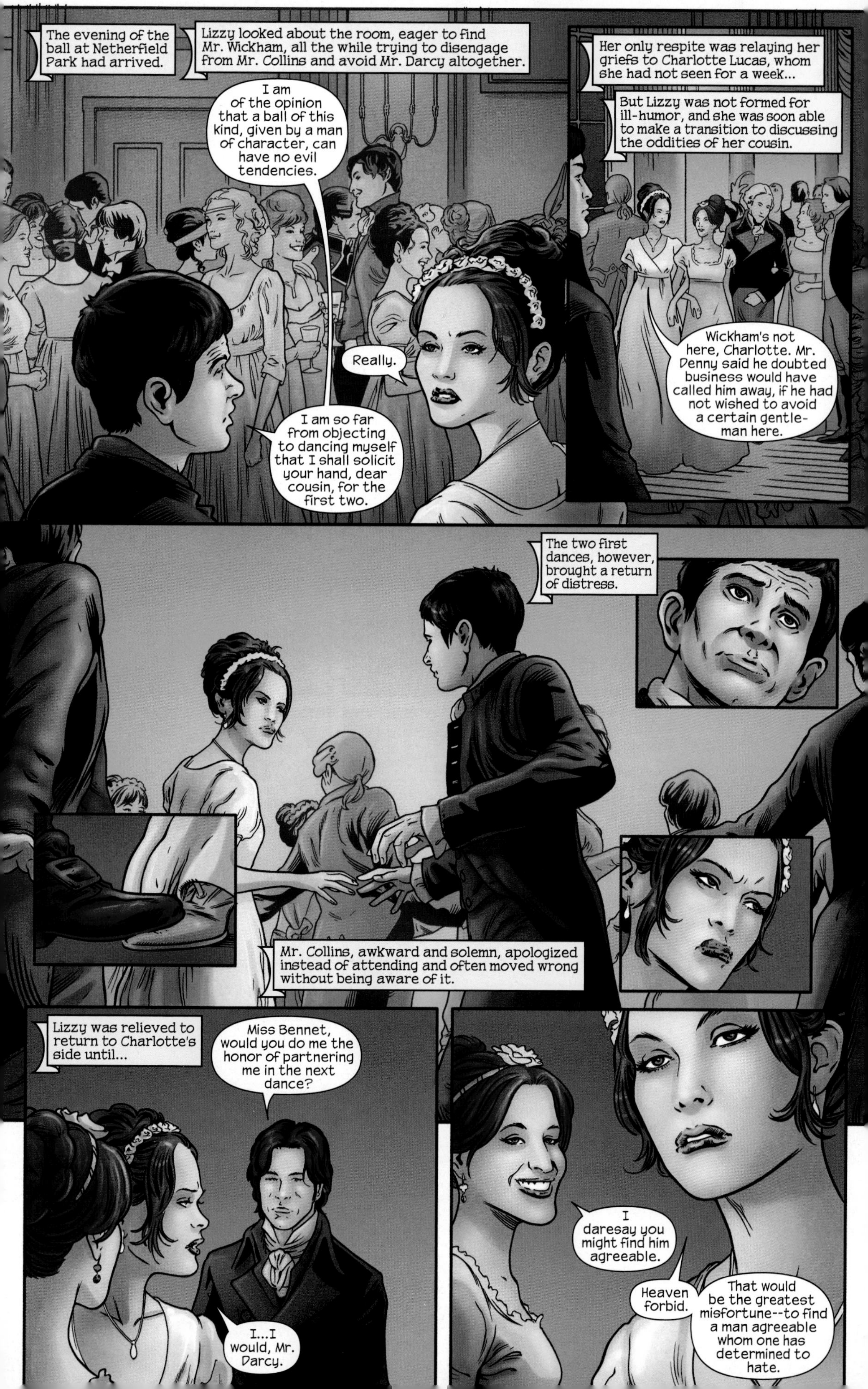
The evening of the ball at Netherfield Park had arrived.
Lizzy looked about the room, eager to find Mr. Wickham, all the while trying to disengage from Mr. Collins and avoid Mr. Darcy altogether.
I am of the opinion that a ball of this kind, given by a man of character, can have no evil tendencies.
Really.
I am so far from objecting to dancing myself that I shall solicit your hand, dear cousin, for the first two.
Her only respite was relaying her griefs to Charlotte Lucas, whom she had not seen for a week...
But Lizzy was not formed for ill-humor, and she was soon able to make a transition to discussing the oddities of her cousin.
Wickham's not here, Charlotte. Mr. Denny said he doubted business would have called him away, if he had not wished to avoid a certain gentleman here.
The two first dances, however, brought a return of distress.
Mr. Collins, awkward and solemn, apologized instead of attending and often moved wrong without being aware of it.
Lizzy was relieved to return to Charlotte's side until...
Miss Bennet, would you do me the honor of partnering me in the next dance?
I...I would, Mr. Darcy.
I daresay you might find him agreeable.
Heaven forbid.
That would be the greatest misfortune--to find a man agreeable whom one has determined to hate.

When the dancing resumed and Darcy came to claim her, Charlotte whispered in Lizzy's ear not to be a simpleton and allow her fancy for Wickham to make her appear unpleasant in the eyes of a man many times his consequence.

Lizzy made no answer, but took her place in the set.

The dancers all seem quite animated tonight.

Now it's your turn to say something, Mr. Darcy. I talked about the dance, now you ought to remark on the size of the room or the number of couples.

I assure you that whatever you wish me to say shall be said.

That reply will do for the present. By and by I may observe that private balls are much pleasanter than public ones. But now we may be silent.

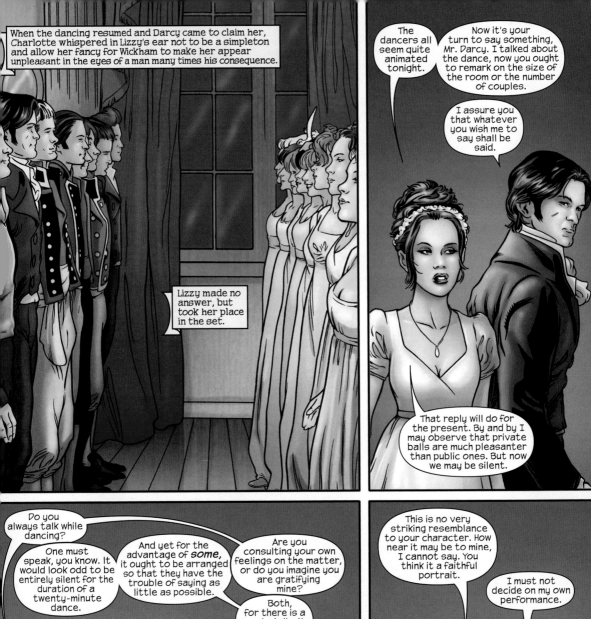

Do you always talk while dancing?

One must speak, you know. It would look odd to be entirely silent for the duration of a twenty-minute dance.

And yet for the advantage of *some*, it ought to be arranged so that they have the trouble of saying as little as possible.

Are you consulting your own feelings on the matter, or do you imagine you are gratifying mine?

Both, for there is a great similarity in our turn of minds.

We are each of a taciturn, unsociable disposition, unwilling to speak... unless we expect to say something that will amaze the whole room.

This is no very striking resemblance to your character. How near it may be to mine, I cannot say. You think it a faithful portrait.

I must not decide on my own performance.

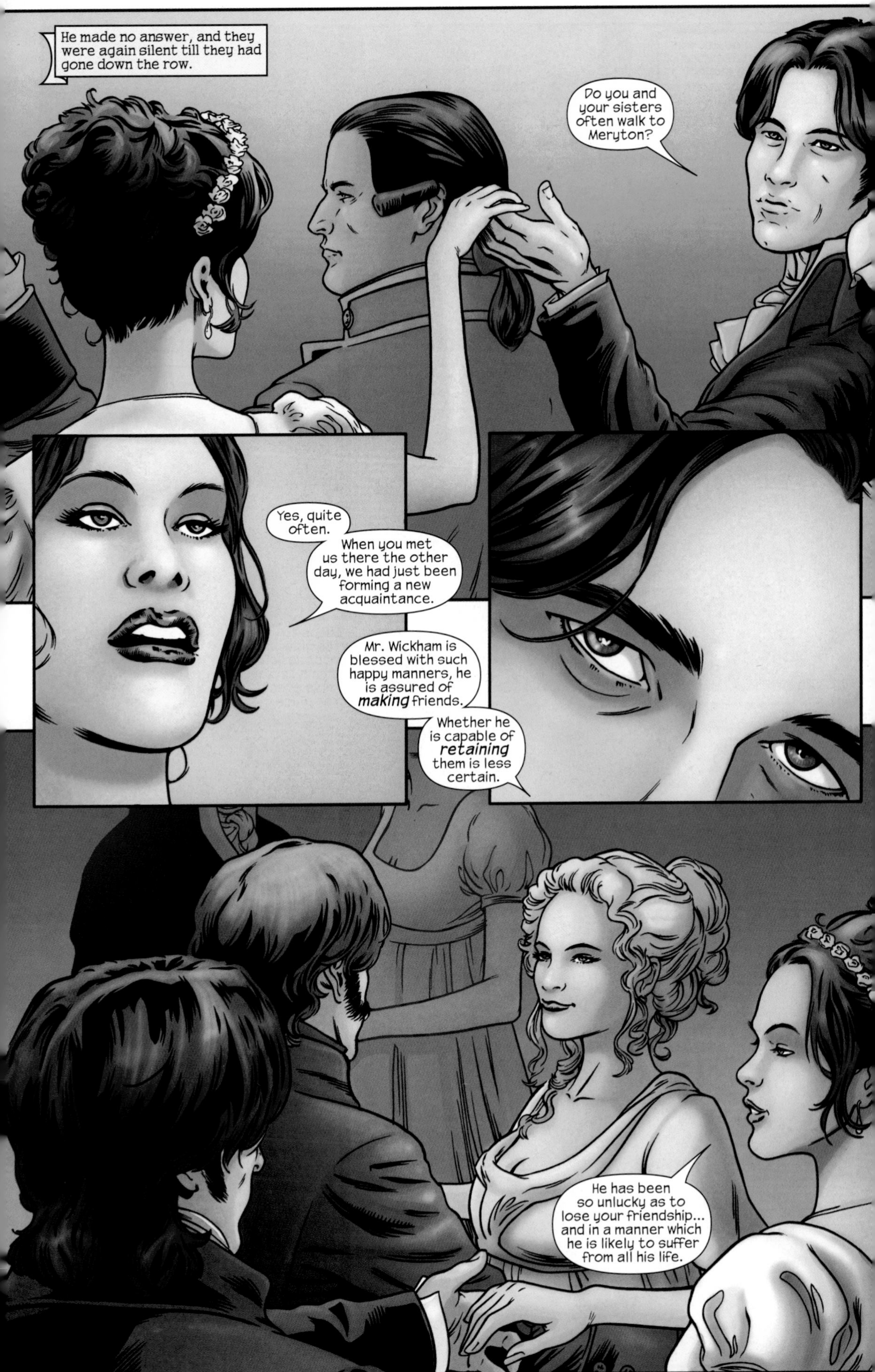
He made no answer, and they were again silent till they had gone down the row.
Do you and your sisters often walk to Meryton?
Yes, quite often.
When you met us there the other day, we had just been forming a new acquaintance.
Mr. Wickham is blessed with such happy manners, he is assured of *making* friends.
Whether he is capable of *retaining* them is less certain.
He has been so unlucky as to lose your friendship... and in a manner which he is likely to suffer from all his life.

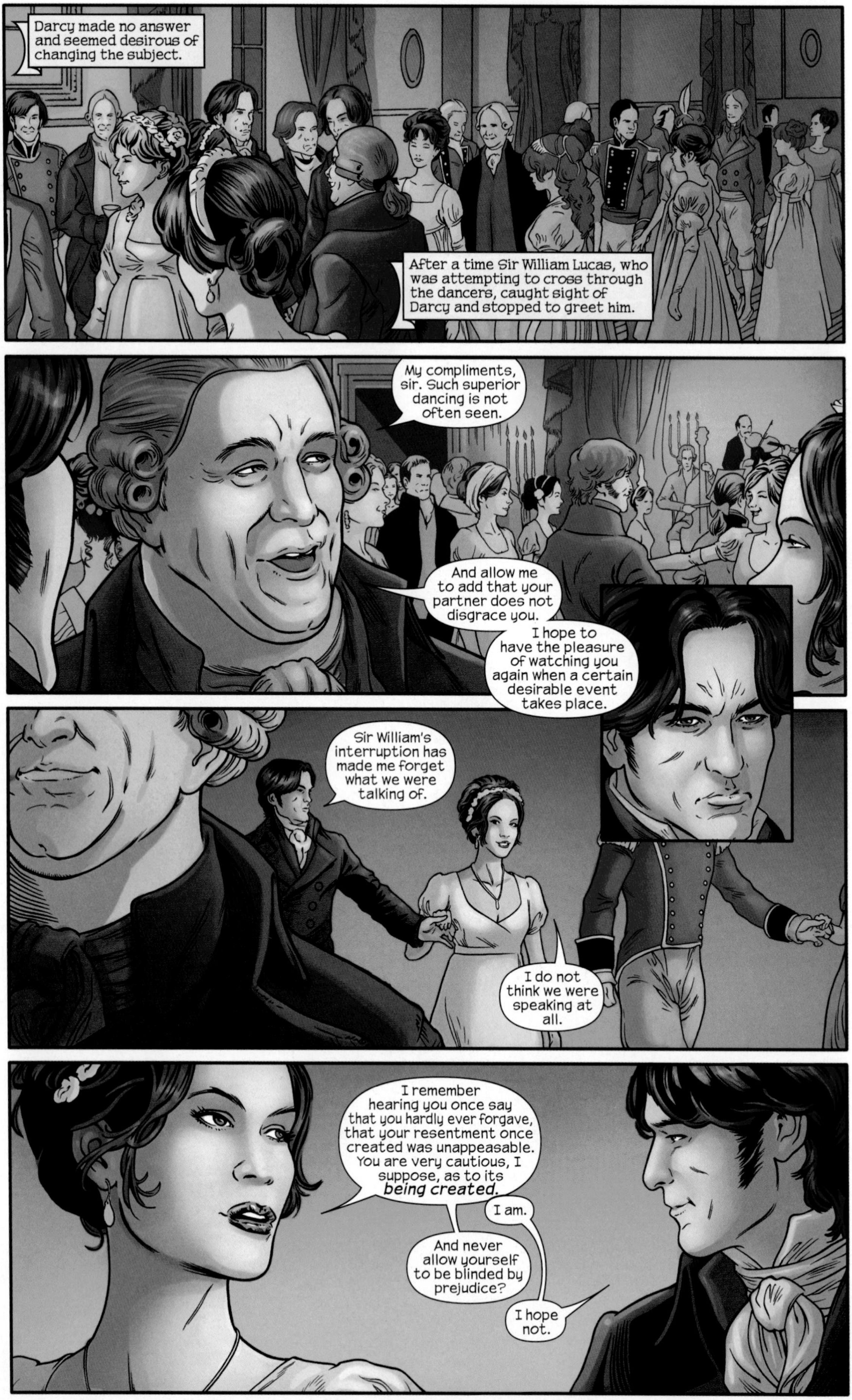
Darcy made no answer and seemed desirous of changing the subject.
After a time Sir William Lucas, who was attempting to cross through the dancers, caught sight of Darcy and stopped to greet him.
My compliments, sir. Such superior dancing is not often seen.
And allow me to add that your partner does not disgrace you.
I hope to have the pleasure of watching you again when a certain desirable event takes place.
Sir William's interruption has made me forget what we were talking of.
I do not think we were speaking at all.
I remember hearing you once say that you hardly ever forgave, that your resentment once created was unappeasable. You are very cautious, I suppose, as to its *being created.*
I am.
And never allow yourself to be blinded by prejudice?
I hope not.

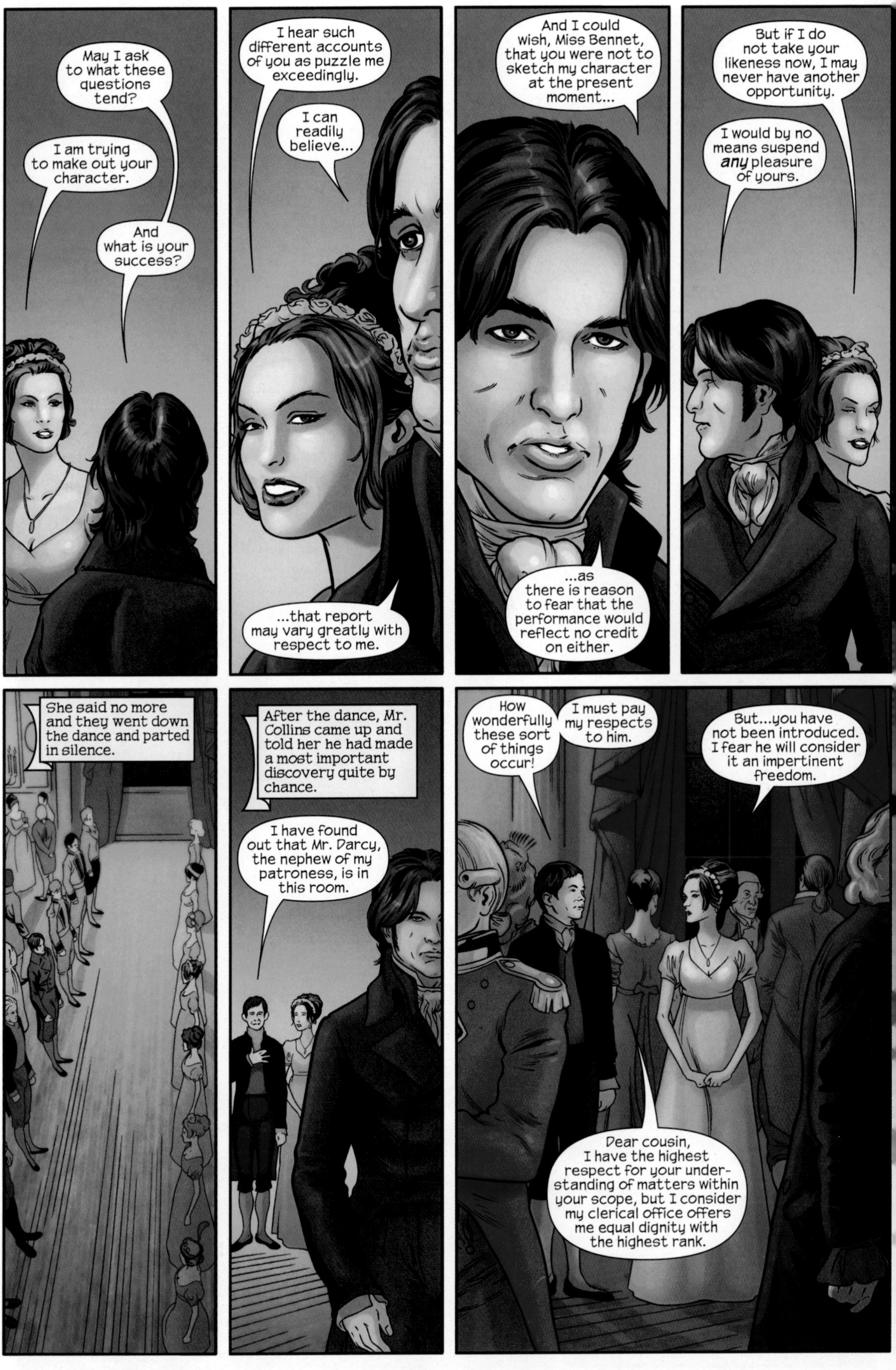
May I ask to what these questions tend?
I am trying to make out your character.
And what is your success?
I hear such different accounts of you as puzzle me exceedingly.
I can readily believe...
...that report may vary greatly with respect to me.
And I could wish, Miss Bennet, that you were not to sketch my character at the present moment...
...as there is reason to fear that the performance would reflect no credit on either.
But if I do not take your likeness now, I may never have another opportunity.
I would by no means suspend any pleasure of yours.
She said no more and they went down the dance and parted in silence.
After the dance, Mr. Collins came up and told her he had made a most important discovery quite by chance.
I have found out that Mr. Darcy, the nephew of my patroness, is in this room.
How wonderfully these sort of things occur!
I must pay my respects to him.
But...you have not been introduced. I fear he will consider it an impertinent freedom.
Dear cousin, I have the highest respect for your understanding of matters within your scope, but I consider my clerical office offers me equal dignity with the highest rank.

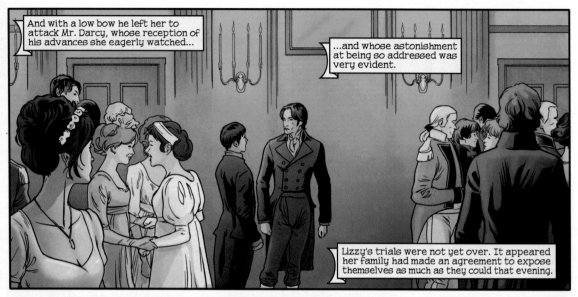

And with a low bow he left her to attack Mr. Darcy, whose reception of his advances she eagerly watched...

...and whose astonishment at being so addressed was very evident.

Lizzy's trials were not yet over. It appeared her family had made an agreement to expose themselves as much as they could that evening.

Her mother grew giddy with wine and spoke openly about the expected betrothal of Jane to Mr. Bingley...

...and Bingley will no doubt find rich suitors for Jane's sisters...

She had the mortification of watching her sister Mary several times display her weak skills at the pianoforte until her father had to intervene...

That will do extremely well, child.

Let the other ladies have time to exhibit.

And Mr. Collins continued perseveringly at her side until, to her relief, Charlotte engaged him in conversation.

Lizzy escaped outside for a breath of air, only to be greeted by the sight of her youngest sisters making lively with the officers.

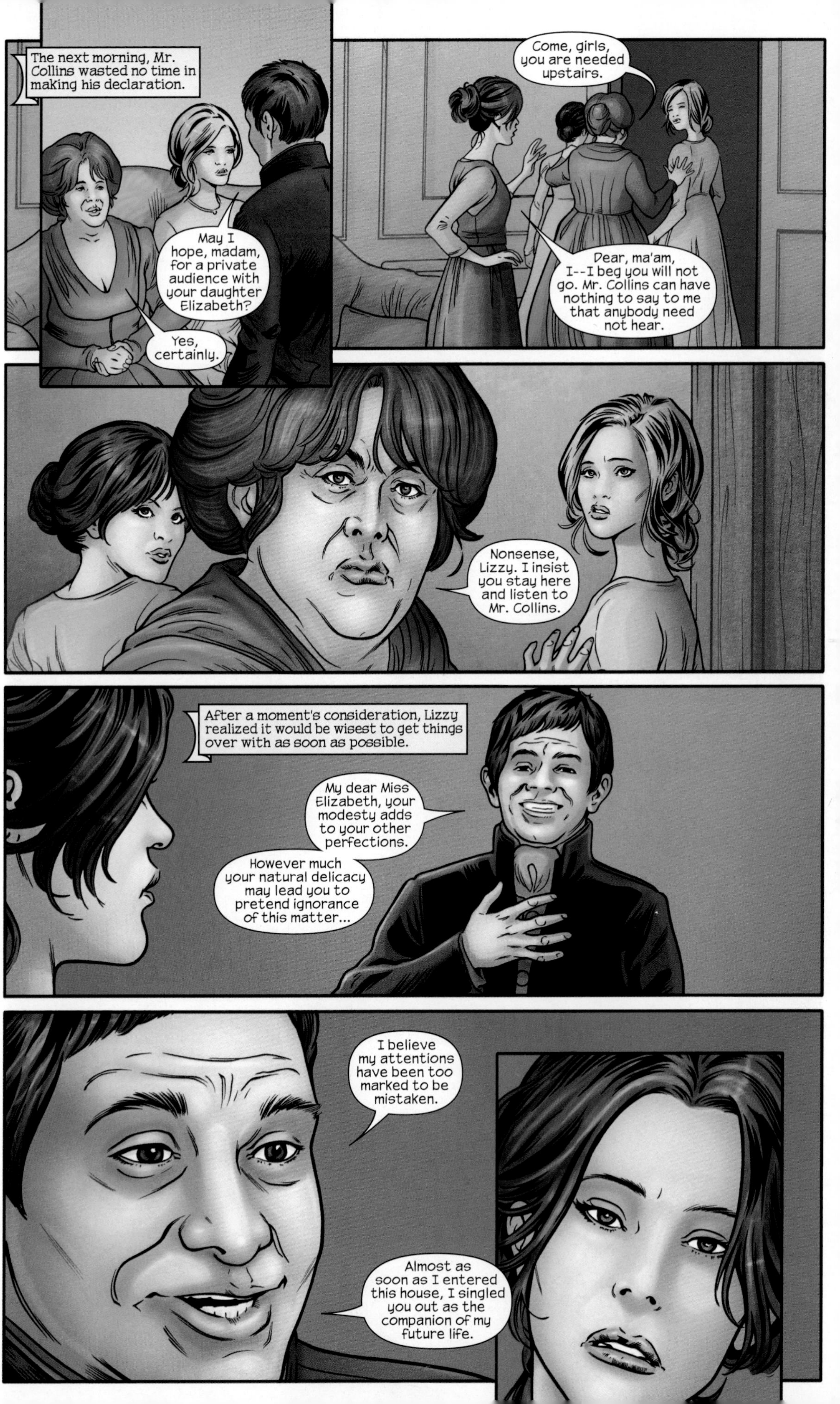
The next morning, Mr. Collins wasted no time in making his declaration.
May I hope, madam, for a private audience with your daughter Elizabeth?
Yes, certainly.
Come, girls, you are needed upstairs.
Dear, ma'am, I--I beg you will not go. Mr. Collins can have nothing to say to me that anybody need not hear.
Nonsense, Lizzy. I insist you stay here and listen to Mr. Collins.
After a moment's consideration, Lizzy realized it would be wisest to get things over with as soon as possible.
My dear Miss Elizabeth, your modesty adds to your other perfections.
However much your natural delicacy may lead you to pretend ignorance of this matter...
I believe my attentions have been too marked to be mistaken.
Almost as soon as I entered this house, I singled you out as the companion of my future life.

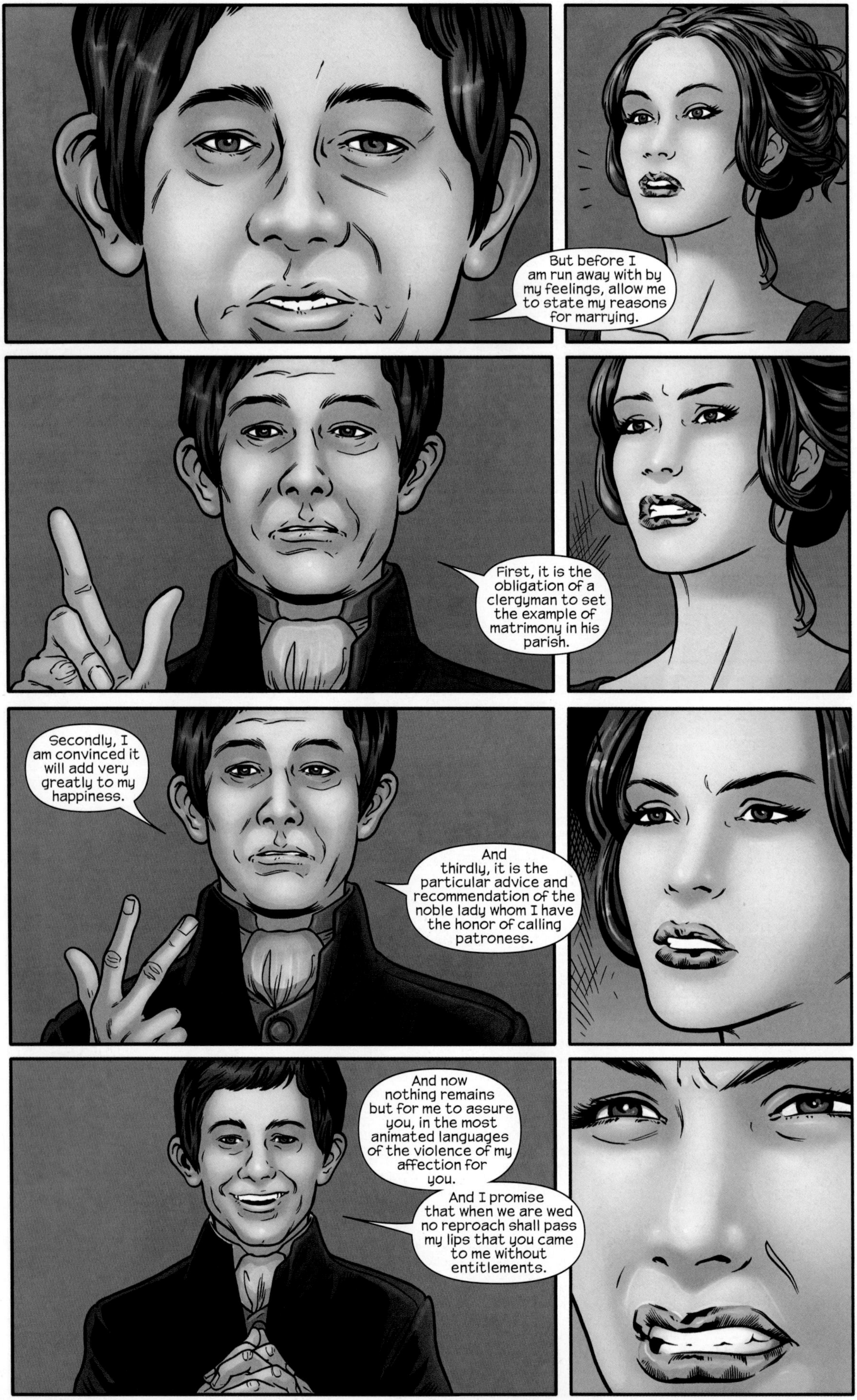
But before I am run away with by my feelings, allow me to state my reasons for marrying.
First, it is the obligation of a clergyman to set the example of matrimony in his parish.
Secondly, I am convinced it will add very greatly to my happiness.
And thirdly, it is the particular advice and recommendation of the noble lady whom I have the honor of calling patroness.
And now nothing remains but for me to assure you, in the most animated languages of the violence of my affection for you.
And I promise that when we are wed no reproach shall pass my lips that you came to me without entitlements.

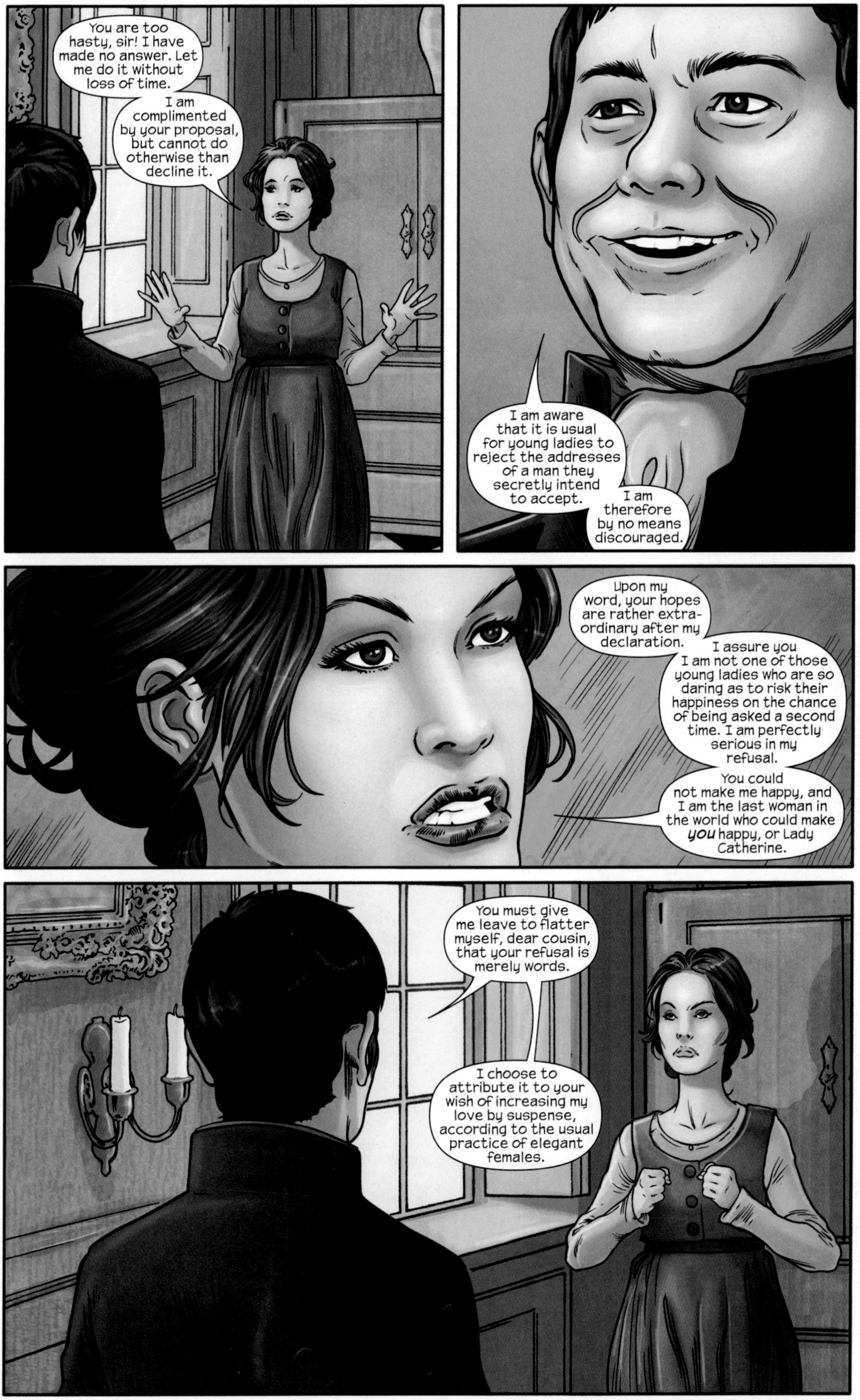
You are too hasty, sir! I have made no answer. Let me do it without loss of time.
I am complimented by your proposal, but cannot do otherwise than decline it.
I am aware that it is usual for young ladies to reject the addresses of a man they secretly intend to accept.
I am therefore by no means discouraged.
Upon my word, your hopes are rather extra-ordinary after my declaration.
I assure you I am not one of those young ladies who are so daring as to risk their happiness on the chance of being asked a second time. I am perfectly serious in my refusal.
You could not make me happy, and I am the last woman in the world who could make *you* happy, or Lady Catherine.
You must give me leave to flatter myself, dear cousin, that your refusal is merely words.
I choose to attribute it to your wish of increasing my love by suspense, according to the usual practice of elegant females.

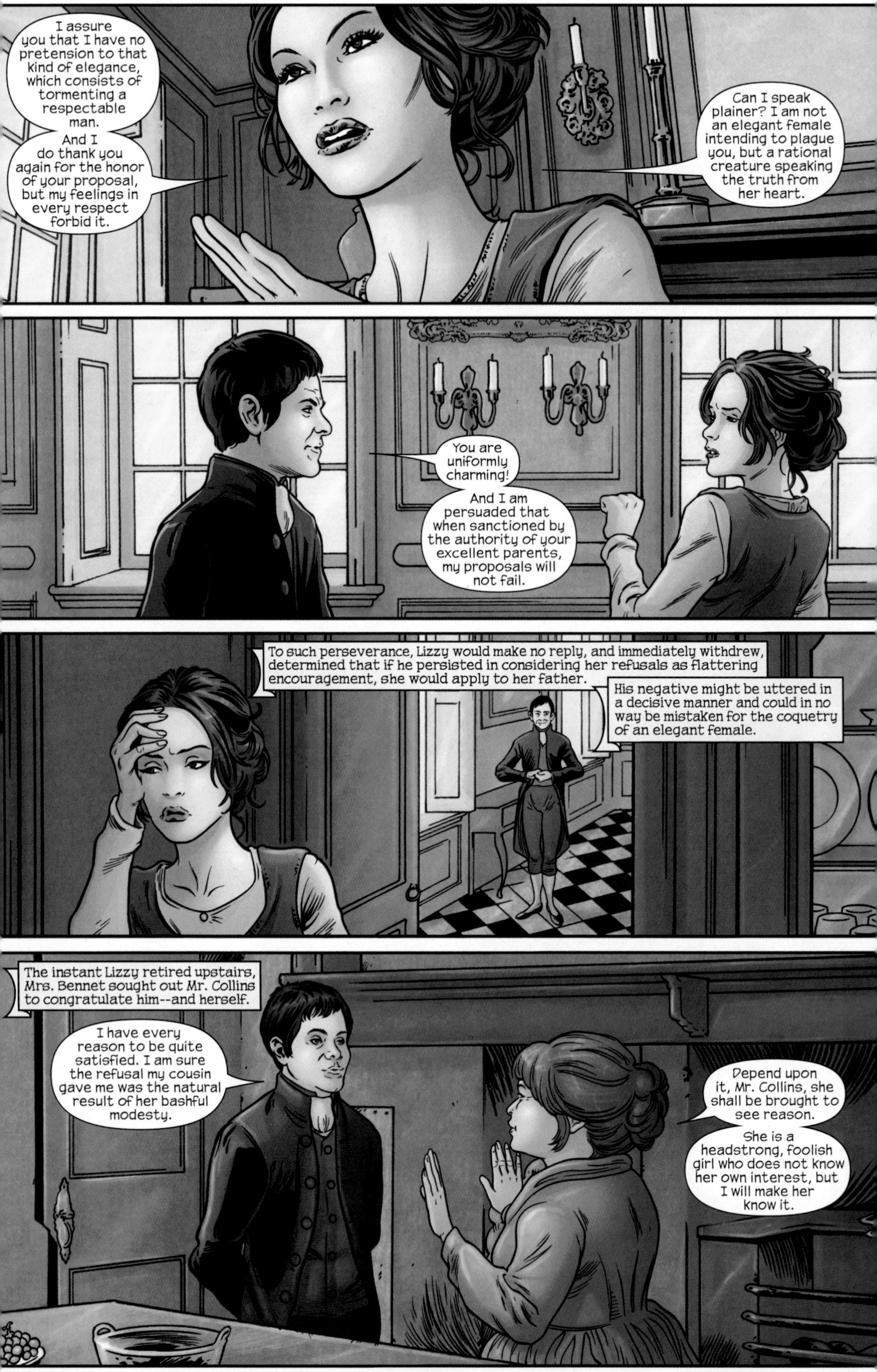
I assure you that I have no pretension to that kind of elegance, which consists of tormenting a respectable man.
And I do thank you again for the honor of your proposal, but my feelings in every respect forbid it.
Can I speak plainer? I am not an elegant female intending to plague you, but a rational creature speaking the truth from her heart.
You are uniformly charming!
And I am persuaded that when sanctioned by the authority of your excellent parents, my proposals will not fail.
To such perseverance, Lizzy would make no reply, and immediately withdrew, determined that if he persisted in considering her refusals as flattering encouragement, she would apply to her father.
His negative might be uttered in a decisive manner and could in no way be mistaken for the coquetry of an elegant female.
The instant Lizzy retired upstairs, Mrs. Bennet sought out Mr. Collins to congratulate him--and herself.
I have every reason to be quite satisfied. I am sure the refusal my cousin gave me was the natural result of her bashful modesty.
Depend upon it, Mr. Collins, she shall be brought to see reason.
She is a headstrong, foolish girl who does not know her own interest, but I will make her know it.

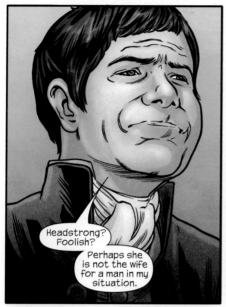

Foolish only in matters such as these. In other respects she is good-natured a girl as ever lived.

Headstrong? Foolish? Perhaps she is not the wife for a man in my situation.

Mr. Bennet and I will soon settle it with her.

Oh, Mr. Bennet! We are all in an uproar!

You must come and make Lizzy marry Mr. Collins.

She vows she will not have him and if you do not make haste, he might change his mind and not have *her*.

I do not have the pleasure of understanding you. Of what are you talking?

Of Mr. Collins and Lizzy.

Lizzy declares she will not have him, and now Mr. Collins is beginning to say he will not have Lizzy.

What am I to do? It seems a hopeless business.

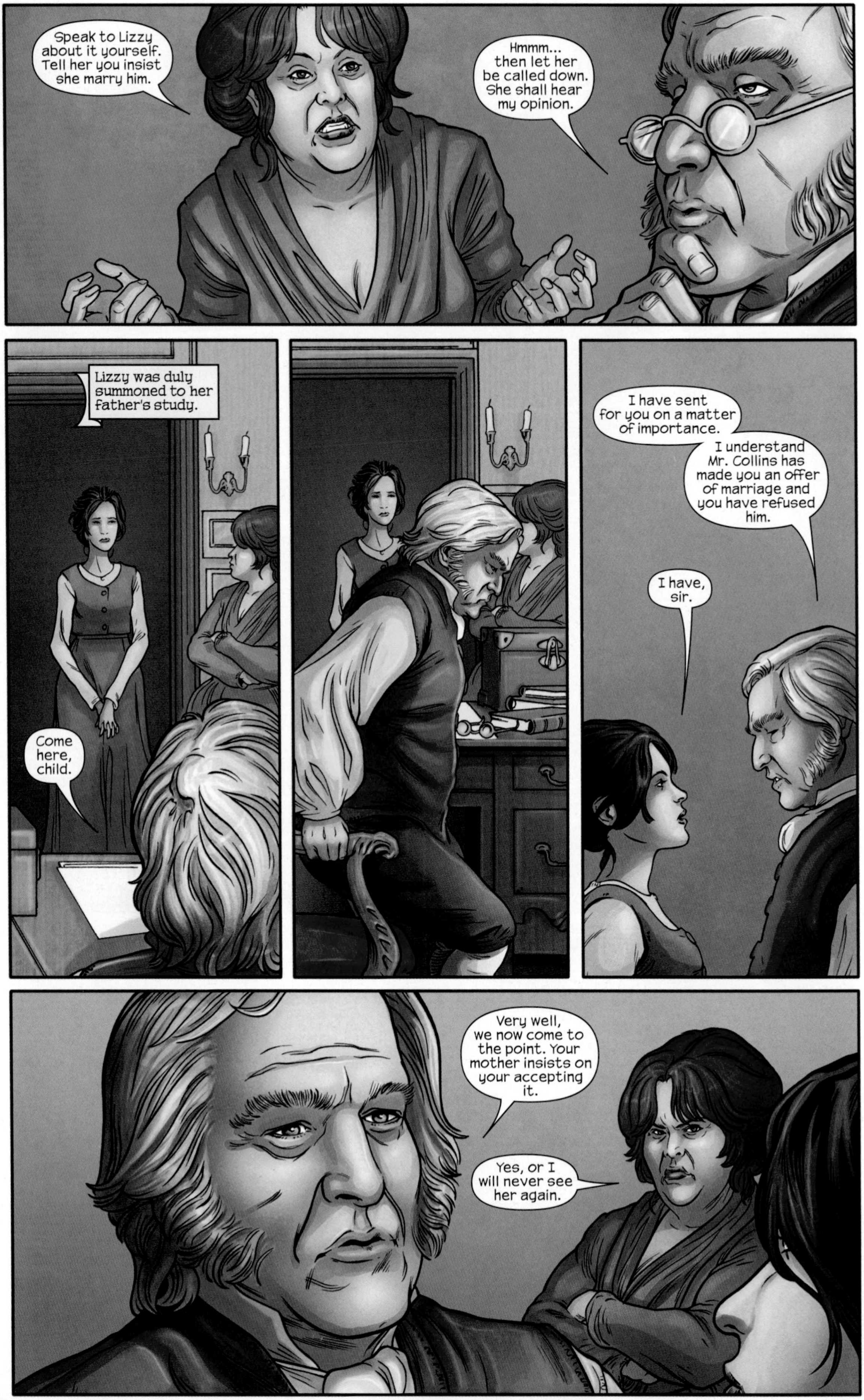
Speak to Lizzy about it yourself. Tell her you insist she marry him.
Hmmm... then let her be called down. She shall hear my opinion.
Lizzy was duly summoned to her father's study.
Come here, child.
I have sent for you on a matter of importance.
I understand Mr. Collins has made you an offer of marriage and you have refused him.
I have, sir.
Very well, we now come to the point. Your mother insists on your accepting it.
Yes, or I will never see her again.

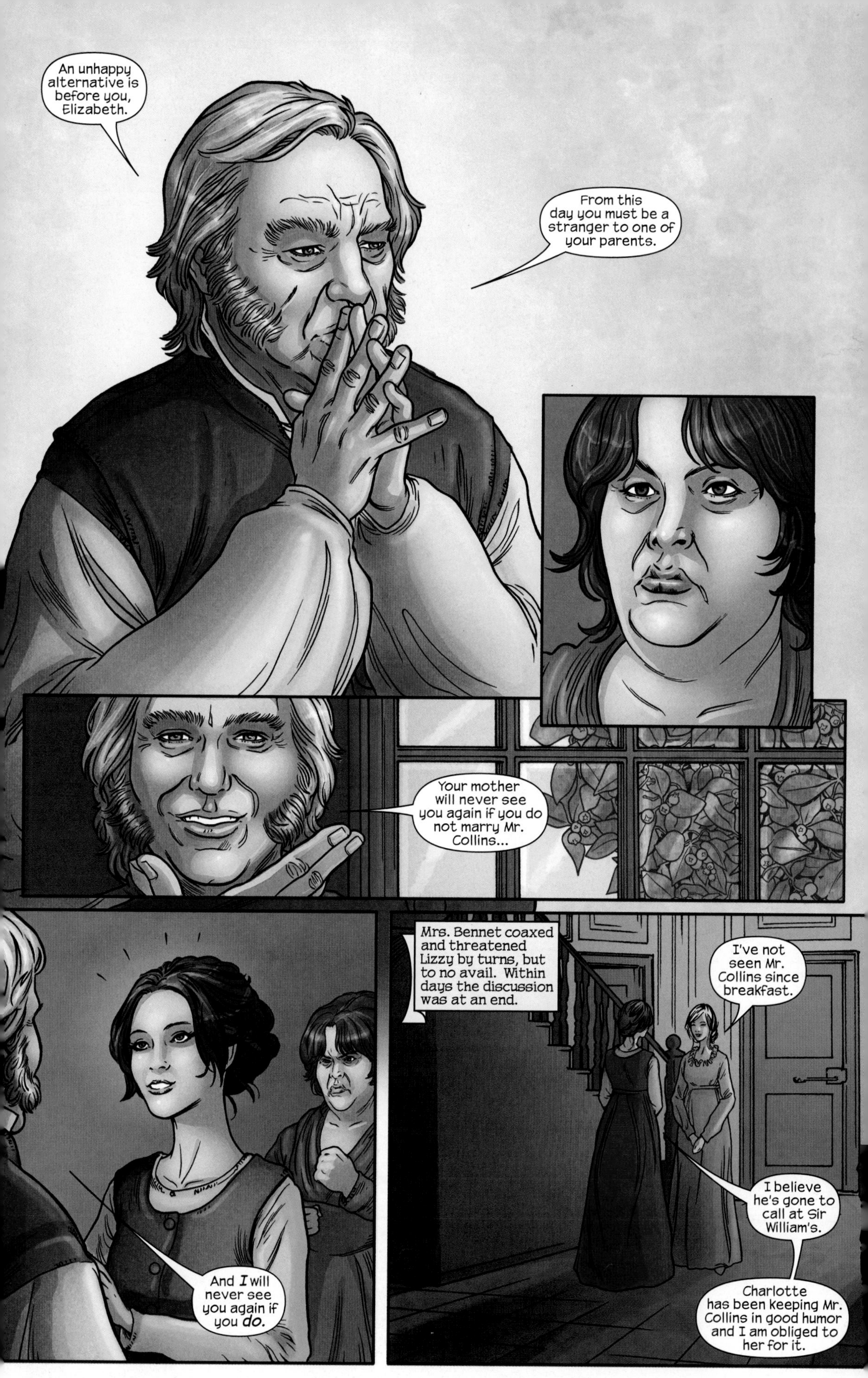
An unhappy alternative is before you, Elizabeth.
From this day you must be a stranger to one of your parents.
Your mother will never see you again if you do not marry Mr. Collins...
And *I* will never see you again if you *do.*
Mrs. Bennet coaxed and threatened Lizzy by turns, but to no avail. Within days the discussion was at an end.
I've not seen Mr. Collins since breakfast.
I believe he's gone to call at Sir William's.
Charlotte has been keeping Mr. Collins in good humor and I am obliged to her for it.

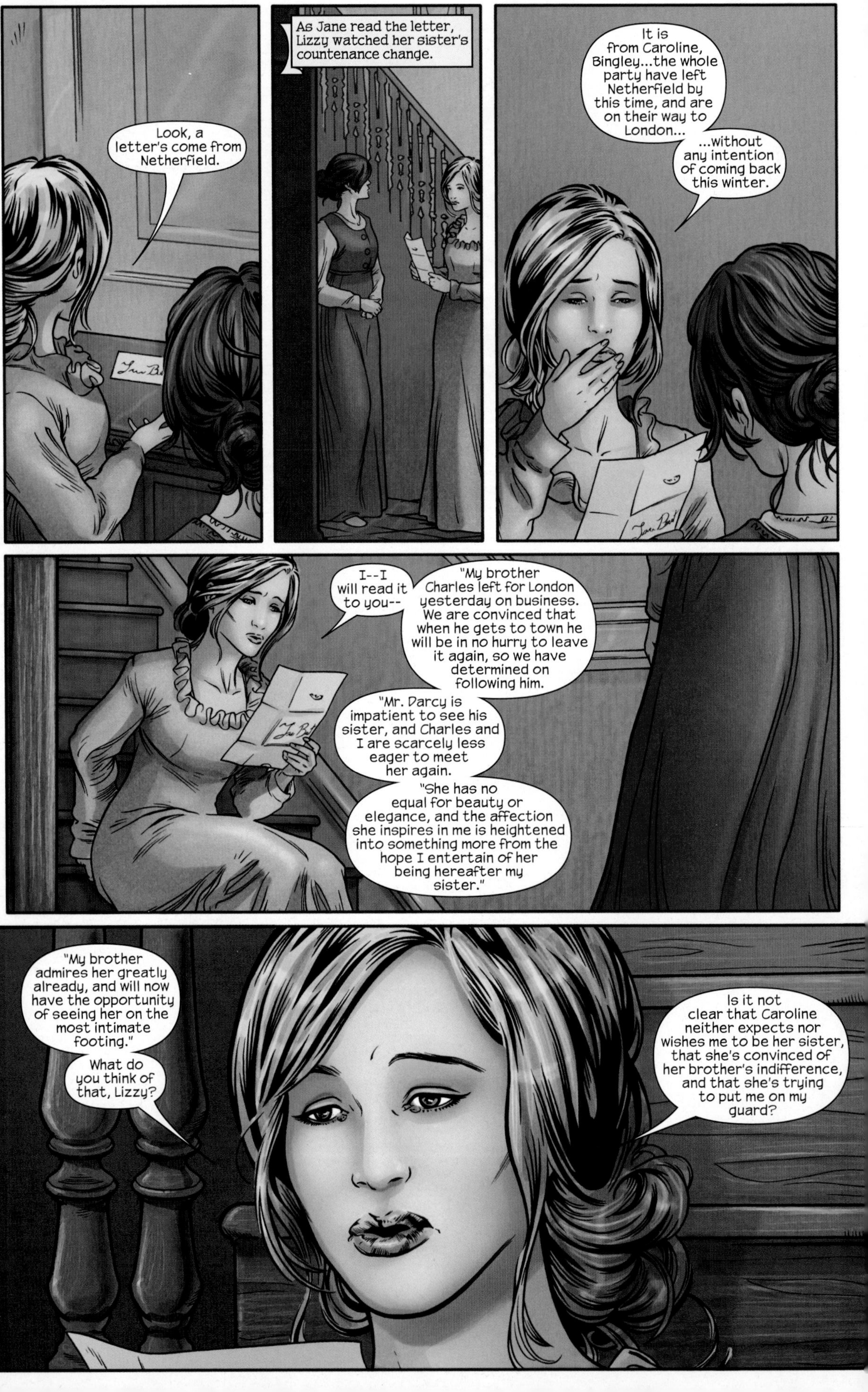

Look, a letter's come from Netherfield.
As Jane read the letter, Lizzy watched her sister's countenance change.
It is from Caroline, Bingley...the whole party have left Netherfield by this time, and are on their way to London...
...without any intention of coming back this winter.
I--I will read it to you--
"My brother Charles left for London yesterday on business. We are convinced that when he gets to town he will be in no hurry to leave it again, so we have determined on following him.
"Mr. Darcy is impatient to see his sister, and Charles and I are scarcely less eager to meet her again.
"She has no equal for beauty or elegance, and the affection she inspires in me is heightened into something more from the hope I entertain of her being hereafter my sister."
"My brother admires her greatly already, and will now have the opportunity of seeing her on the most intimate footing."
What do you think of that, Lizzy?
Is it not clear that Caroline neither expects nor wishes me to be her sister, that she's convinced of her brother's indifference, and that she's trying to put me on my guard?

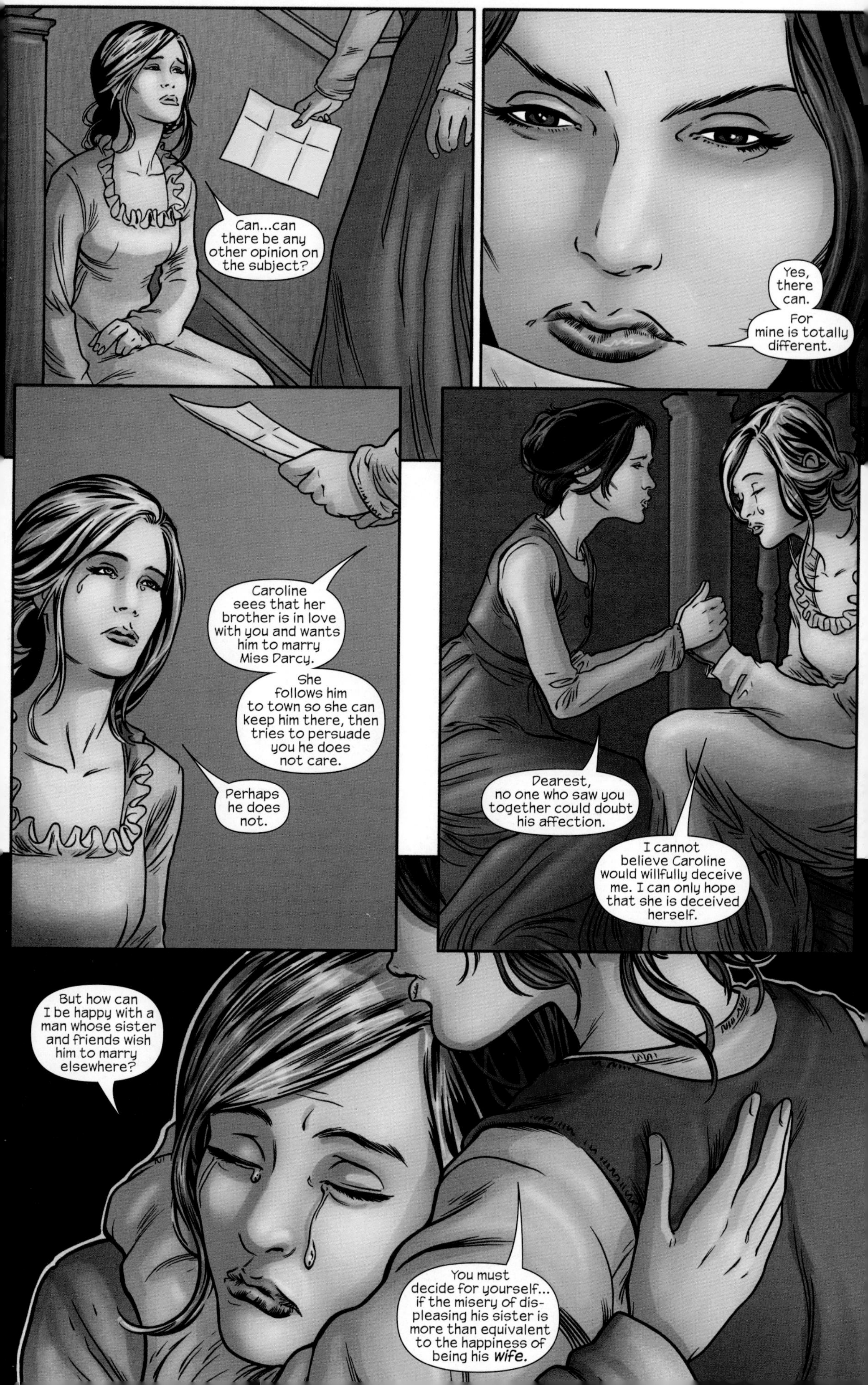
Can...can there be any other opinion on the subject?
Yes, there can.
For mine is totally different.
Caroline sees that her brother is in love with you and wants him to marry Miss Darcy.
She follows him to town so she can keep him there, then tries to persuade you he does not care.
Perhaps he does not.
Dearest, no one who saw you together could doubt his affection.
I cannot believe Caroline would willfully deceive me. I can only hope that she is deceived herself.
But how can I be happy with a man whose sister and friends wish him to marry elsewhere?
You must decide for yourself... if the misery of dis-pleasing his sister is more than equivalent to the happiness of being his *wife.*

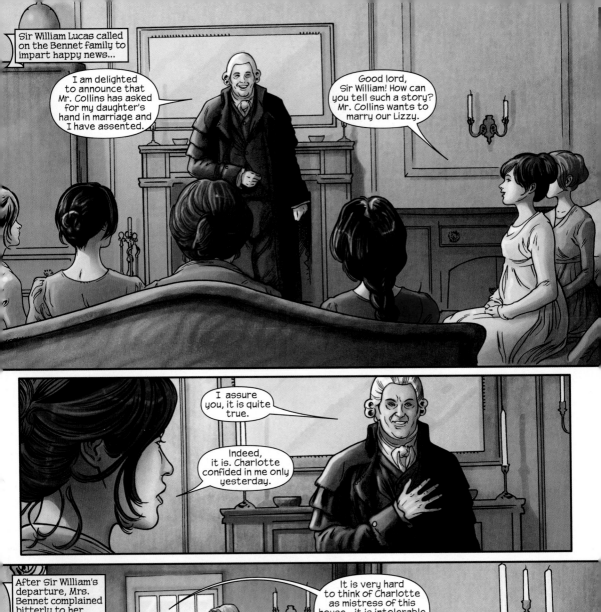

Sir William Lucas called on the Bennet family to impart happy news...

I am delighted to announce that Mr. Collins has asked for my daughter's hand in marriage and I have assented.

Good lord, Sir William! How can you tell such a story? Mr. Collins wants to marry our Lizzy.

I assure you, it is quite true.

Indeed, it is. Charlotte confided in me only yesterday.

After Sir William's departure, Mrs. Bennet complained bitterly to her husband.

It is very hard to think of Charlotte as mistress of this house...it is intolerable that *I* should be forced to make way for *her*.

Don't dwell on gloomy thoughts, my dear. Let us hope for better things.

Let us flatter ourselves that I may be the survivor.

How anyone could entail an estate away from one's own daughters is beyond my understanding.

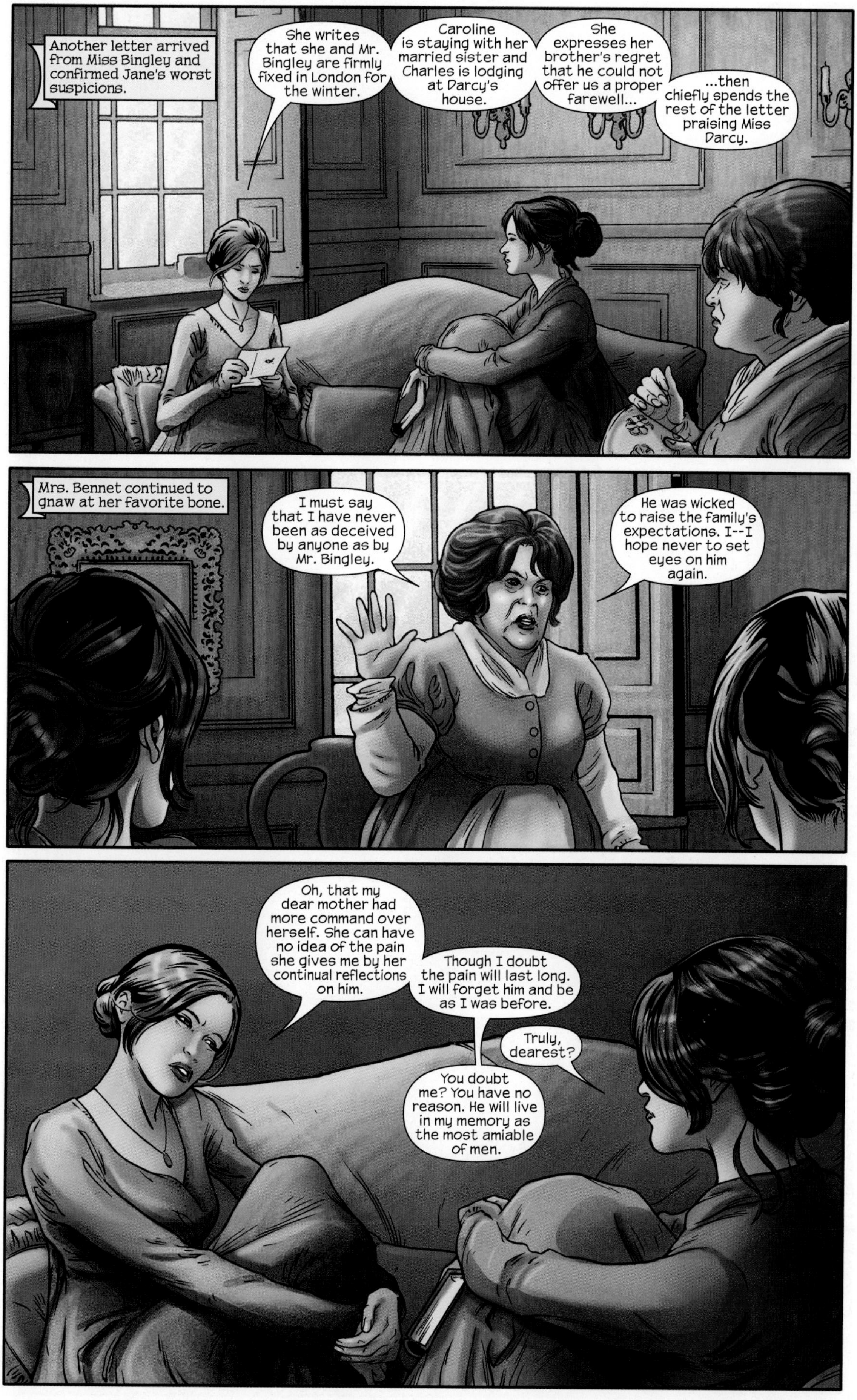

Another letter arrived from Miss Bingley and confirmed Jane's worst suspicions.
She writes that she and Mr. Bingley are firmly fixed in London for the winter.
Caroline is staying with her married sister and Charles is lodging at Darcy's house.
She expresses her brother's regret that he could not offer us a proper farewell...
...then chiefly spends the rest of the letter praising Miss Darcy.
Mrs. Bennet continued to gnaw at her favorite bone.
I must say that I have never been as deceived by anyone as by Mr. Bingley.
He was wicked to raise the family's expectations. I--I hope never to set eyes on him again.
Oh, that my dear mother had more command over herself. She can have no idea of the pain she gives me by her continual reflections on him.
Though I doubt the pain will last long. I will forget him and be as I was before.
Truly, dearest?
You doubt me? You have no reason. He will live in my memory as the most amiable of men.

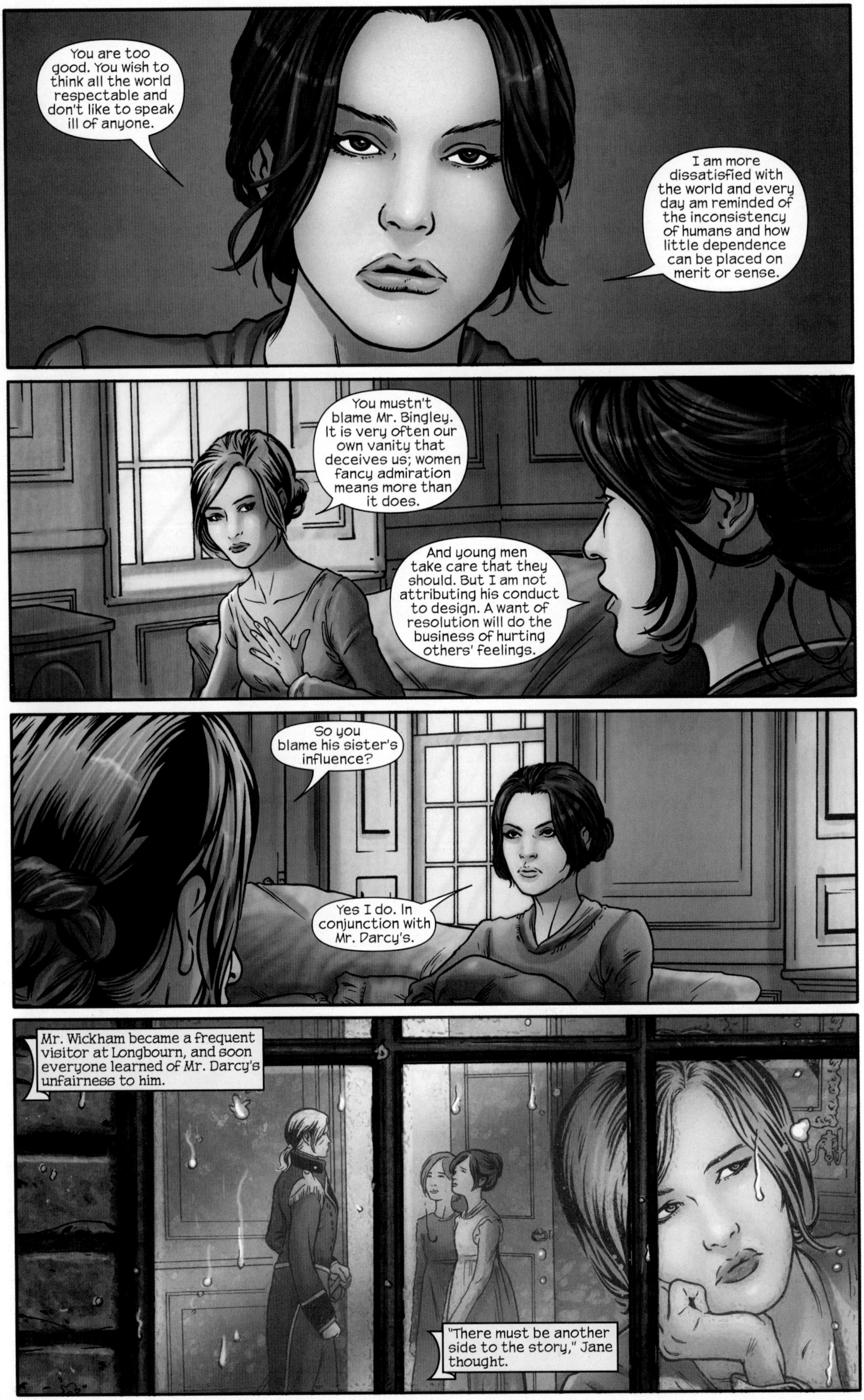
You are too good. You wish to think all the world respectable and don't like to speak ill of anyone.
I am more dissatisfied with the world and every day am reminded of the inconsistency of humans and how little dependence can be placed on merit or sense.
You mustn't blame Mr. Bingley. It is very often our own vanity that deceives us; women fancy admiration means more than it does.
And young men take care that they should. But I am not attributing his conduct to design. A want of resolution will do the business of hurting others' feelings.
So you blame his sister's influence?
Yes I do. In conjunction with Mr. Darcy's.
Mr. Wickham became a frequent visitor at Longbourn, and soon everyone learned of Mr. Darcy's unfairness to him.
"There must be another side to the story," Jane thought.

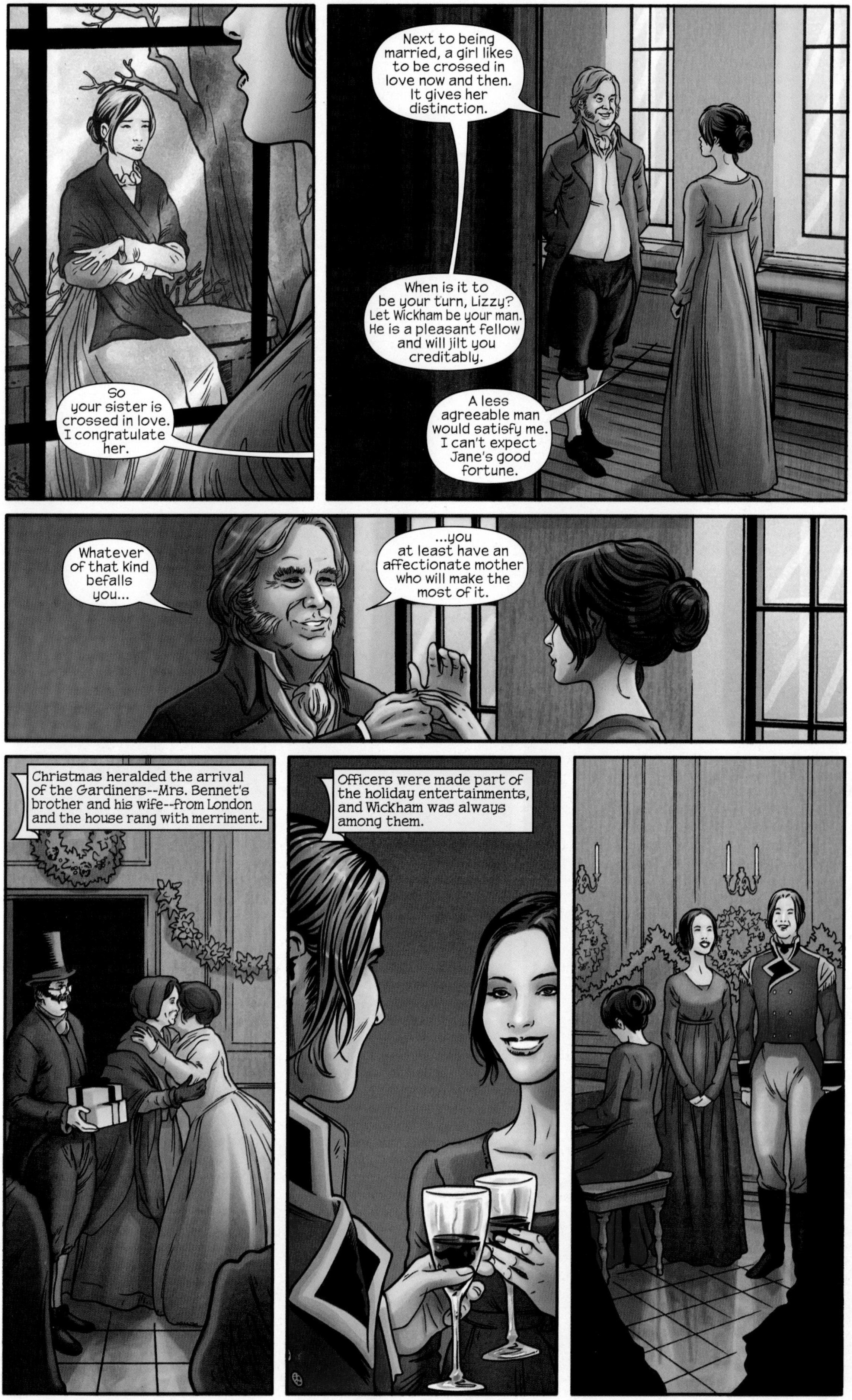

So your sister is crossed in love. I congratulate her.
Next to being married, a girl likes to be crossed in love now and then. It gives her distinction.
When is it to be your turn, Lizzy? Let Wickham be your man. He is a pleasant fellow and will jilt you creditably.
A less agreeable man would satisfy me. I can't expect Jane's good fortune.
Whatever of that kind befalls you...
...you at least have an affectionate mother who will make the most of it.
Christmas heralded the arrival of the Gardiners--Mrs. Bennet's brother and his wife--from London and the house rang with merriment.
Officers were made part of the holiday entertainments, and Wickham was always among them.

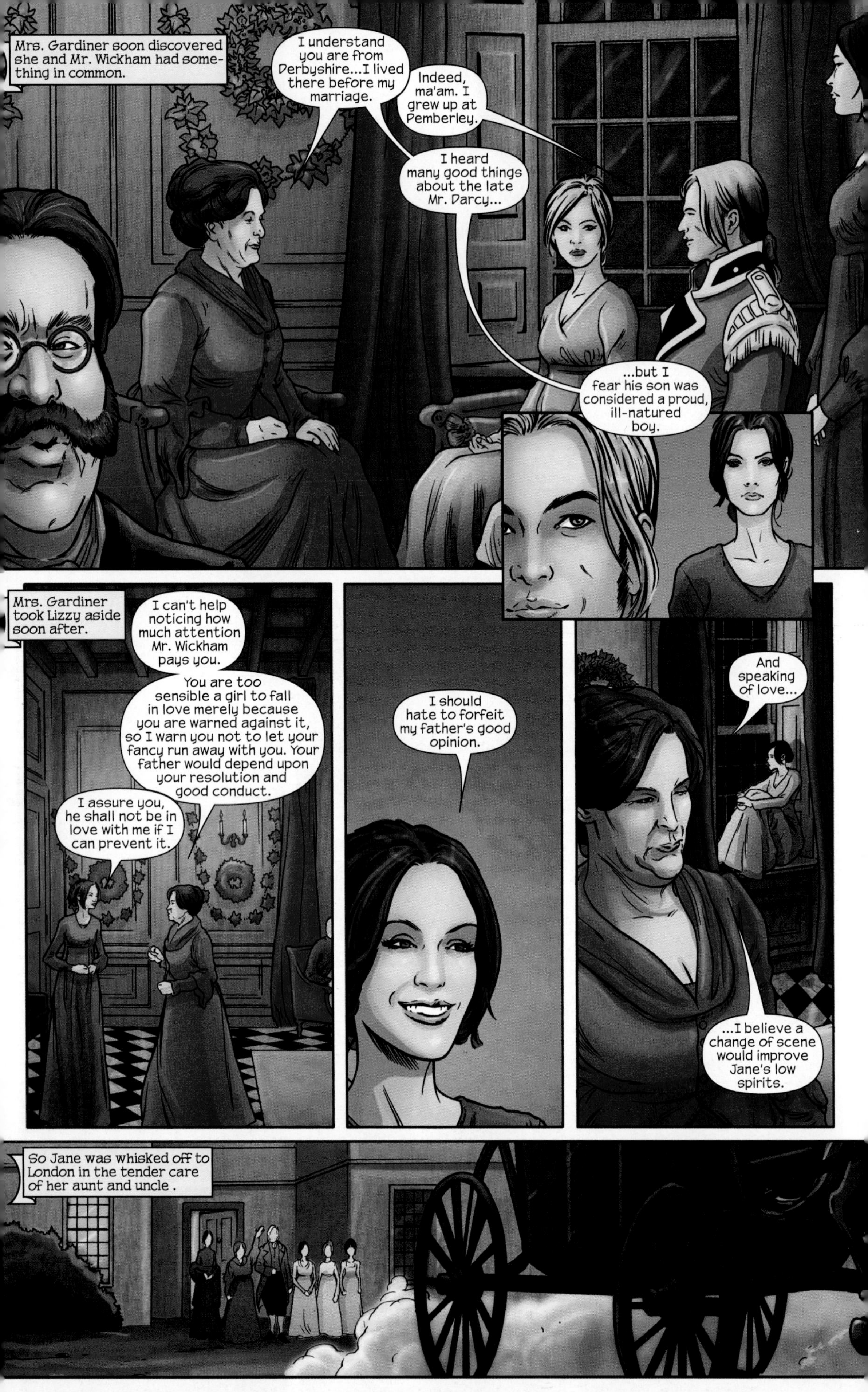
Mrs. Gardiner soon discovered she and Mr. Wickham had something in common.
I understand you are from Derbyshire...I lived there before my marriage.
Indeed, ma'am. I grew up at Pemberley.
I heard many good things about the late Mr. Darcy...
...but I fear his son was considered a proud, ill-natured boy.
Mrs. Gardiner took Lizzy aside soon after.
I can't help noticing how much attention Mr. Wickham pays you.
You are too sensible a girl to fall in love merely because you are warned against it, so I warn you not to let your fancy run away with you. Your father would depend upon your resolution and good conduct.
I assure you, he shall not be in love with me if I can prevent it.
I should hate to forfeit my father's good opinion.
And speaking of love...
...I believe a change of scene would improve Jane's low spirits.
So Jane was whisked off to London in the tender care of her aunt and uncle .

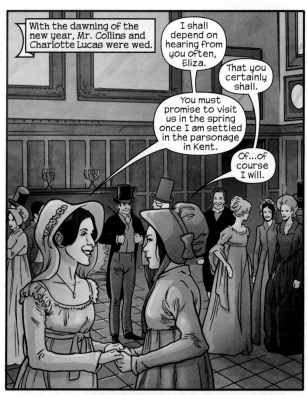

With the dawning of the new year, Mr. Collins and Charlotte Lucas were wed.

I shall depend on hearing from you often, Eliza.

That you certainly shall.

You must promise to visit us in the spring once I am settled in the parsonage in Kent.

Of...of course I will.

Not long after, Lizzy was shopping with her Aunt Phillips in Meryton.

Who is that with Mr. Wickham?

She is a Miss King, an heiress recently come into ten thousand pounds.

Mr. Wickham seems quite taken with her.

How fortunate I listened to my Aunt Gardiner.

I am quite sure I am not in love with him.

Miss Bingley called upon Jane in London...

I'm sorry it took me so long to respond to your note. One finds so many delightful things to do in Town.

Your brother is well?

Of course. He adores London.

And speaking of Charles, I must be off. He is expecting me to dine with him at the Darcys.

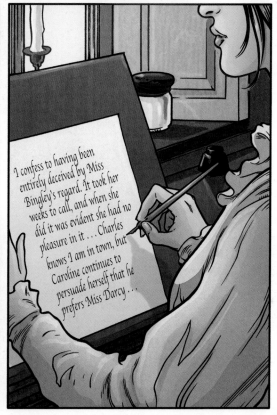

I confess to having been entirely deceived by Miss Bingley's regard. It took her weeks to call, and when she did it was evident she had no pleasure in it... Charles knows I am in town, but Caroline continues to persuade herself that he prefers Miss Darcy...

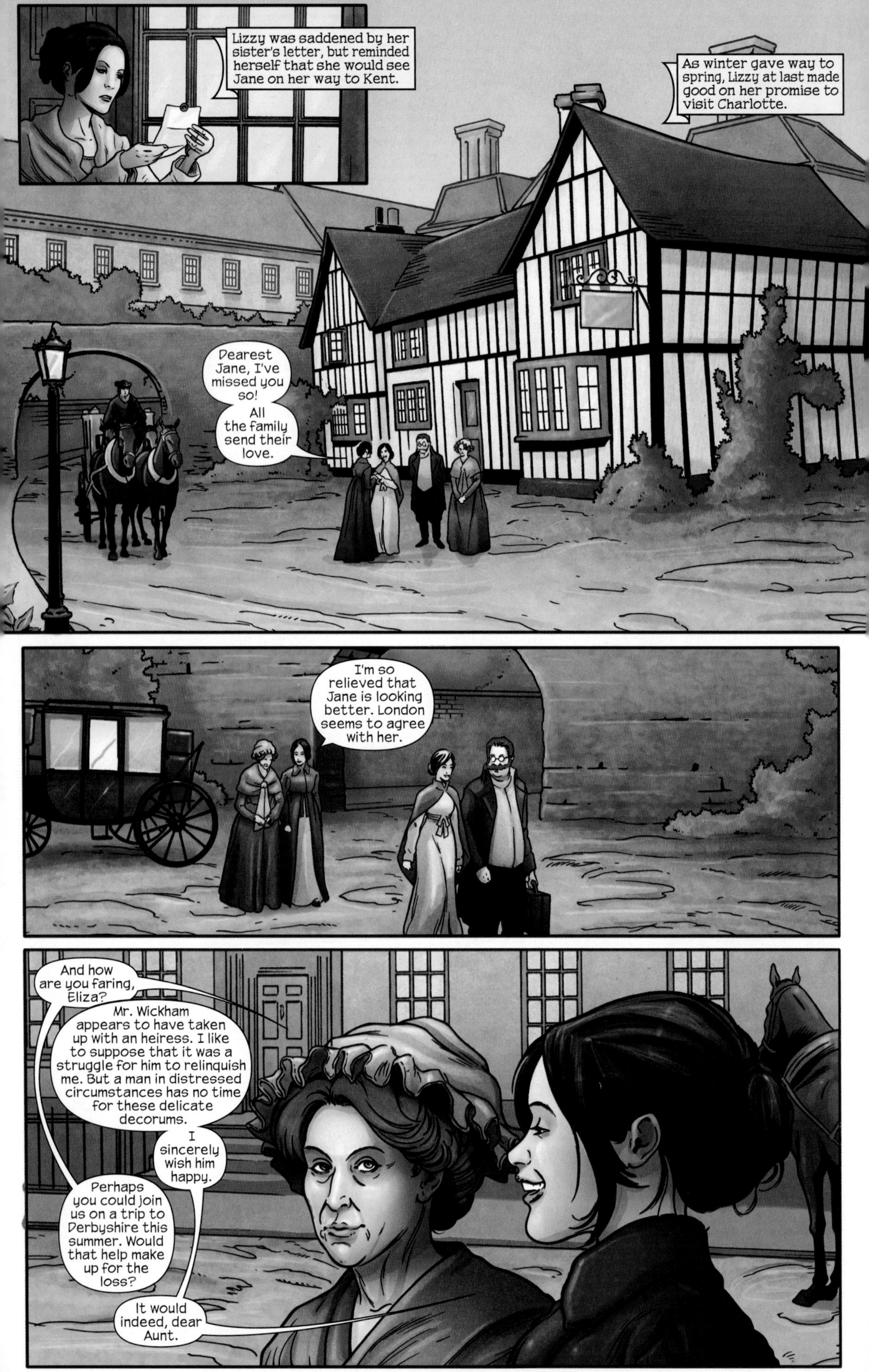
Lizzy was saddened by her sister's letter, but reminded herself that she would see Jane on her way to Kent.
As winter gave way to spring, Lizzy at last made good on her promise to visit Charlotte.
Dearest Jane, I've missed you so!
All the family send their love.
I'm so relieved that Jane is looking better. London seems to agree with her.
And how are you faring, Eliza?
Mr. Wickham appears to have taken up with an heiress. I like to suppose that it was a struggle for him to relinquish me. But a man in distressed circumstances has no time for these delicate decorums.
I sincerely wish him happy.
Perhaps you could join us on a trip to Derbyshire this summer. Would that help make up for the loss?
It would indeed, dear Aunt.

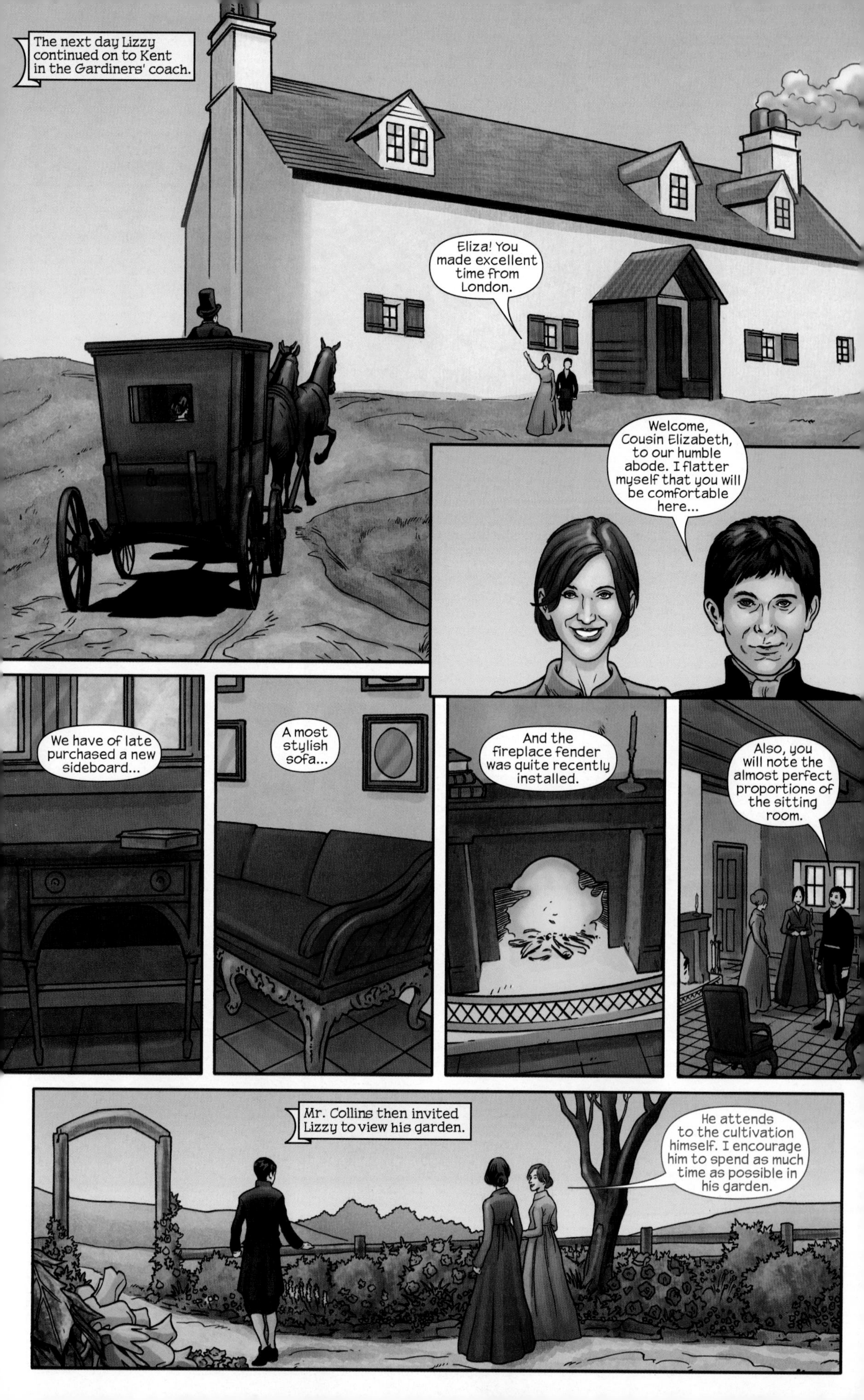
The next day Lizzy continued on to Kent in the Gardiners' coach.
Eliza! You made excellent time from London.
Welcome, Cousin Elizabeth, to our humble abode. I flatter myself that you will be comfortable here...
We have of late purchased a new sideboard...
A most stylish sofa...
And the fireplace fender was quite recently installed.
Also, you will note the almost perfect proportions of the sitting room.
Mr. Collins then invited Lizzy to view his garden.
He attends to the cultivation himself. I encourage him to spend as much time as possible in his garden.

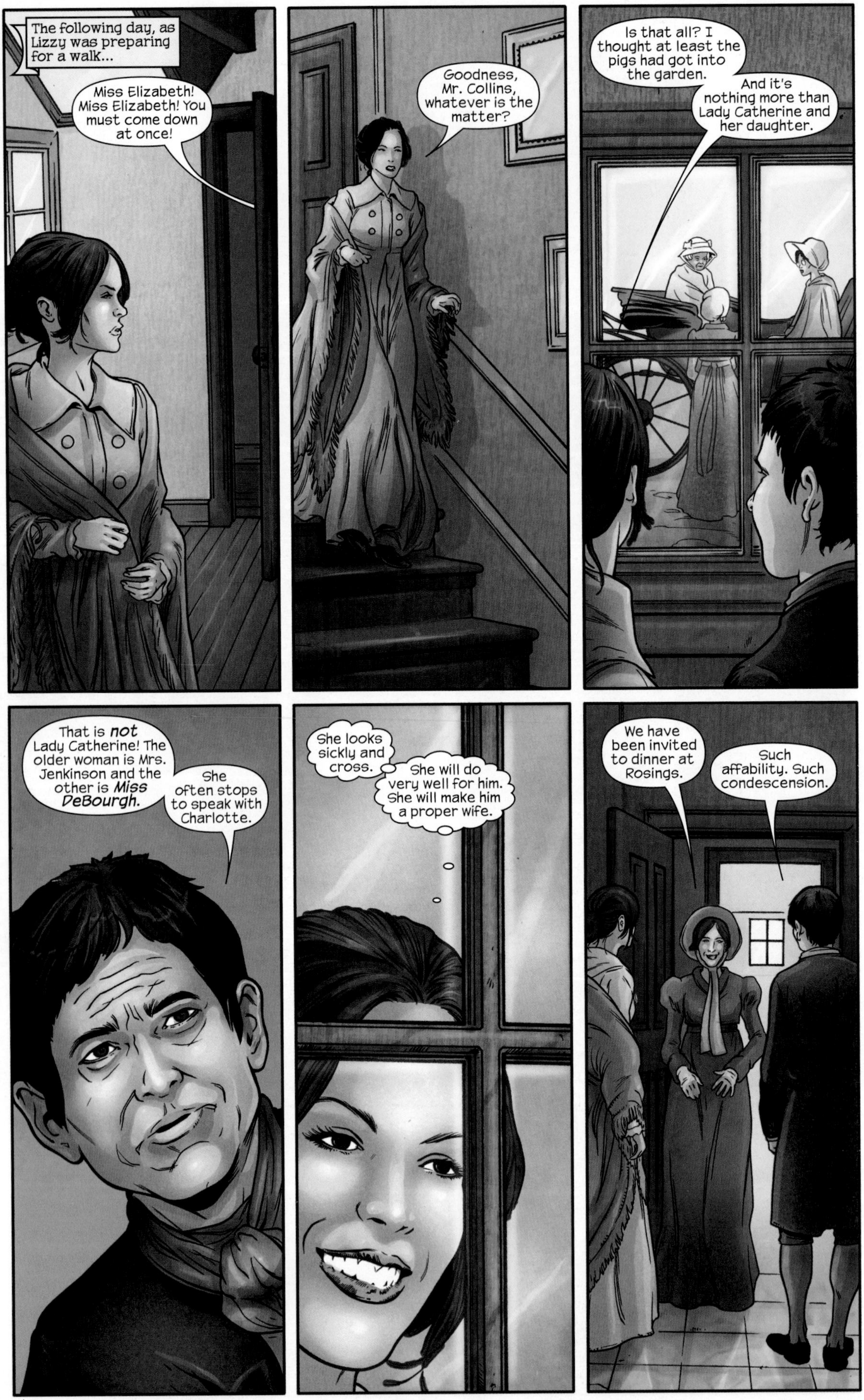
The following day, as Lizzy was preparing for a walk...
Miss Elizabeth! Miss Elizabeth! You must come down at once!
Goodness, Mr. Collins, whatever is the matter?
Is that all? I thought at least the pigs had got into the garden.
And it's nothing more than Lady Catherine and her daughter.
That is *not* Lady Catherine! The older woman is Mrs. Jenkinson and the other is *Miss DeBourgh.*
She often stops to speak with Charlotte.
She looks sickly and cross.
She will do very well for him. She will make him a proper wife.
We have been invited to dinner at Rosings.
Such affability. Such condescension.

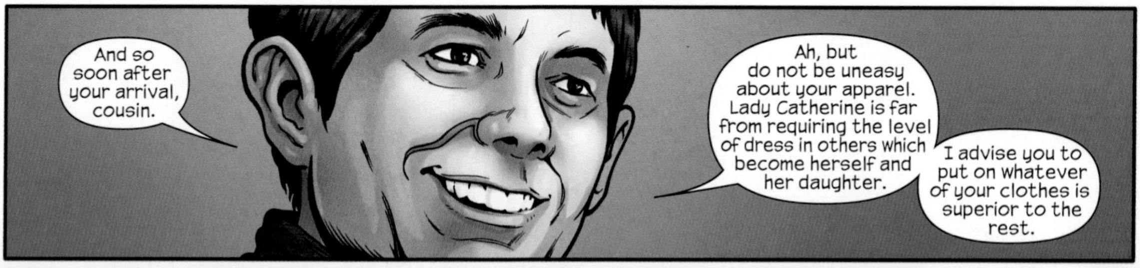
And so soon after your arrival, cousin.
Ah, but do not be uneasy about your apparel. Lady Catherine is far from requiring the level of dress in others which become herself and her daughter.
I advise you to put on whatever of your clothes is superior to the rest.

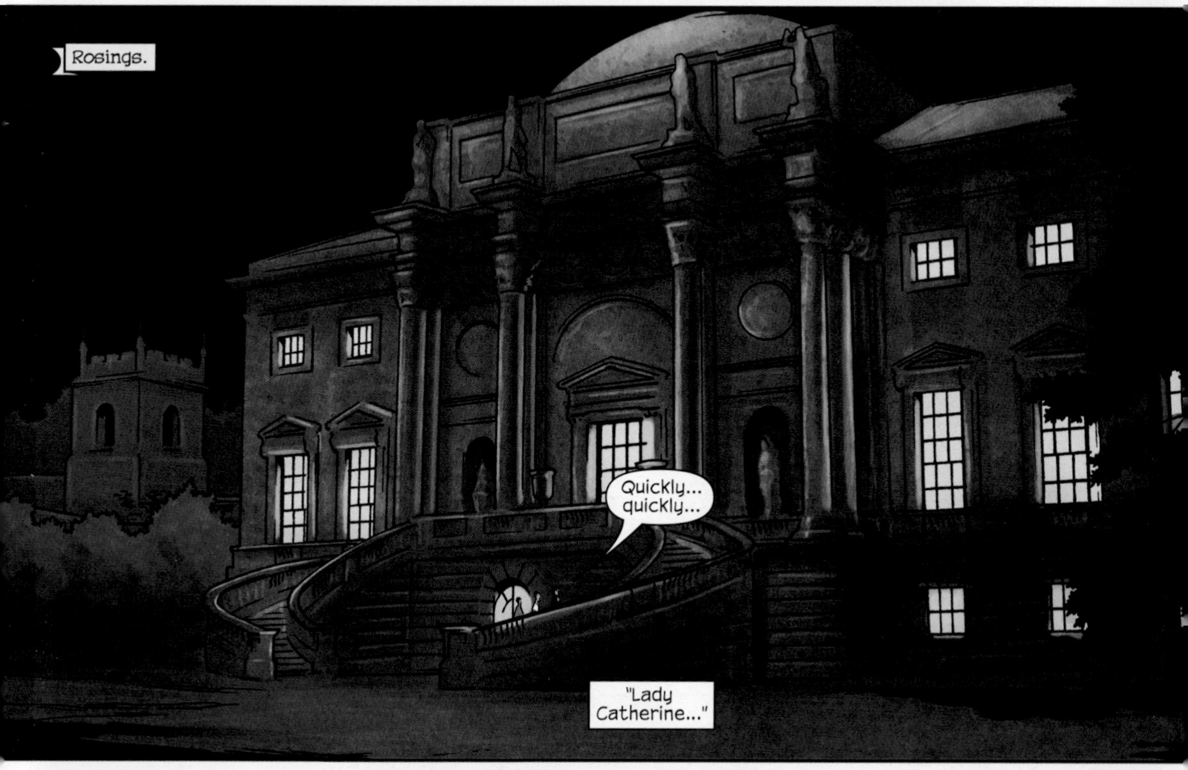
Rosings.
Quickly... quickly...
"Lady Catherine..."

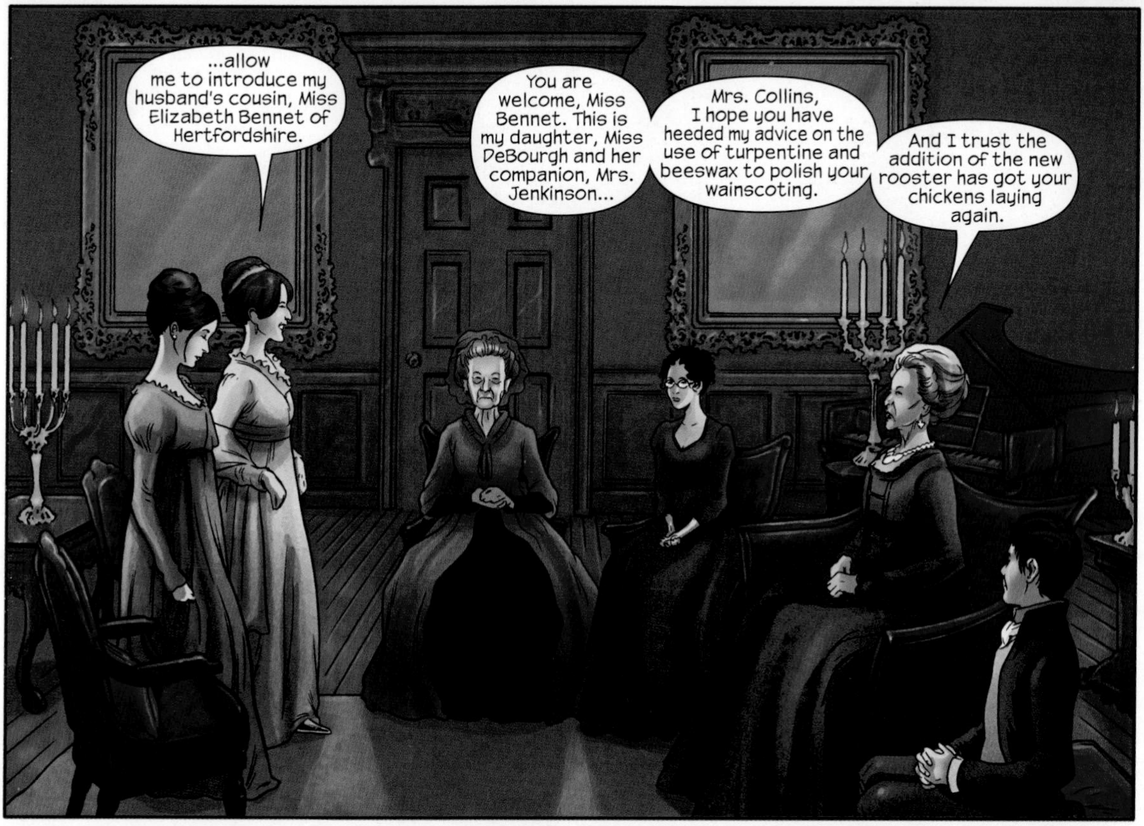
...allow me to introduce my husband's cousin, Miss Elizabeth Bennet of Hertfordshire.
You are welcome, Miss Bennet. This is my daughter, Miss DeBourgh and her companion, Mrs. Jenkinson...
Mrs. Collins, I hope you have heeded my advice on the use of turpentine and beeswax to polish your wainscoting.
And I trust the addition of the new rooster has got your chickens laying again.

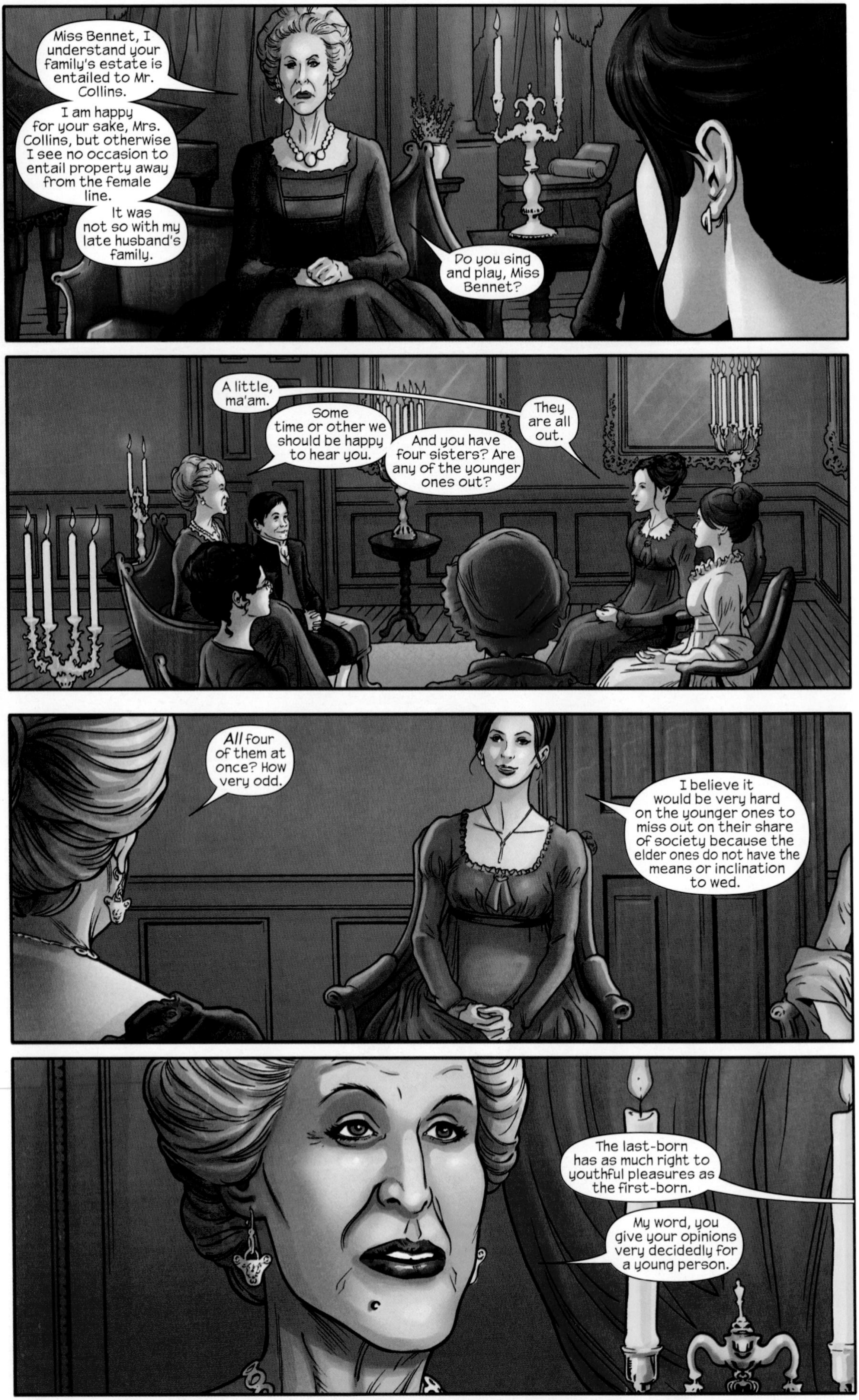
Miss Bennet, I understand your family's estate is entailed to Mr. Collins.
I am happy for your sake, Mrs. Collins, but otherwise I see no occasion to entail property away from the female line.
It was not so with my late husband's family.
Do you sing and play, Miss Bennet?
A little, ma'am.
Some time or other we should be happy to hear you.
And you have four sisters? Are any of the younger ones out?
They are all out.
All four of them at once? How very odd.
I believe it would be very hard on the younger ones to miss out on their share of society because the elder ones do not have the means or inclination to wed.
The last-born has as much right to youthful pleasures as the first-born.
My word, you give your opinions very decidedly for a young person.

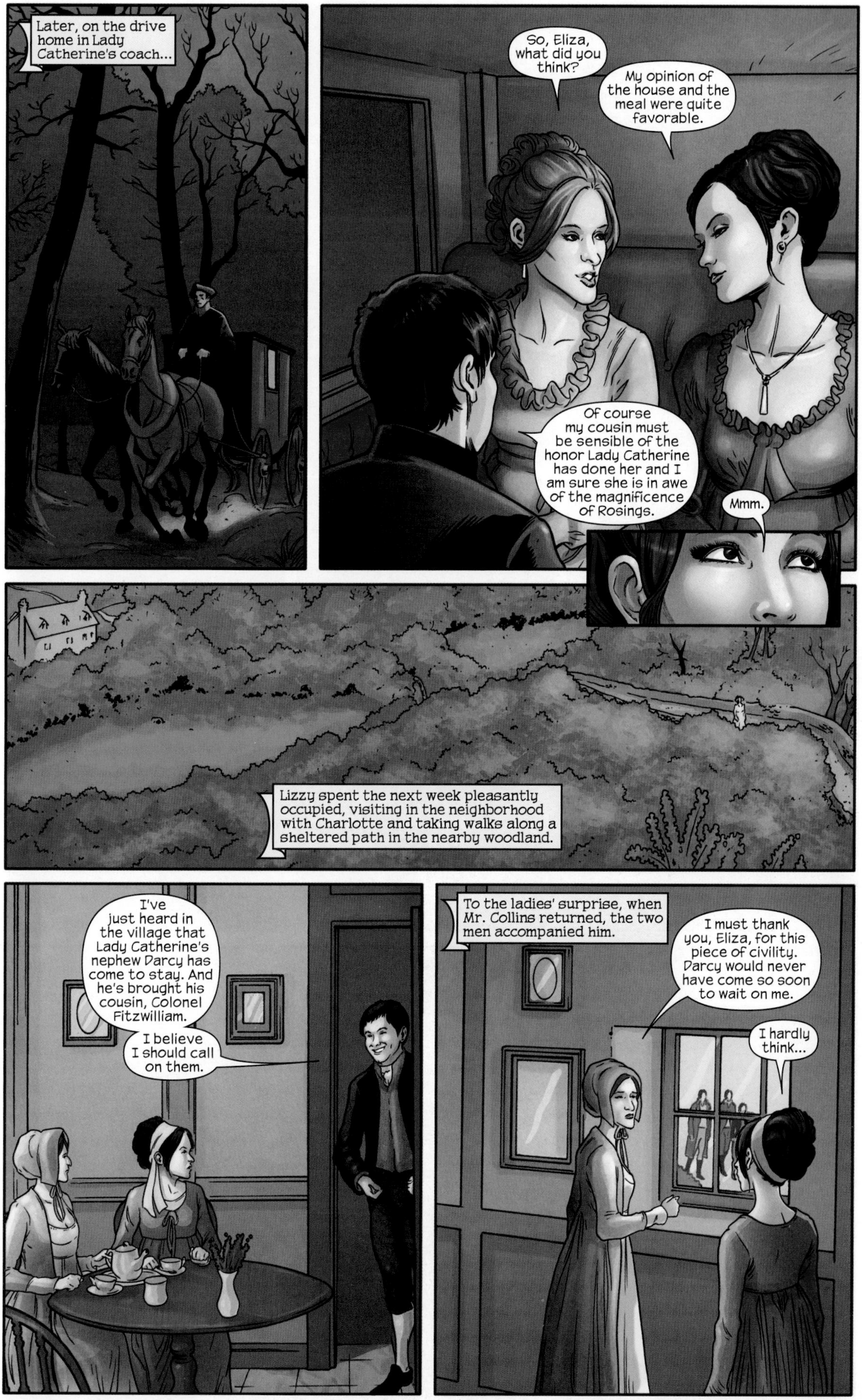
Later, on the drive home in Lady Catherine's coach...
So, Eliza, what did you think?
My opinion of the house and the meal were quite favorable.
Of course my cousin must be sensible of the honor Lady Catherine has done her and I am sure she is in awe of the magnificence of Rosings.
Mmm.
Lizzy spent the next week pleasantly occupied, visiting in the neighborhood with Charlotte and taking walks along a sheltered path in the nearby woodland.
I've just heard in the village that Lady Catherine's nephew Darcy has come to stay. And he's brought his cousin, Colonel Fitzwilliam.
I believe I should call on them.
To the ladies' surprise, when Mr. Collins returned, the two men accompanied him.
I must thank you, Eliza, for this piece of civility. Darcy would never have come so soon to wait on me.
I hardly think...

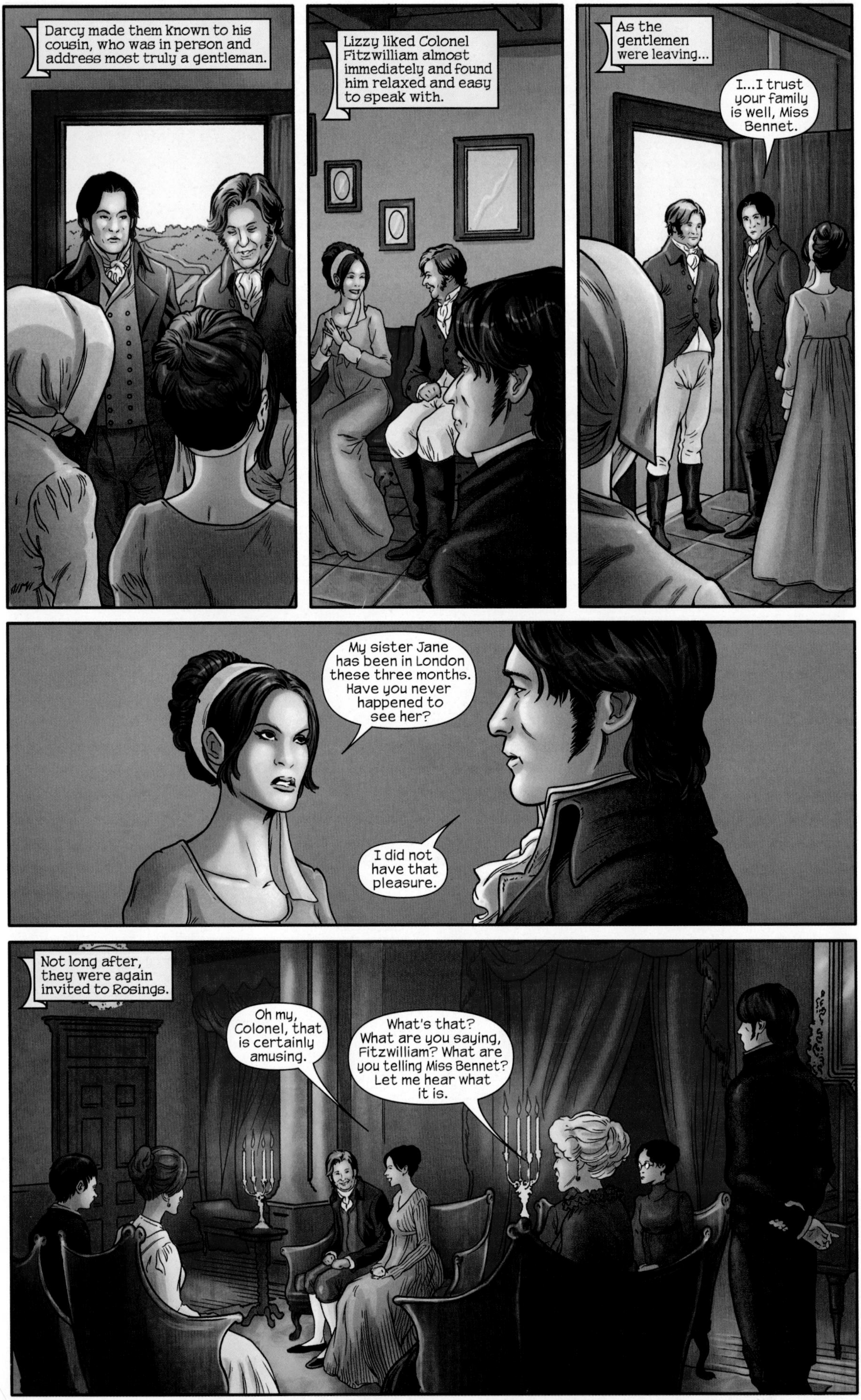
Darcy made them known to his cousin, who was in person and address most truly a gentleman.
Lizzy liked Colonel Fitzwilliam almost immediately and found him relaxed and easy to speak with.
As the gentlemen were leaving...
I...I trust your family is well, Miss Bennet.
My sister Jane has been in London these three months. Have you never happened to see her?
I did not have that pleasure.
Not long after, they were again invited to Rosings.
Oh my, Colonel, that is certainly amusing.
What's that? What are you saying, Fitzwilliam? What are you telling Miss Bennet? Let me hear what it is.

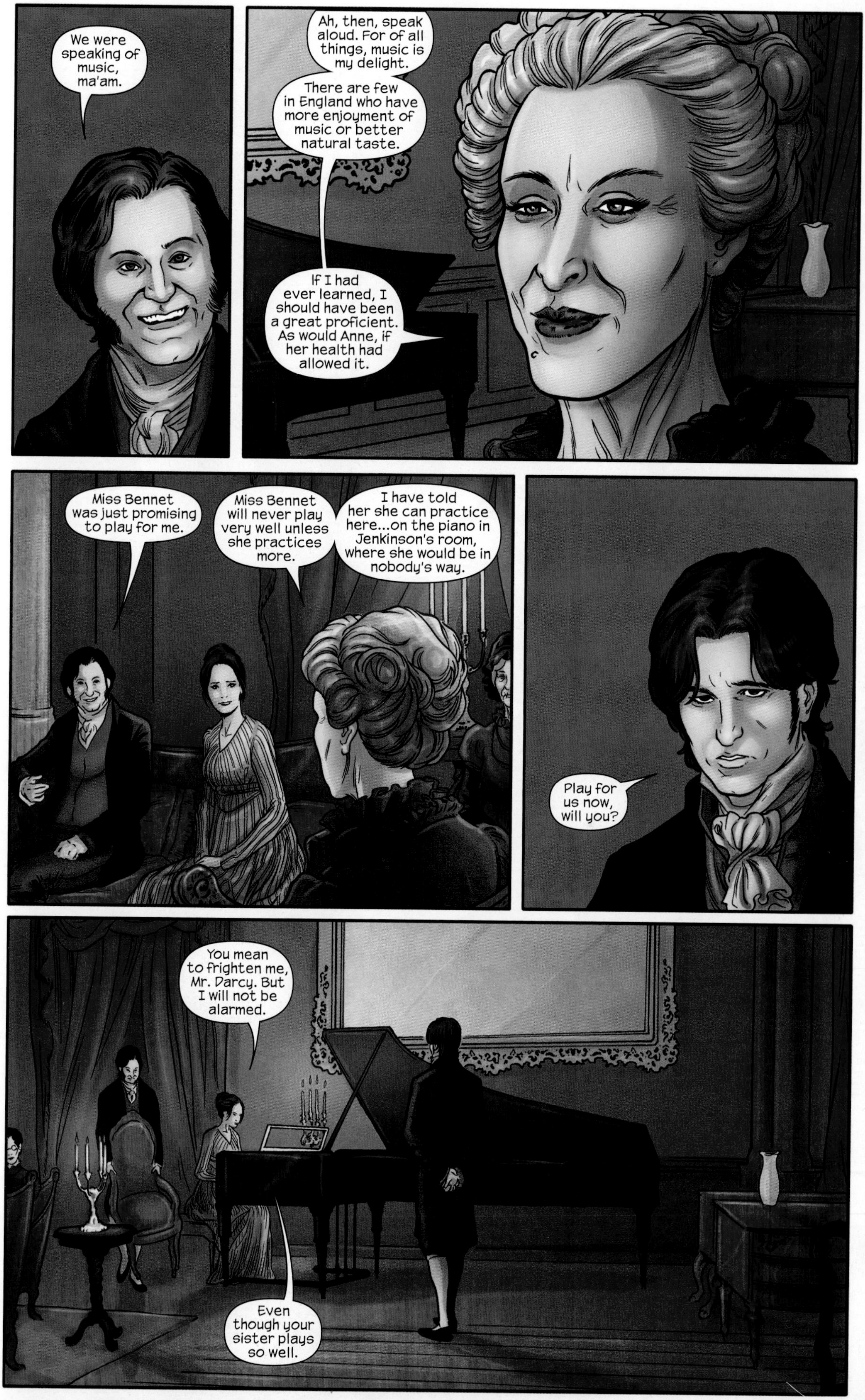
We were speaking of music, ma'am.
Ah, then, speak aloud. For of all things, music is my delight.
There are few in England who have more enjoyment of music or better natural taste.
If I had ever learned, I should have been a great proficient. As would Anne, if her health had allowed it.
Miss Bennet was just promising to play for me.
Miss Bennet will never play very well unless she practices more.
I have told her she can practice here...on the piano in Jenkinson's room, where she would be in nobody's way.
Play for us now, will you?
You mean to frighten me, Mr. Darcy. But I will not be alarmed.
Even though your sister plays so well.

There is a stubbornness about me that can never bear to be frightened at the will of others.

My courage always rises with every attempt to intimidate me.

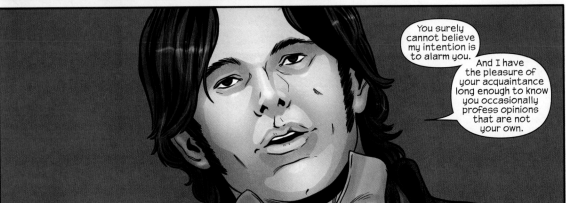

You surely cannot believe my intention is to alarm you. And I have the pleasure of your acquaintance long enough to know you occasionally profess opinions that are not your own.

Colonel, your cousin will teach you not to believe anything I say.

Mr. Darcy, don't provoke me to retaliate, or such things may come out as will shock your relations to hear.

I am not afraid of you.

Pray, tell us what you have to accuse him of. I'd like to know how he behaves among strangers.

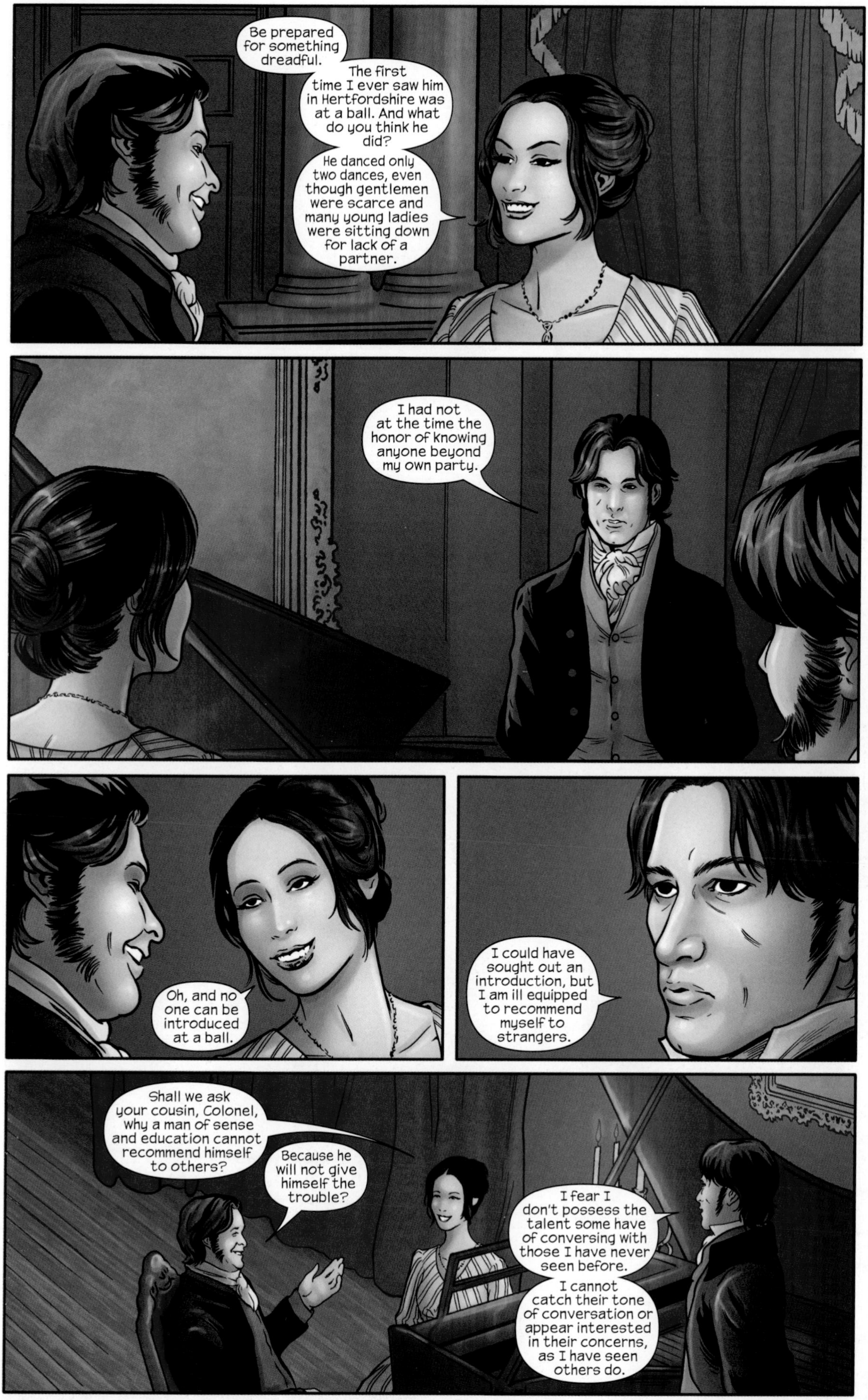
Be prepared for something dreadful.
The first time I ever saw him in Hertfordshire was at a ball. And what do you think he did?
He danced only two dances, even though gentlemen were scarce and many young ladies were sitting down for lack of a partner.
I had not at the time the honor of knowing anyone beyond my own party.
Oh, and no one can be introduced at a ball.
I could have sought out an introduction, but I am ill equipped to recommend myself to strangers.
Shall we ask your cousin, Colonel, why a man of sense and education cannot recommend himself to others?
Because he will not give himself the trouble?
I fear I don't possess the talent some have of conversing with those I have never seen before.
I cannot catch their tone of conversation or appear interested in their concerns, as I have seen others do.

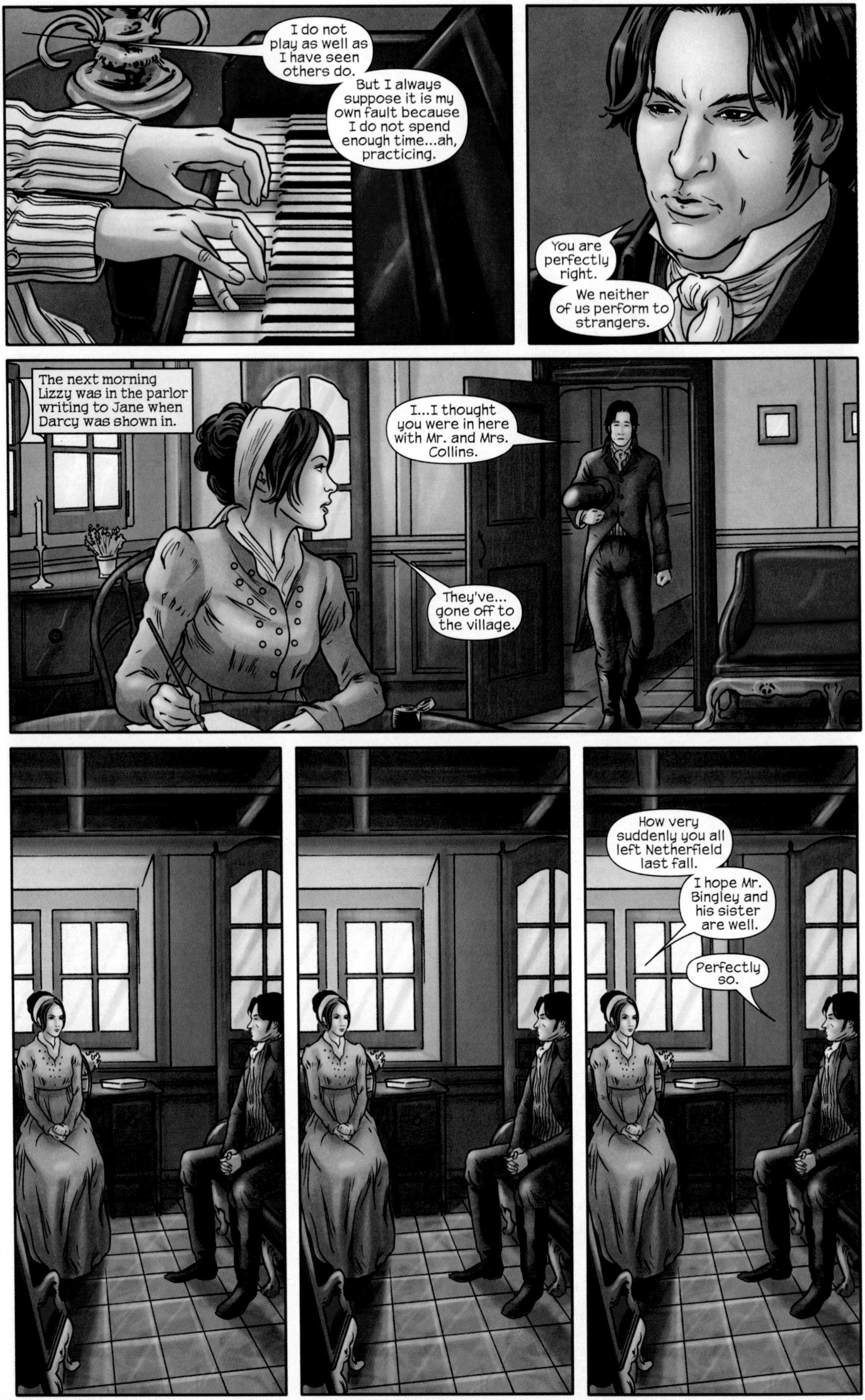
I do not play as well as I have seen others do.
But I always suppose it is my own fault because I do not spend enough time...ah, practicing.
You are perfectly right.
We neither of us perform to strangers.
The next morning Lizzy was in the parlor writing to Jane when Darcy was shown in.
I...I thought you were in here with Mr. and Mrs. Collins.
They've... gone off to the village.
How very suddenly you all left Netherfield last fall.
I hope Mr. Bingley and his sister are well.
Perfectly so.

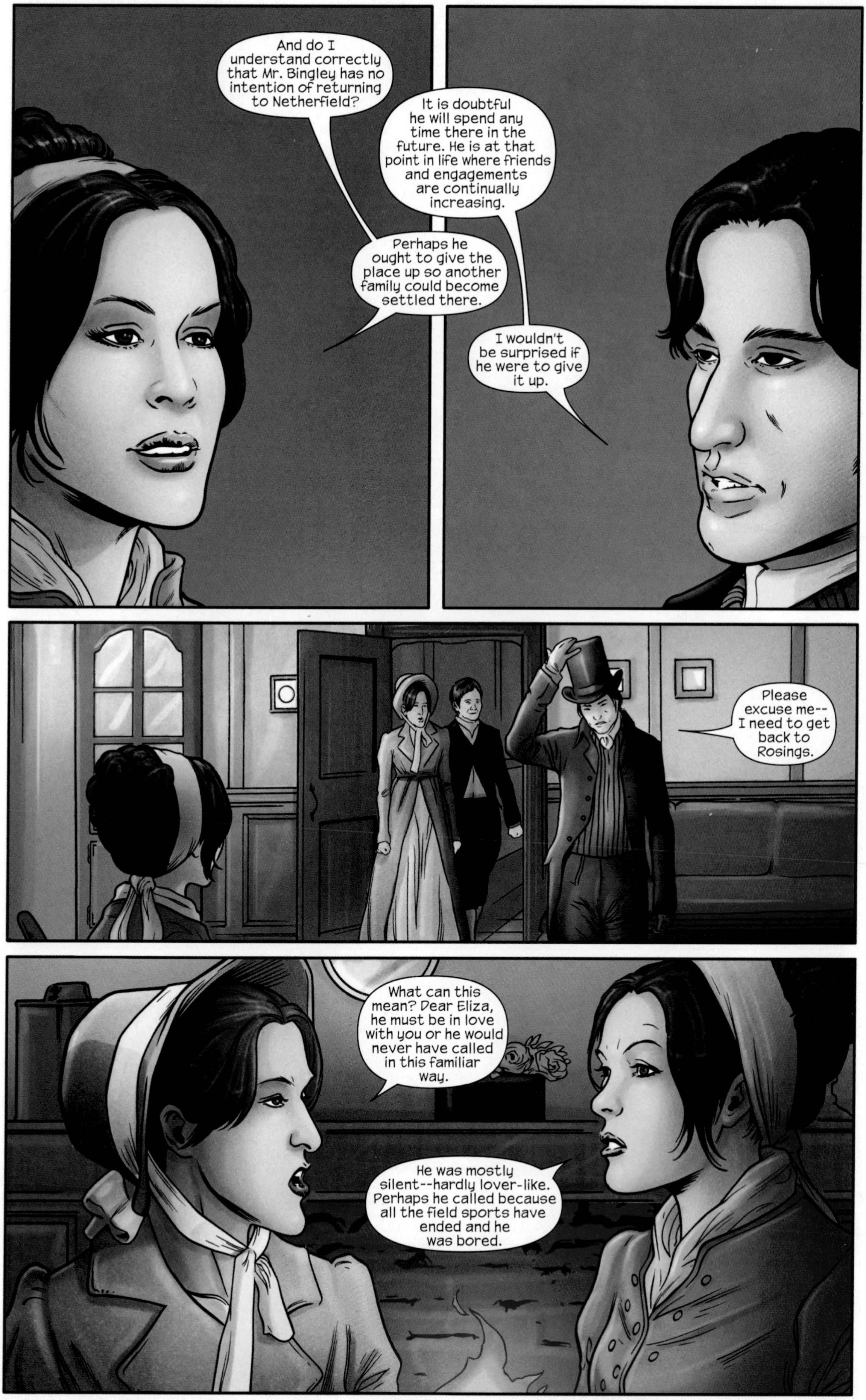
And do I understand correctly that Mr. Bingley has no intention of returning to Netherfield?
It is doubtful he will spend any time there in the future. He is at that point in life where friends and engagements are continually increasing.
Perhaps he ought to give the place up so another family could become settled there.
I wouldn't be surprised if he were to give it up.
Please excuse me-- I need to get back to Rosings.
What can this mean? Dear Eliza, he must be in love with you or he would never have called in this familiar way.
He was mostly silent--hardly lover-like. Perhaps he called because all the field sports have ended and he was bored.

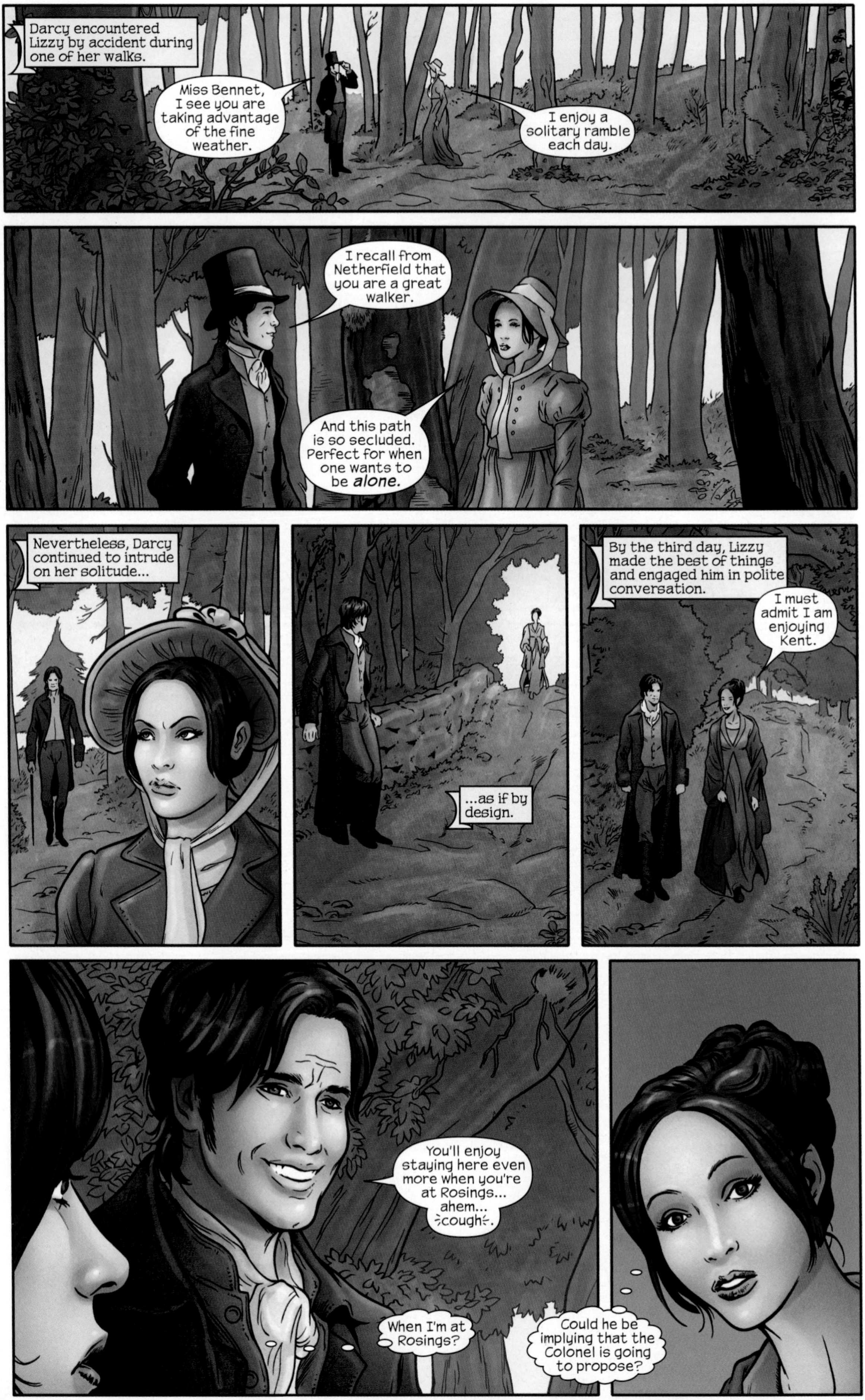
Darcy encountered Lizzy by accident during one of her walks.
Miss Bennet, I see you are taking advantage of the fine weather.
I enjoy a solitary ramble each day.
I recall from Netherfield that you are a great walker.
And this path is so secluded. Perfect for when one wants to be *alone.*
Nevertheless, Darcy continued to intrude on her solitude...
...as if by design.
By the third day, Lizzy made the best of things and engaged him in polite conversation.
I must admit I am enjoying Kent.
You'll enjoy staying here even more when you're at Rosings... ahem... cough.
When I'm at Rosings?
Could he be implying that the Colonel is going to propose?

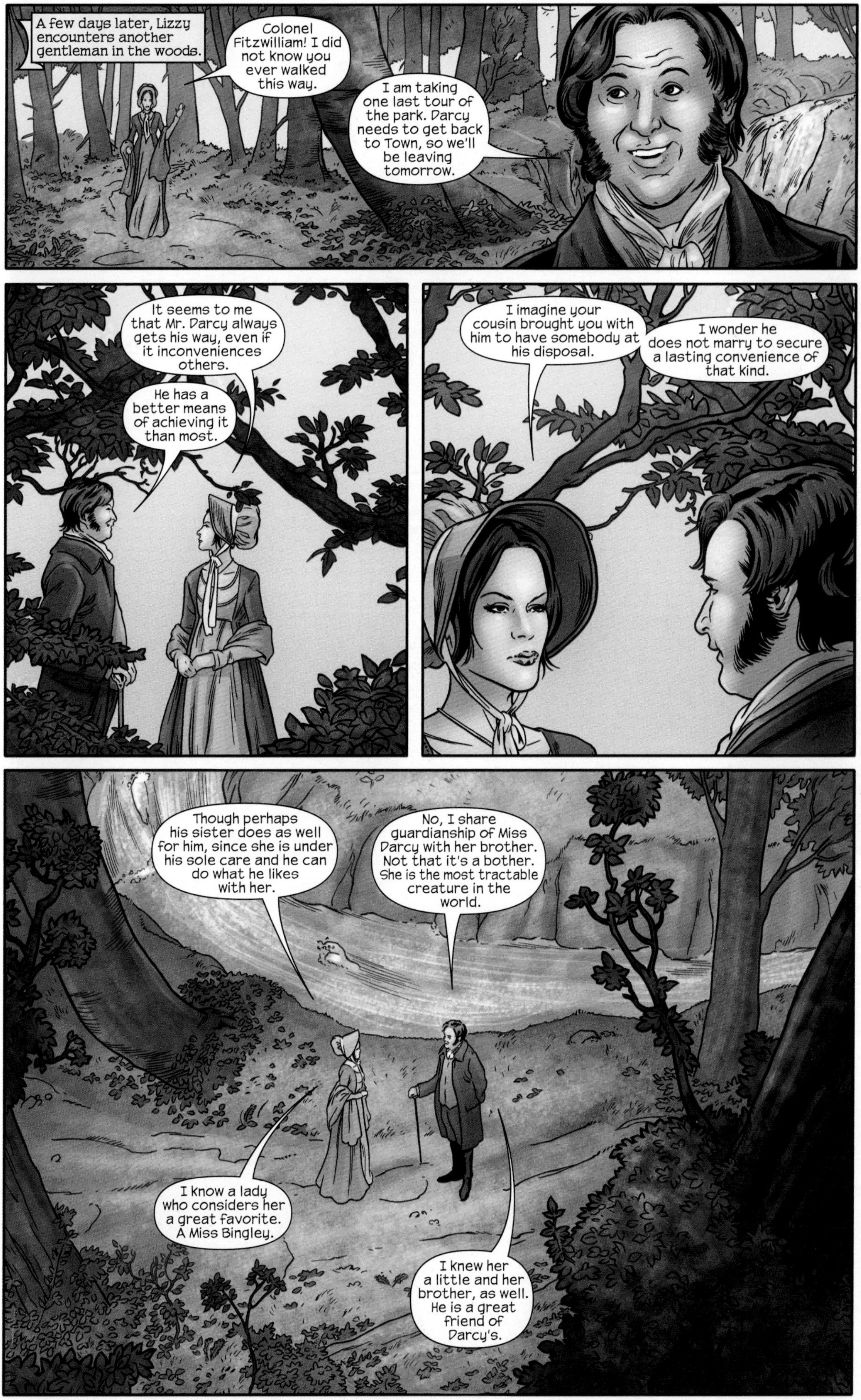
A few days later, Lizzy encounters another gentleman in the woods.
Colonel Fitzwilliam! I did not know you ever walked this way.
I am taking one last tour of the park. Darcy needs to get back to Town, so we'll be leaving tomorrow.
It seems to me that Mr. Darcy always gets his way, even if it inconveniences others.
He has a better means of achieving it than most.
I imagine your cousin brought you with him to have somebody at his disposal.
I wonder he does not marry to secure a lasting convenience of that kind.
Though perhaps his sister does as well for him, since she is under his sole care and he can do what he likes with her.
No, I share guardianship of Miss Darcy with her brother. Not that it's a bother. She is the most tractable creature in the world.
I know a lady who considers her a great favorite. A Miss Bingley.
I knew her a little and her brother, as well. He is a great friend of Darcy's.

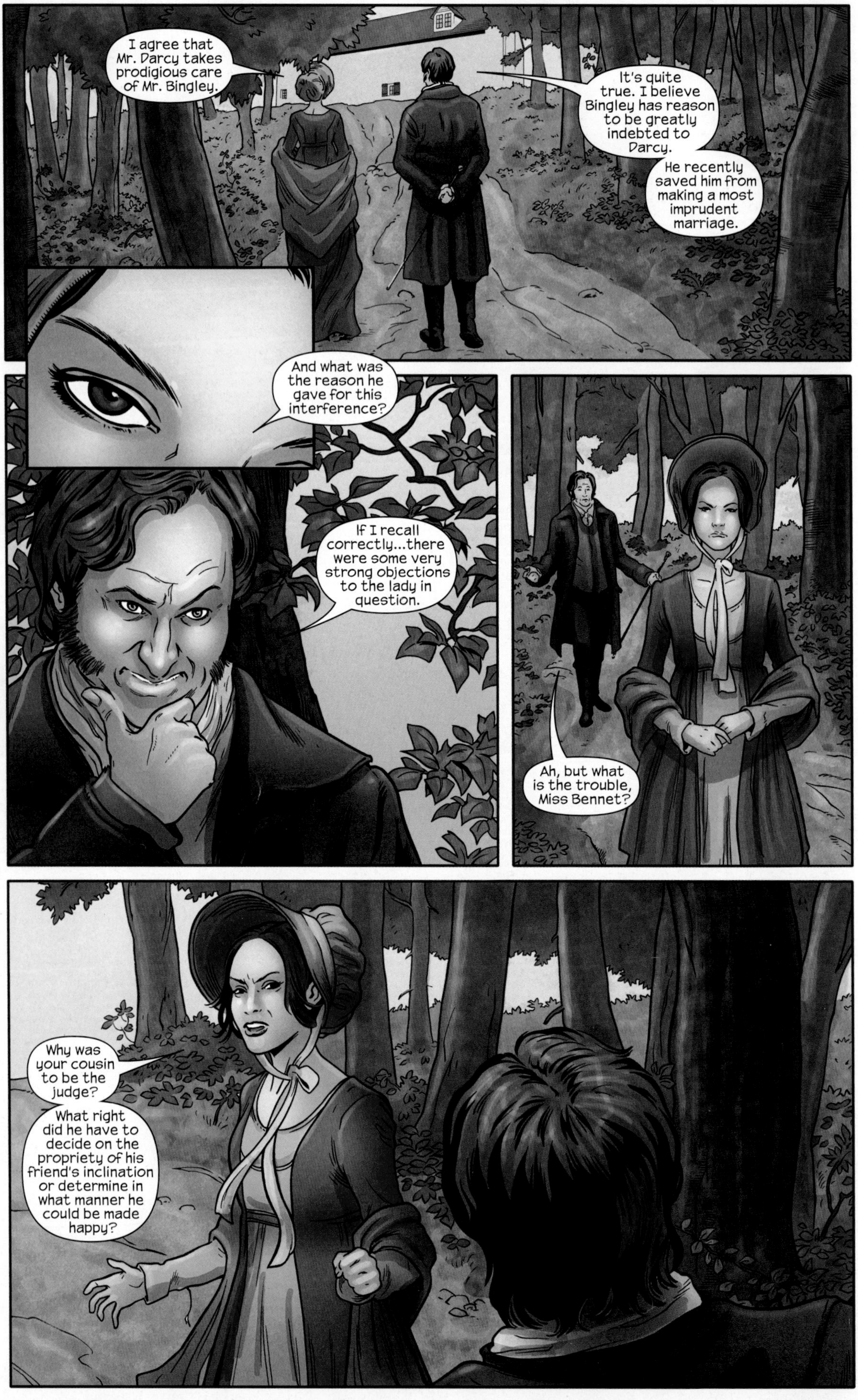
I agree that Mr. Darcy takes prodigious care of Mr. Bingley.
It's quite true. I believe Bingley has reason to be greatly indebted to Darcy.
He recently saved him from making a most imprudent marriage.
And what was the reason he gave for this interference?
If I recall correctly...there were some very strong objections to the lady in question.
Ah, but what is the trouble, Miss Bennet?
Why was your cousin to be the judge?
What right did he have to decide on the propriety of his friend's inclination or determine in what manner he could be made happy?

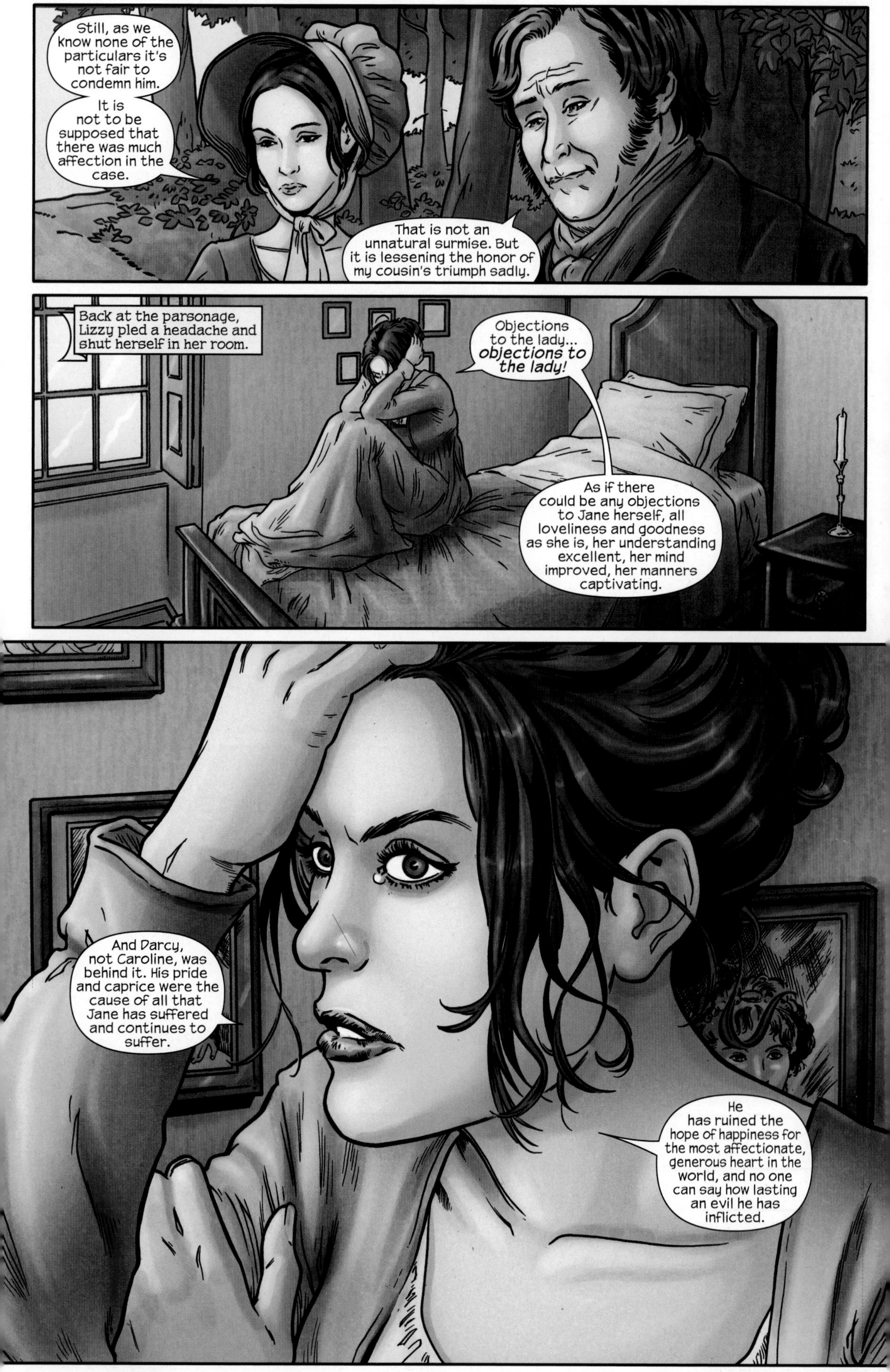
Still, as we know none of the particulars it's not fair to condemn him.
It is not to be supposed that there was much affection in the case.
That is not an unnatural surmise. But it is lessening the honor of my cousin's triumph sadly.
Back at the parsonage, Lizzy pled a headache and shut herself in her room.
Objections to the lady... *objections to the lady!*
As if there could be any objections to Jane herself, all loveliness and goodness as she is, her understanding excellent, her mind improved, her manners captivating.
And Darcy, not Caroline, was behind it. His pride and caprice were the cause of all that Jane has suffered and continues to suffer.
He has ruined the hope of happiness for the most affectionate, generous heart in the world, and no one can say how lasting an evil he has inflicted.

Lizzy was still too upset over Colonel Fitzwilliam's revelation at Rosings that night and so pleaded a headache.

But less than an hour later...

Mr. Darcy to see you, miss.

I trust you are well, Miss Bennet.

Well enough.

In vain have I struggled. It will not do. My feelings will not be repressed.

You must allow me to tell you...

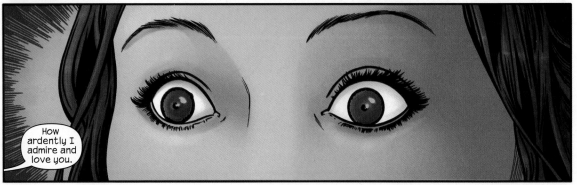

How ardently I admire and love you.

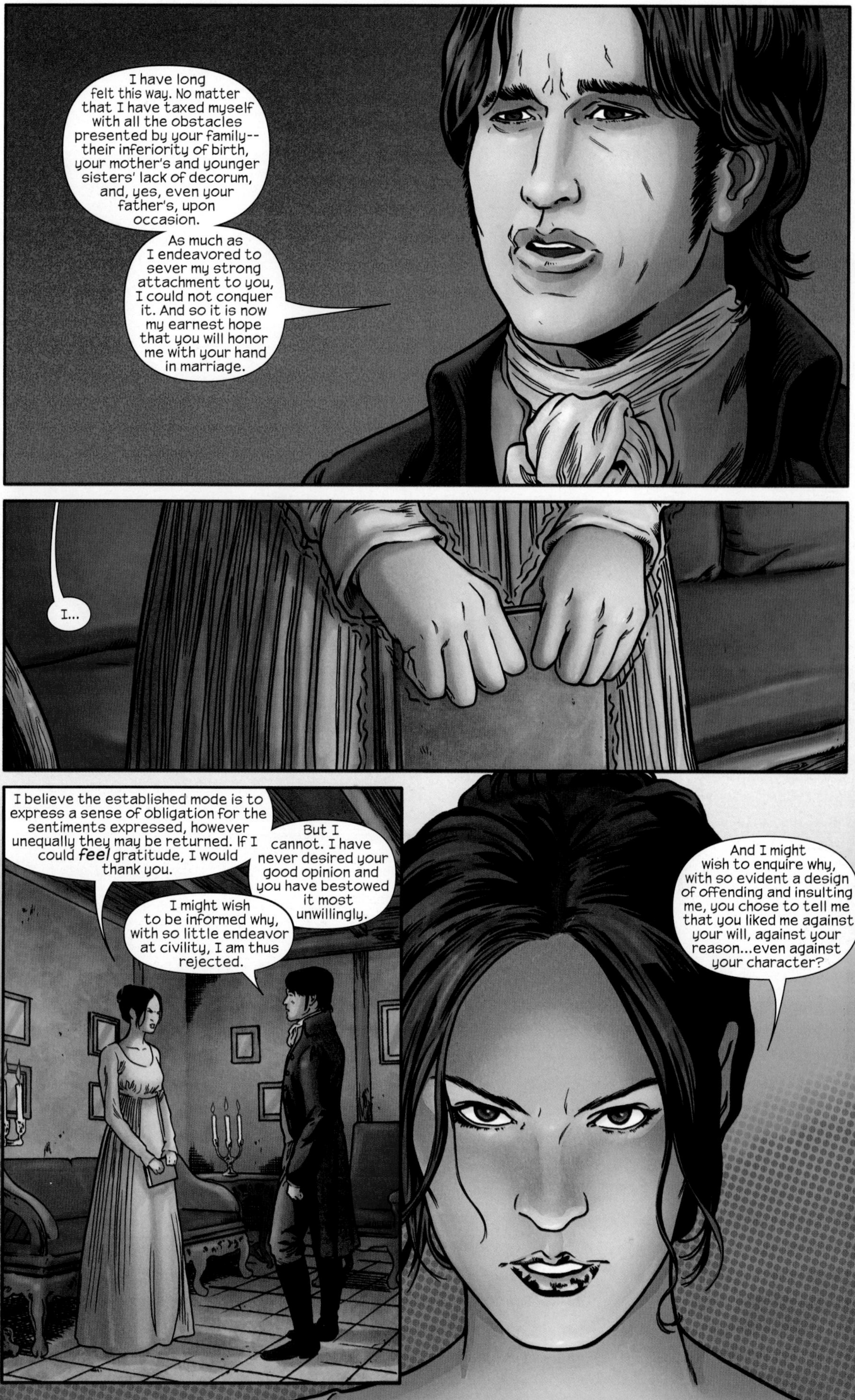
I have long felt this way. No matter that I have taxed myself with all the obstacles presented by your family--their inferiority of birth, your mother's and younger sisters' lack of decorum, and, yes, even your father's, upon occasion.
As much as I endeavored to sever my strong attachment to you, I could not conquer it. And so it is now my earnest hope that you will honor me with your hand in marriage.
I...
I believe the established mode is to express a sense of obligation for the sentiments expressed, however unequally they may be returned. If I could *feel* gratitude, I would thank you.
But I cannot. I have never desired your good opinion and you have bestowed it most unwillingly.
I might wish to be informed why, with so little endeavor at civility, I am thus rejected.
And I might wish to enquire why, with so evident a design of offending and insulting me, you chose to tell me that you liked me against your will, against your reason...even against your character?

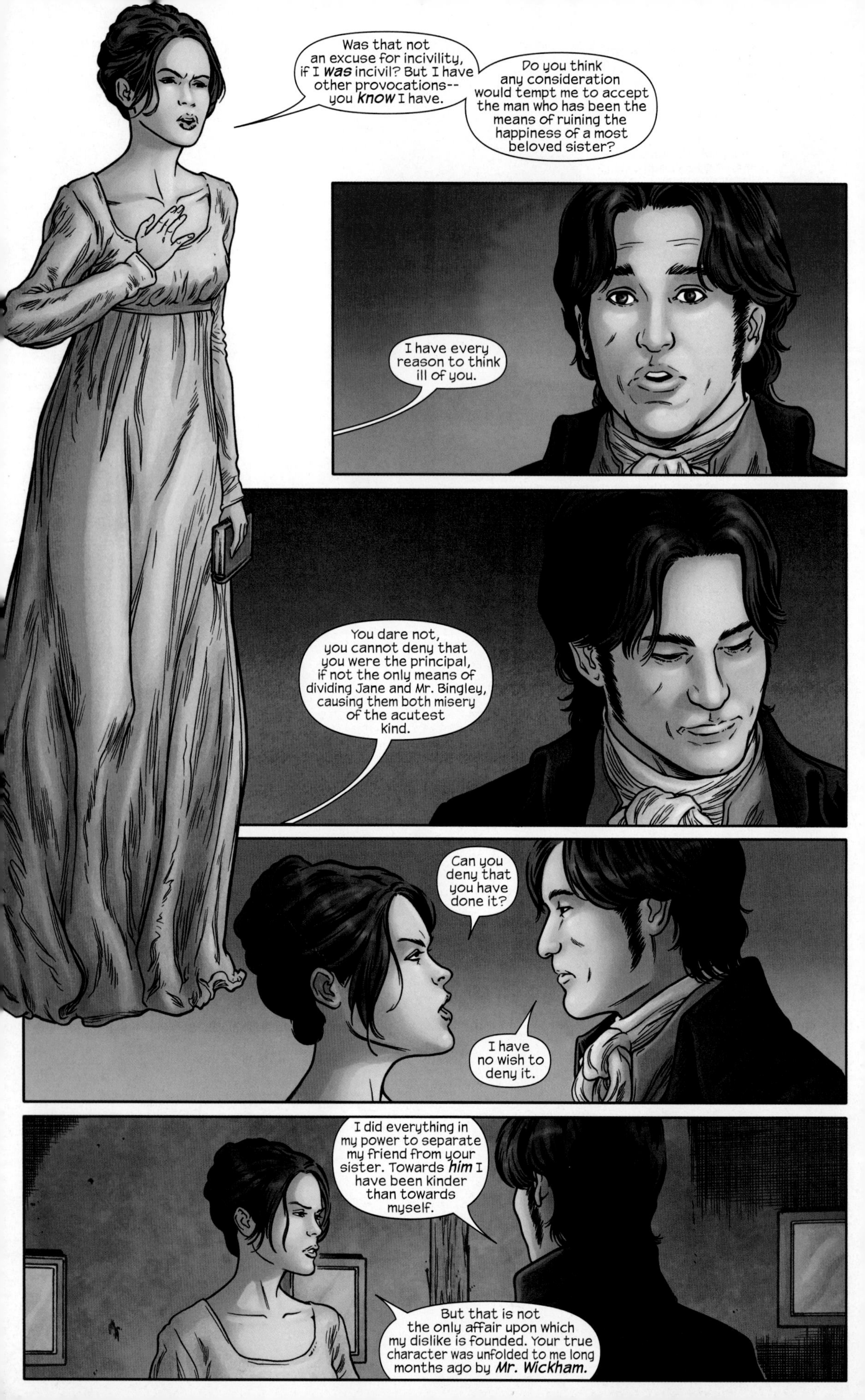
Was that not an excuse for incivility, if I *was* incivil? But I have other provocations-- you *know* I have.
Do you think any consideration would tempt me to accept the man who has been the means of ruining the happiness of a most beloved sister?
I have every reason to think ill of you.
You dare not, you cannot deny that you were the principal, if not the only means of dividing Jane and Mr. Bingley, causing them both misery of the acutest kind.
Can you deny that you have done it?
I have no wish to deny it.
I did everything in my power to separate my friend from your sister. Towards *him* I have been kinder than towards myself.
But that is not the only affair upon which my dislike is founded. Your true character was unfolded to me long months ago by *Mr. Wickham.*

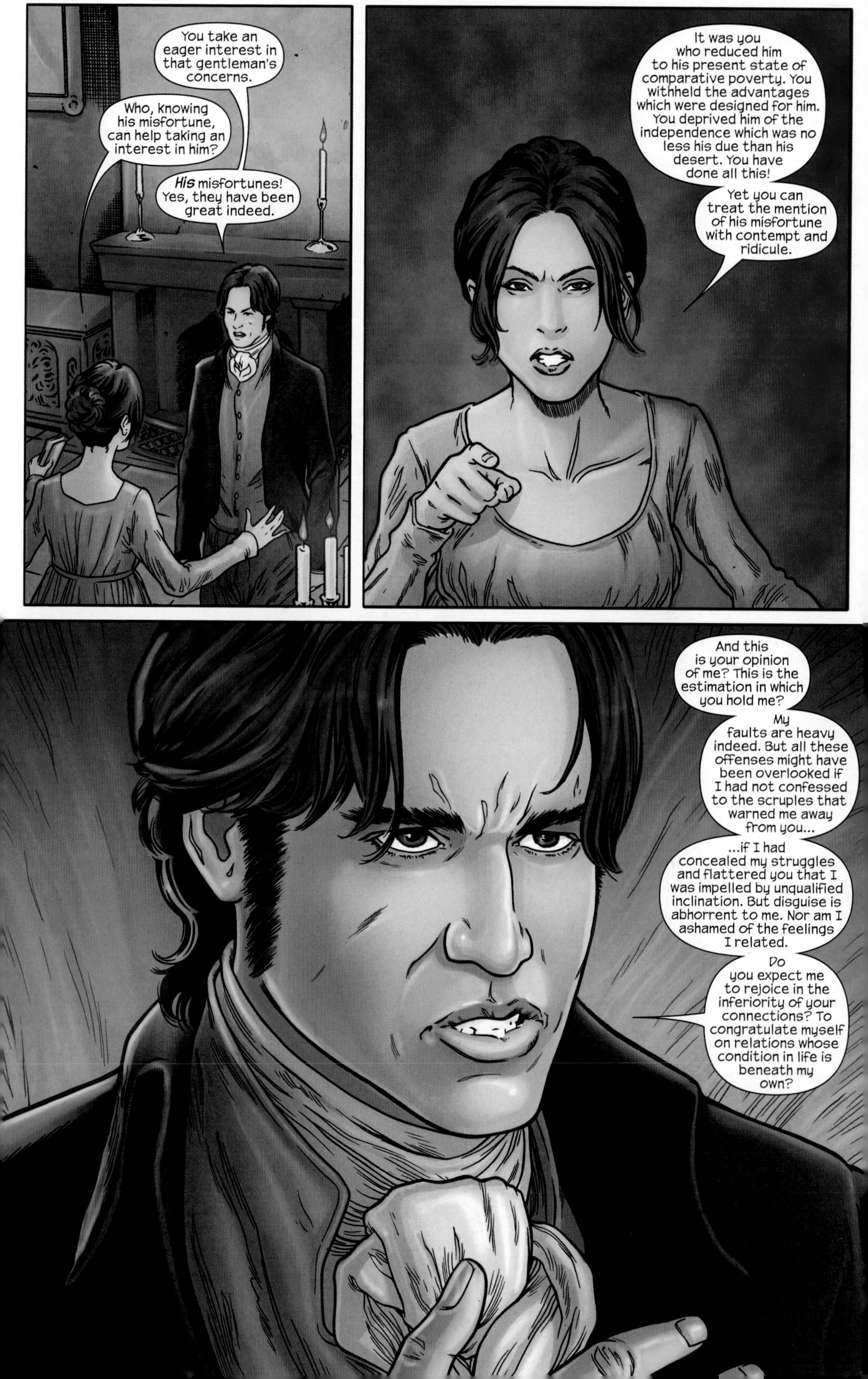
You take an eager interest in that gentleman's concerns.
Who, knowing his misfortune, can help taking an interest in him?
*His* misfortunes! Yes, they have been great indeed.
It was you who reduced him to his present state of comparative poverty. You withheld the advantages which were designed for him. You deprived him of the independence which was no less his due than his desert. You have done all this!
Yet you can treat the mention of his misfortune with contempt and ridicule.
And this is your opinion of me? This is the estimation in which you hold me?
My faults are heavy indeed. But all these offenses might have been overlooked if I had not confessed to the scruples that warned me away from you...
...if I had concealed my struggles and flattered you that I was impelled by unqualified inclination. But disguise is abhorrent to me. Nor am I ashamed of the feelings I related.
Do you expect me to rejoice in the inferiority of your connections? To congratulate myself on relations whose condition in life is beneath my own?

You are mistaken if you suppose that the mode of your declaration affected me in any way, save that it spared me the concern I might have felt in refusing you.

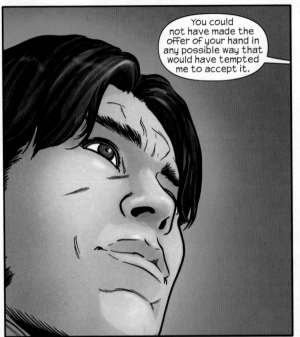

You could not have made the offer of your hand in any possible way that would have tempted me to accept it.

From the very beginning your manners, your conceit, and your selfish disdain for others created such a groundwork of dislike, that I had not known you a month before I felt that you were the last man in the world I would ever marry.

You have said quite enough, madam. I perfectly comprehend your feelings and have only to be ashamed of what my own have been.

Forgive me for taking up your time, and accept my best wishes for your health and happiness.

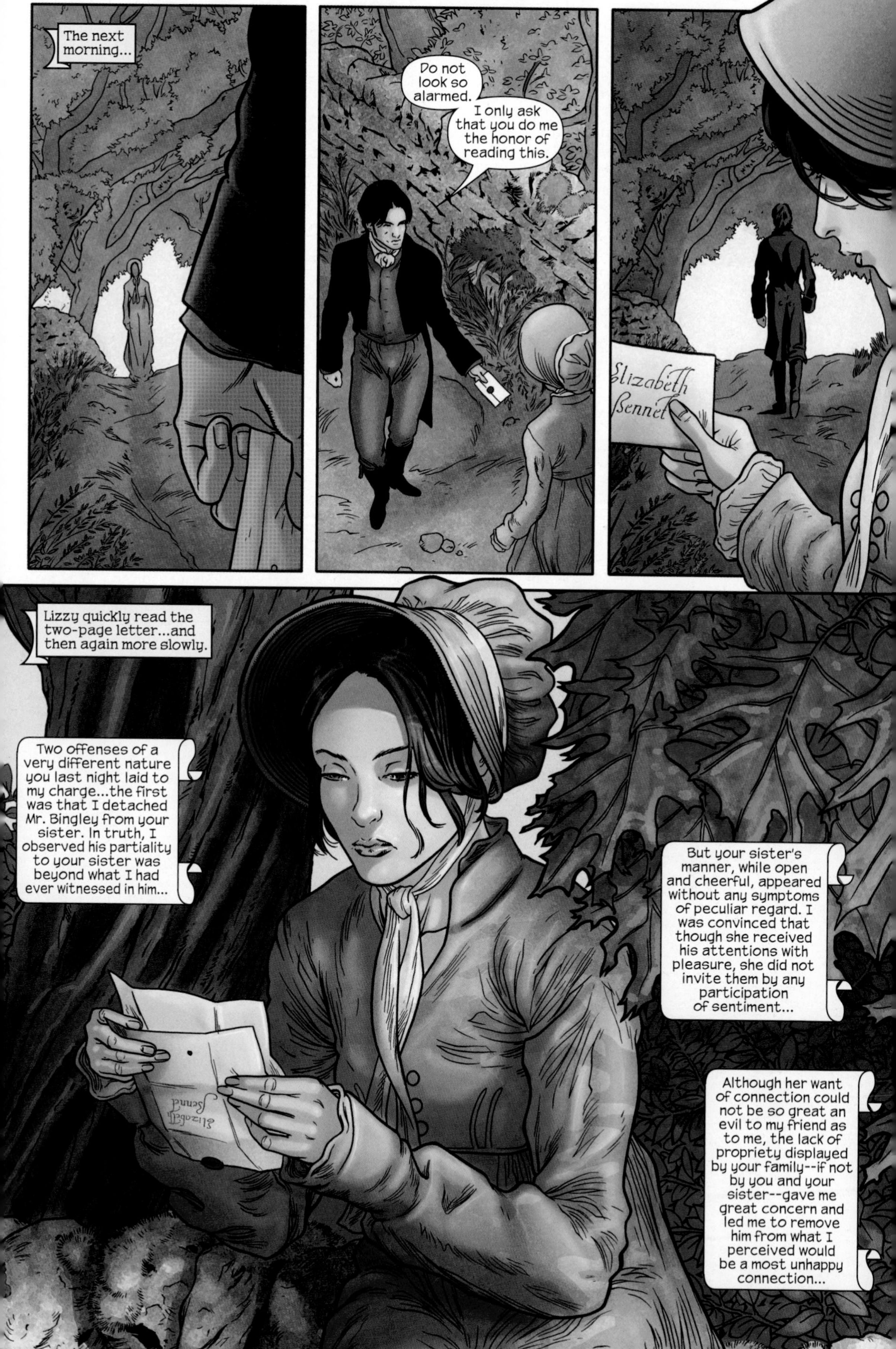
The next morning...
Do not look so alarmed.
I only ask that you do me the honor of reading this.
Elizabeth Bennet
Lizzy quickly read the two-page letter...and then again more slowly.
Two offenses of a very different nature you last night laid to my charge...the first was that I detached Mr. Bingley from your sister. In truth, I observed his partiality to your sister was beyond what I had ever witnessed in him...
But your sister's manner, while open and cheerful, appeared without any symptoms of peculiar regard. I was convinced that though she received his attentions with pleasure, she did not invite them by any participation of sentiment...
Although her want of connection could not be so great an evil to my friend as to me, the lack of propriety displayed by your family--if not by you and your sister--gave me great concern and led me to remove him from what I perceived would be a most unhappy connection...

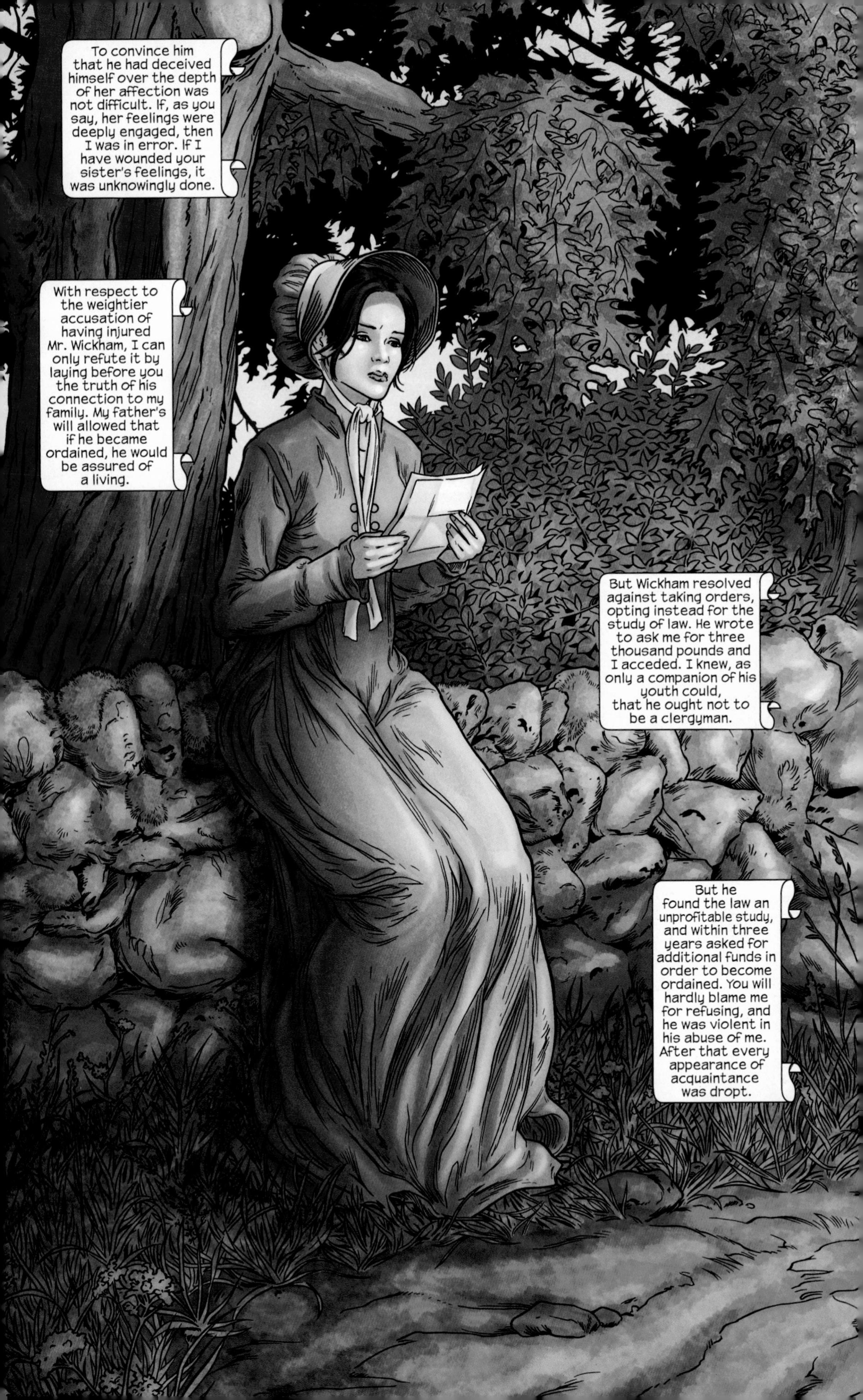
To convince him that he had deceived himself over the depth of her affection was not difficult. If, as you say, her feelings were deeply engaged, then I was in error. If I have wounded your sister's feelings, it was unknowingly done.
With respect to the weightier accusation of having injured Mr. Wickham, I can only refute it by laying before you the truth of his connection to my family. My father's will allowed that if he became ordained, he would be assured of a living.
But Wickham resolved against taking orders, opting instead for the study of law. He wrote to ask me for three thousand pounds and I acceded. I knew, as only a companion of his youth could, that he ought not to be a clergyman.
But he found the law an unprofitable study, and within three years asked for additional funds in order to become ordained. You will hardly blame me for refusing, and he was violent in his abuse of me. After that every appearance of acquaintance was dropt.

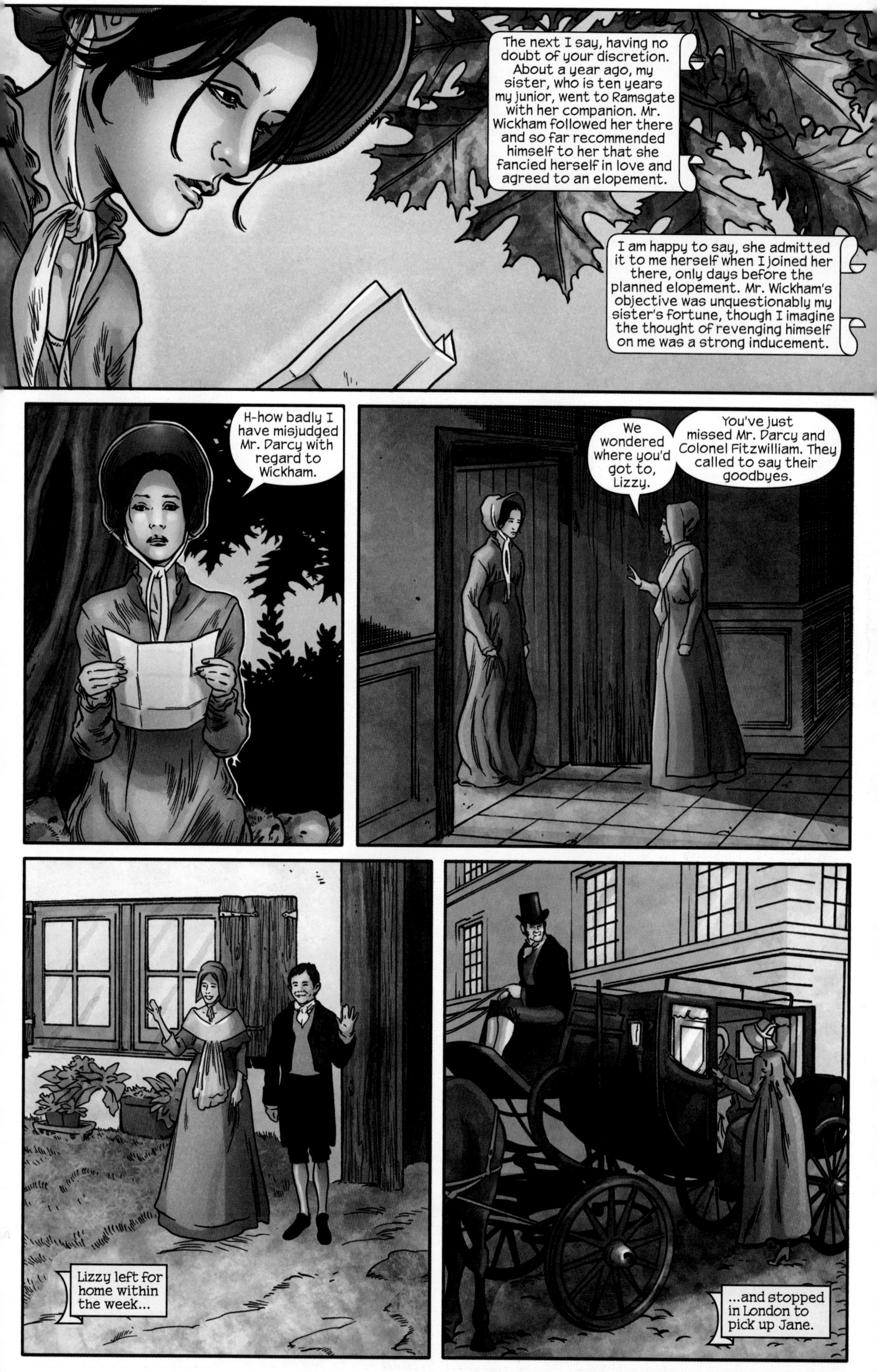
The next I say, having no doubt of your discretion. About a year ago, my sister, who is ten years my junior, went to Ramsgate with her companion. Mr. Wickham followed her there and so far recommended himself to her that she fancied herself in love and agreed to an elopement.
I am happy to say, she admitted it to me herself when I joined her there, only days before the planned elopement. Mr. Wickham's objective was unquestionably my sister's fortune, though I imagine the thought of revenging himself on me was a strong inducement.
H-how badly I have misjudged Mr. Darcy with regard to Wickham.
We wondered where you'd got to, Lizzy.
You've just missed Mr. Darcy and Colonel Fitzwilliam. They called to say their goodbyes.
Lizzy left for home within the week...
...and stopped in London to pick up Jane.

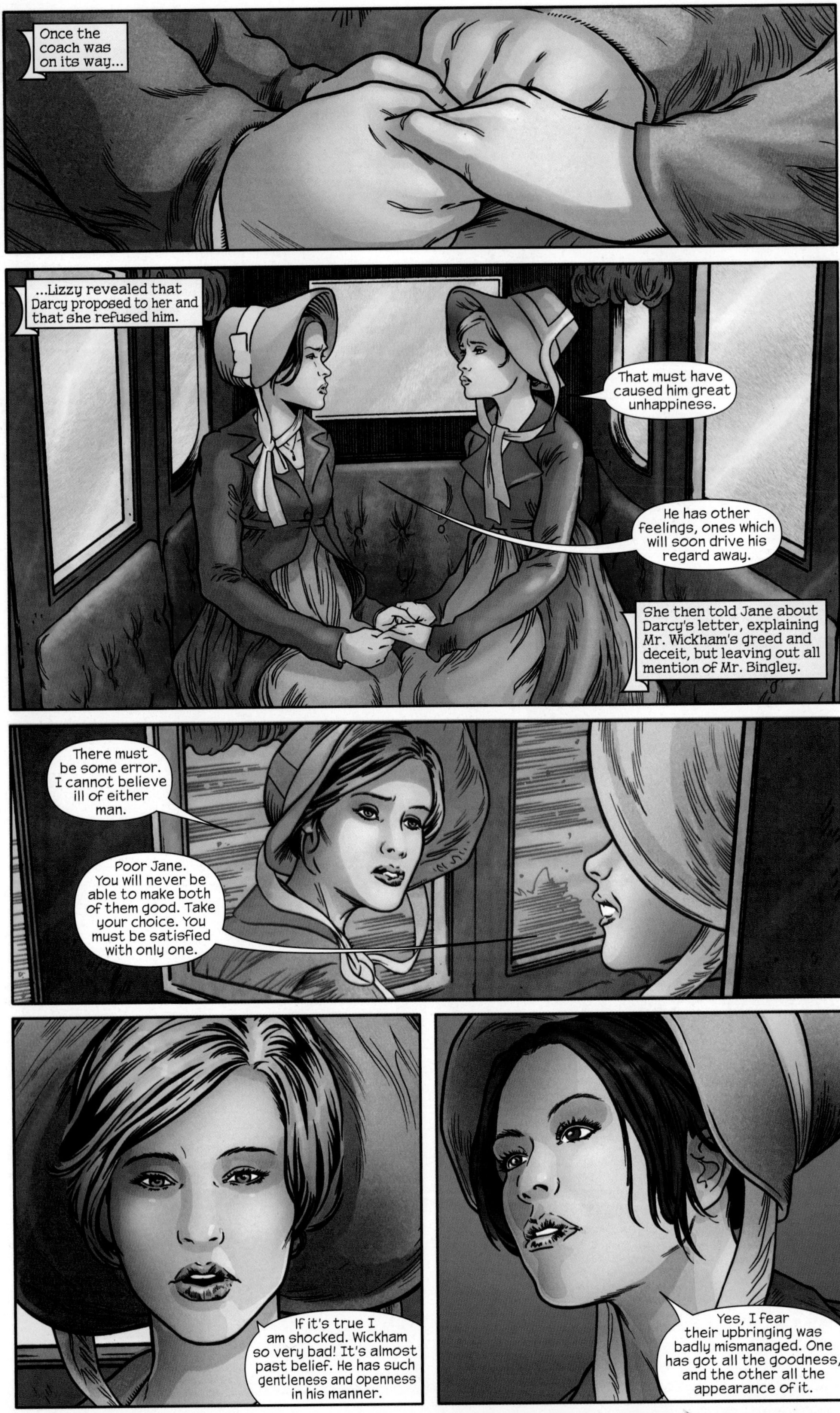
Once the coach was on its way...
...Lizzy revealed that Darcy proposed to her and that she refused him.
That must have caused him great unhappiness.
He has other feelings, ones which will soon drive his regard away.
She then told Jane about Darcy's letter, explaining Mr. Wickham's greed and deceit, but leaving out all mention of Mr. Bingley.
There must be some error. I cannot believe ill of either man.
Poor Jane. You will never be able to make both of them good. Take your choice. You must be satisfied with only one.
If it's true I am shocked. Wickham so very bad! It's almost past belief. He has such gentleness and openness in his manner.
Yes, I fear their upbringing was badly mismanaged. One has got all the goodness, and the other all the appearance of it.

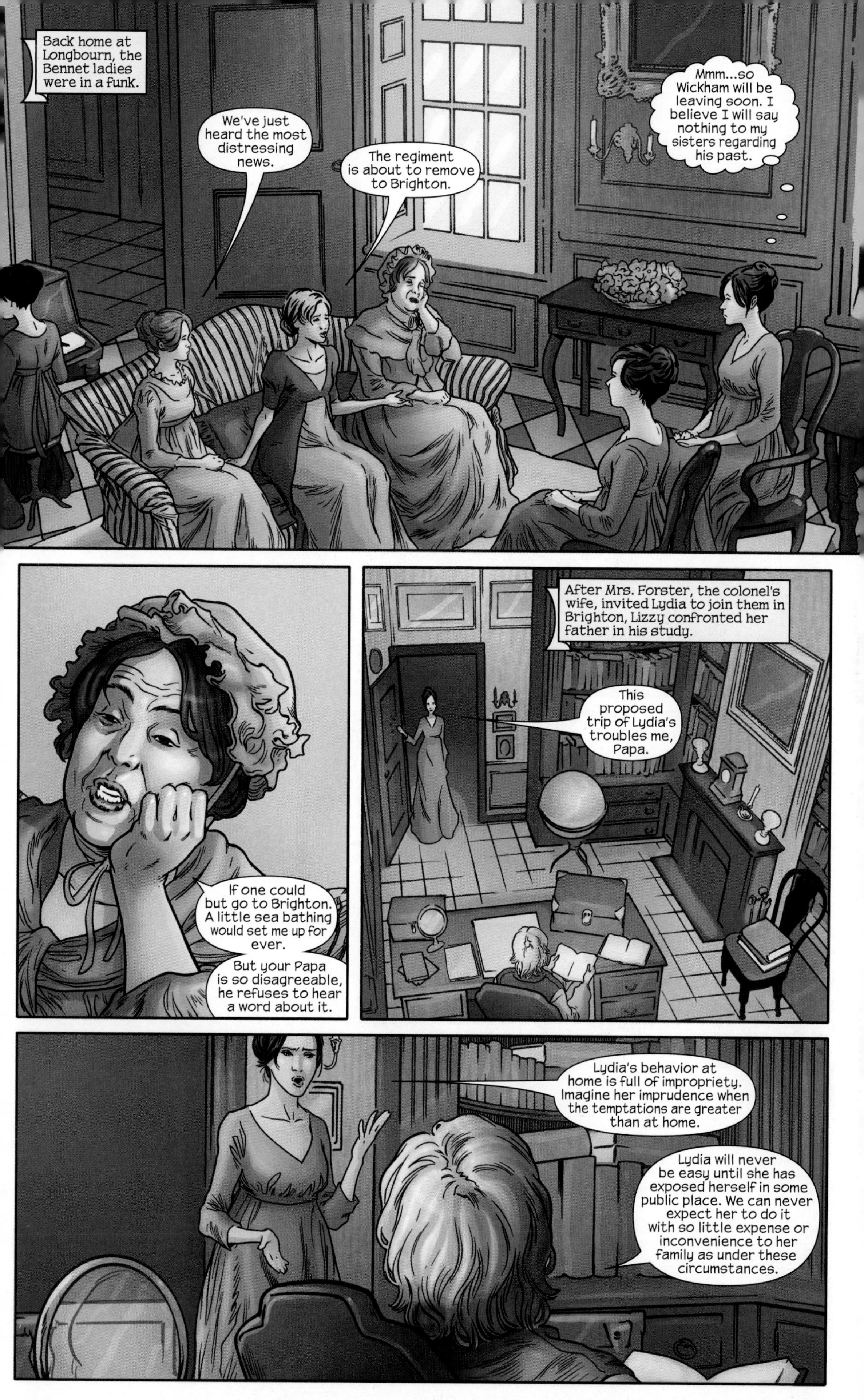
Back home at Longbourn, the Bennet ladies were in a funk.
We've just heard the most distressing news.
The regiment is about to remove to Brighton.
Mmm...so Wickham will be leaving soon. I believe I will say nothing to my sisters regarding his past.
If one could but go to Brighton. A little sea bathing would set me up for ever.
But your Papa is so disagreeable, he refuses to hear a word about it.
After Mrs. Forster, the colonel's wife, invited Lydia to join them in Brighton, Lizzy confronted her father in his study.
This proposed trip of Lydia's troubles me, Papa.
Lydia's behavior at home is full of impropriety. Imagine her imprudence when the temptations are greater than at home.
Lydia will never be easy until she has exposed herself in some public place. We can never expect her to do it with so little expense or inconvenience to her family as under these circumstances.

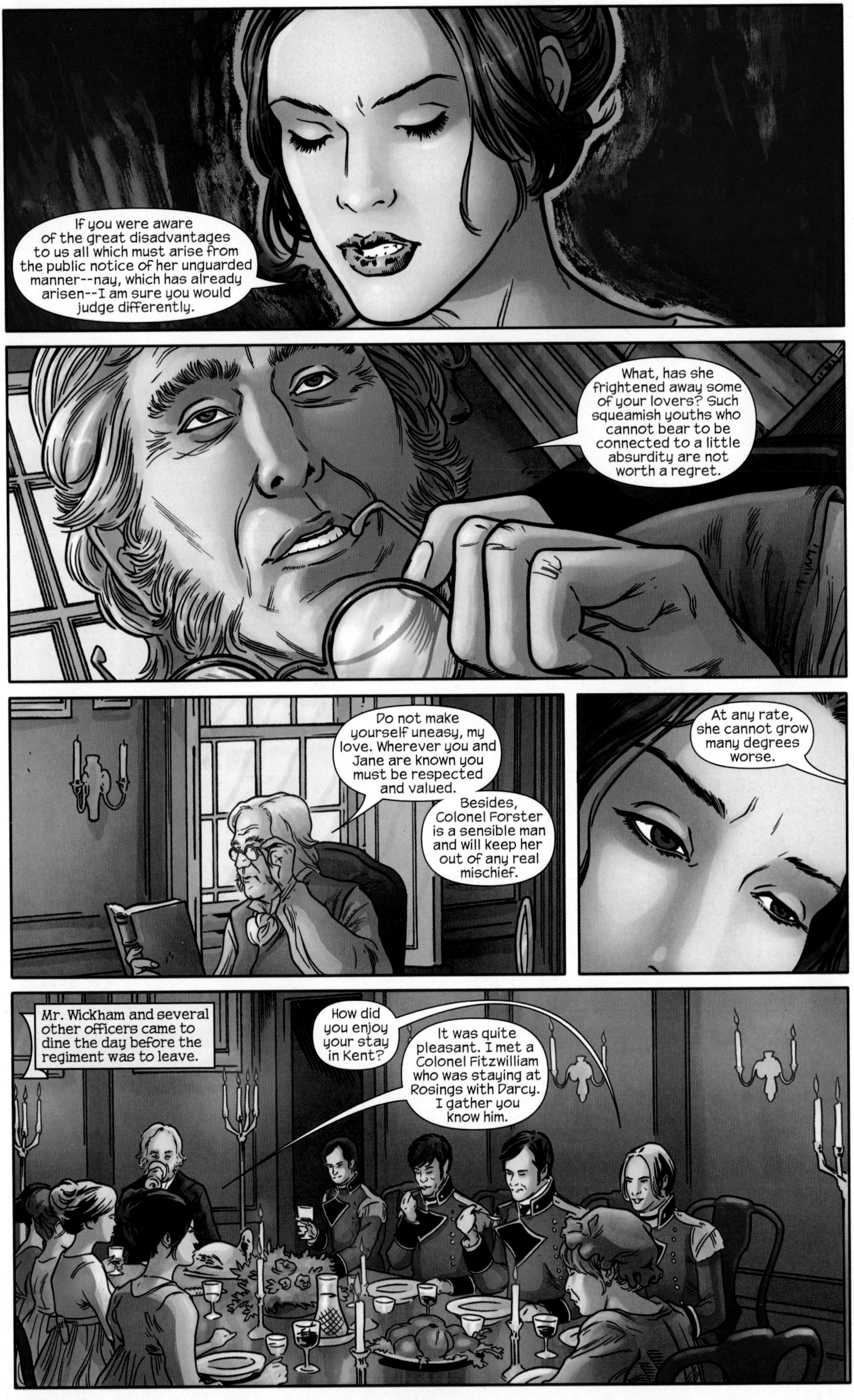

If you were aware of the great disadvantages to us all which must arise from the public notice of her unguarded manner--nay, which has already arisen--I am sure you would judge differently.
What, has she frightened away some of your lovers? Such squeamish youths who cannot bear to be connected to a little absurdity are not worth a regret.
Do not make yourself uneasy, my love. Wherever you and Jane are known you must be respected and valued.
Besides, Colonel Forster is a sensible man and will keep her out of any real mischief.
At any rate, she cannot grow many degrees worse.
Mr. Wickham and several other officers came to dine the day before the regiment was to leave.
How did you enjoy your stay in Kent?
It was quite pleasant. I met a Colonel Fitzwilliam who was staying at Rosings with Darcy. I gather you know him.

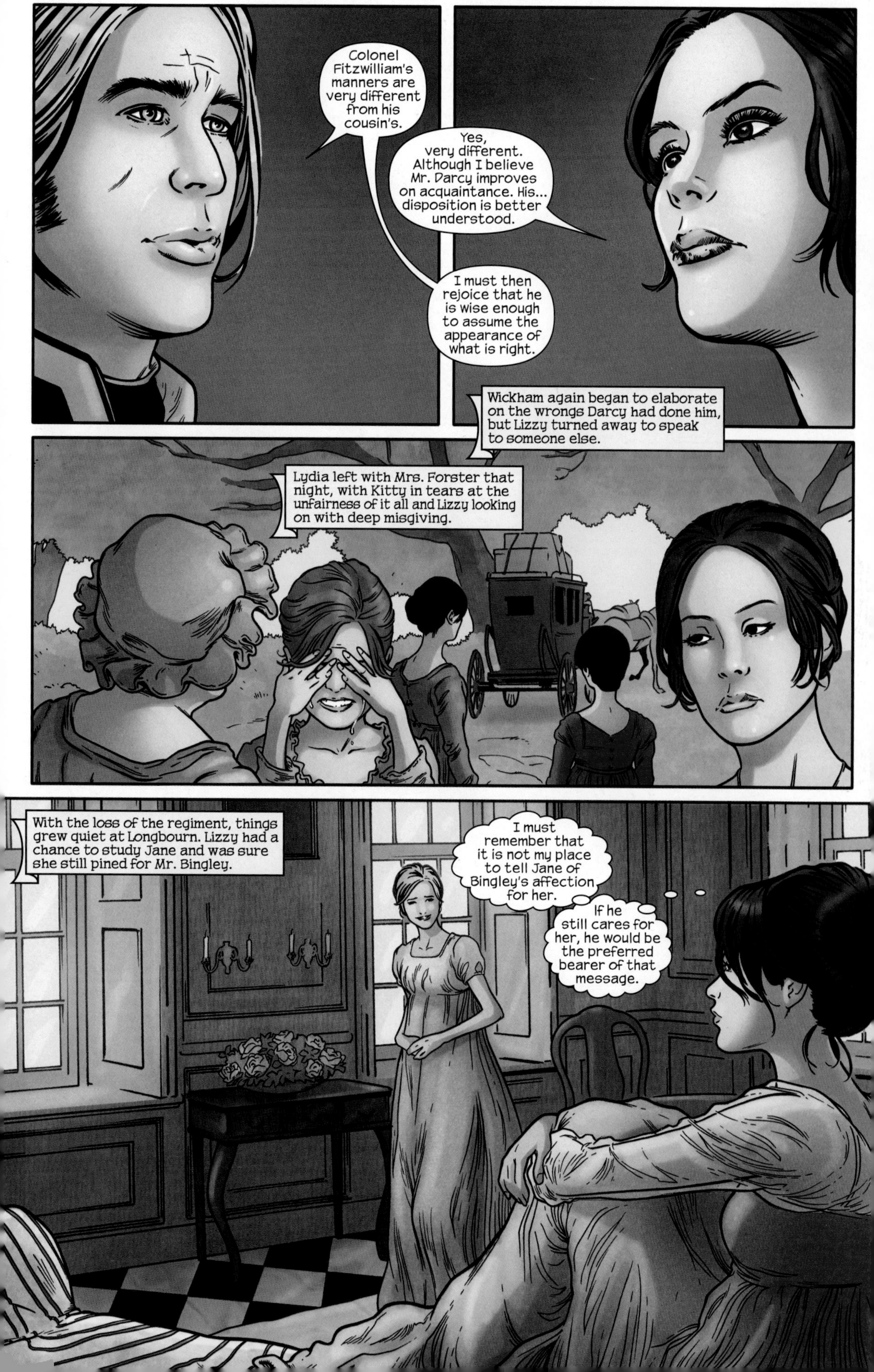
Colonel Fitzwilliam's manners are very different from his cousin's.
Yes, very different. Although I believe Mr. Darcy improves on acquaintance. His... disposition is better understood.
I must then rejoice that he is wise enough to assume the appearance of what is right.
Wickham again began to elaborate on the wrongs Darcy had done him, but Lizzy turned away to speak to someone else.
Lydia left with Mrs. Forster that night, with Kitty in tears at the unfairness of it all and Lizzy looking on with deep misgiving.
With the loss of the regiment, things grew quiet at Longbourn. Lizzy had a chance to study Jane and was sure she still pined for Mr. Bingley.
I must remember that it is not my place to tell Jane of Bingley's affection for her.
If he still cares for her, he would be the preferred bearer of that message.

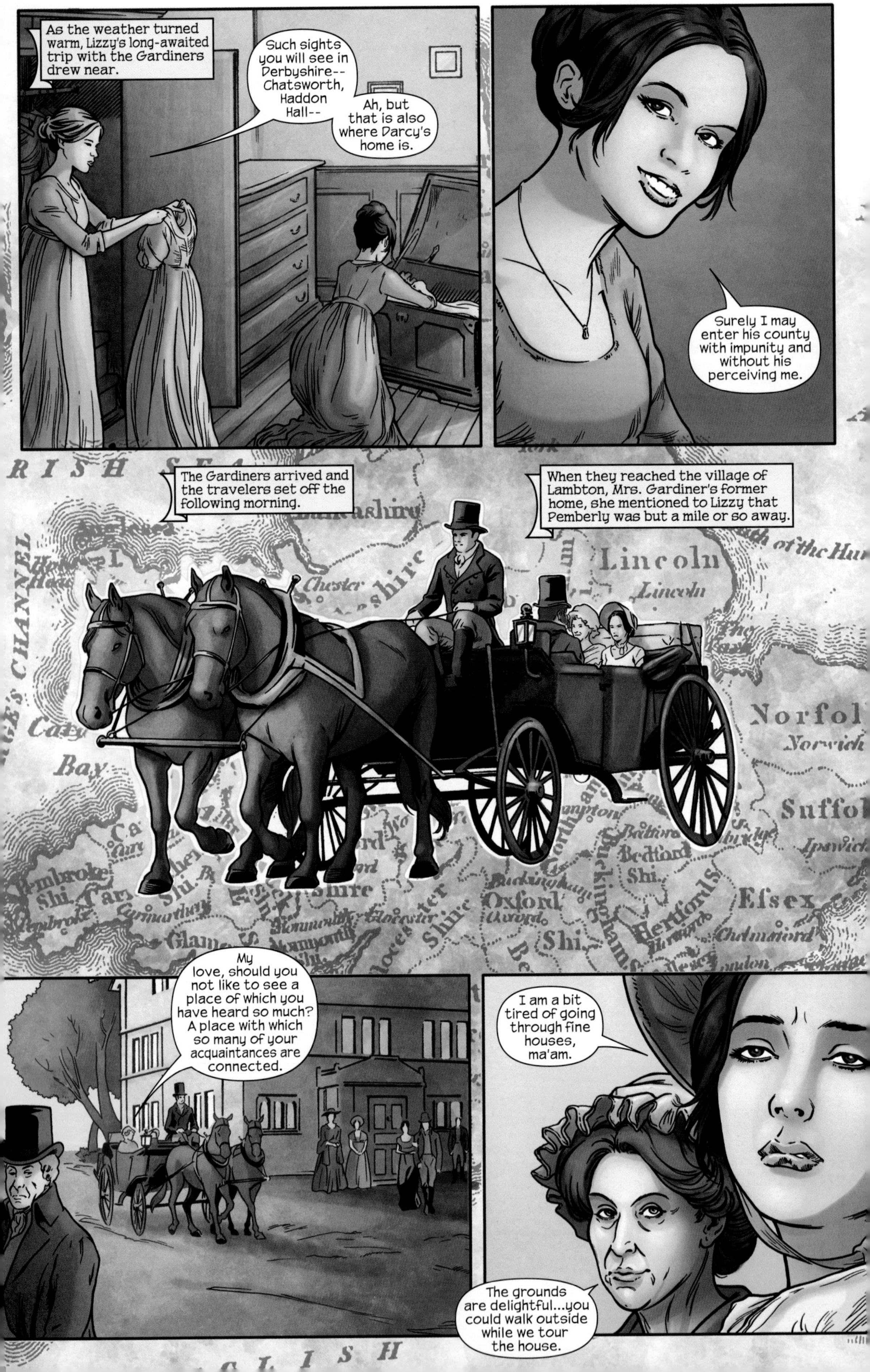
As the weather turned warm, Lizzy's long-awaited trip with the Gardiners drew near.
Such sights you will see in Derbyshire--Chatsworth, Haddon Hall--
Ah, but that is also where Darcy's home is.
Surely I may enter his county with impunity and without his perceiving me.
The Gardiners arrived and the travelers set off the following morning.
When they reached the village of Lambton, Mrs. Gardiner's former home, she mentioned to Lizzy that Pemberly was but a mile or so away.
My love, should you not like to see a place of which you have heard so much? A place with which so many of your acquaintances are connected.
I am a bit tired of going through fine houses, ma'am.
The grounds are delightful...you could walk outside while we tour the house.

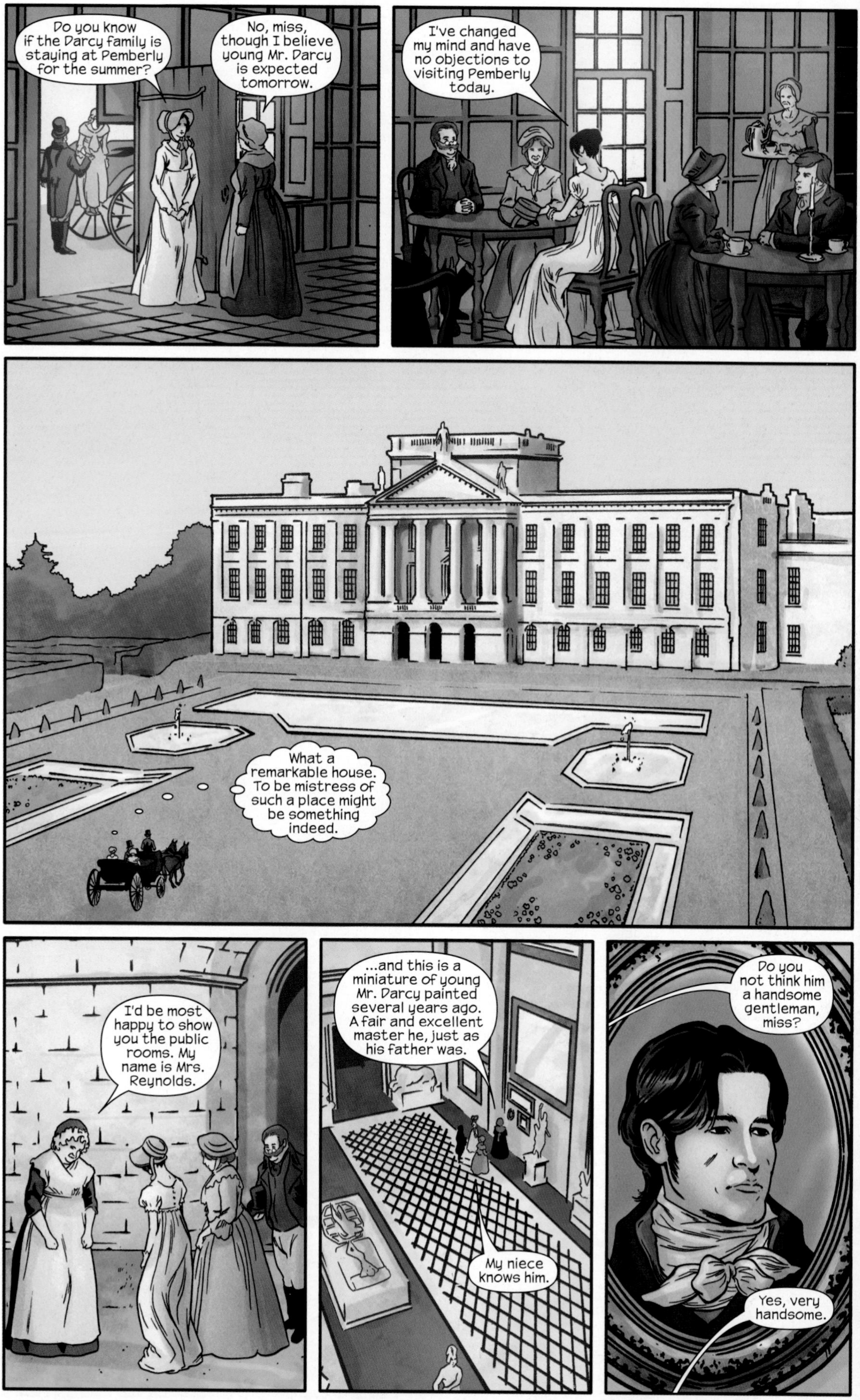
Do you know if the Darcy family is staying at Pemberly for the summer?
No, miss, though I believe young Mr. Darcy is expected tomorrow.
I've changed my mind and have no objections to visiting Pemberly today.
What a remarkable house. To be mistress of such a place might be something indeed.
I'd be most happy to show you the public rooms. My name is Mrs. Reynolds.
...and this is a miniature of young Mr. Darcy painted several years ago. A fair and excellent master he, just as his father was.
My niece knows him.
Do you not think him a handsome gentleman, miss?
Yes, very handsome.

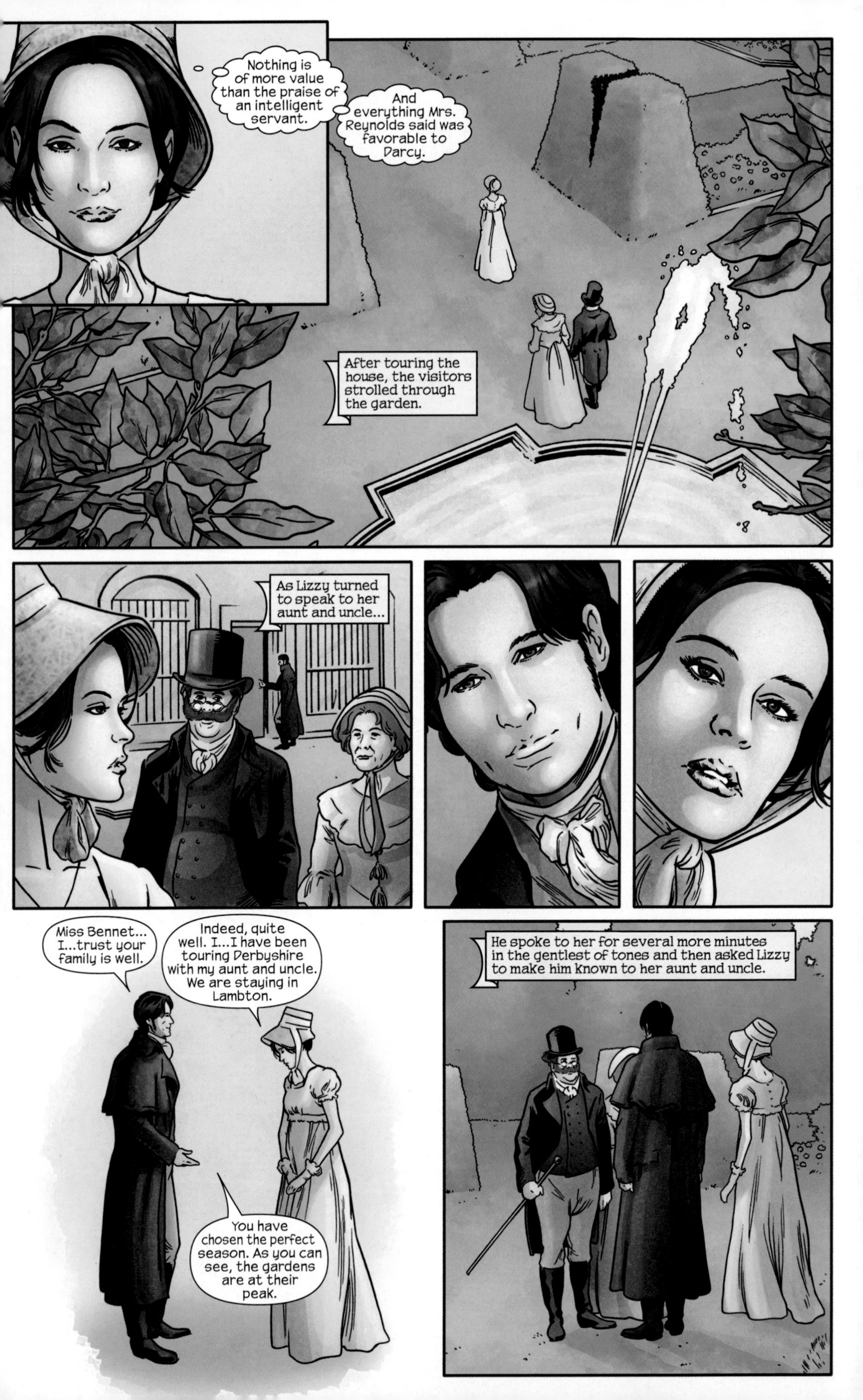
Nothing is of more value than the praise of an intelligent servant.
And everything Mrs. Reynolds said was favorable to Darcy.
After touring the house, the visitors strolled through the garden.
As Lizzy turned to speak to her aunt and uncle...
Miss Bennet... I...trust your family is well.
Indeed, quite well. I...I have been touring Derbyshire with my aunt and uncle. We are staying in Lambton.
You have chosen the perfect season. As you can see, the gardens are at their peak.
He spoke to her for several more minutes in the gentlest of tones and then asked Lizzy to make him known to her aunt and uncle.

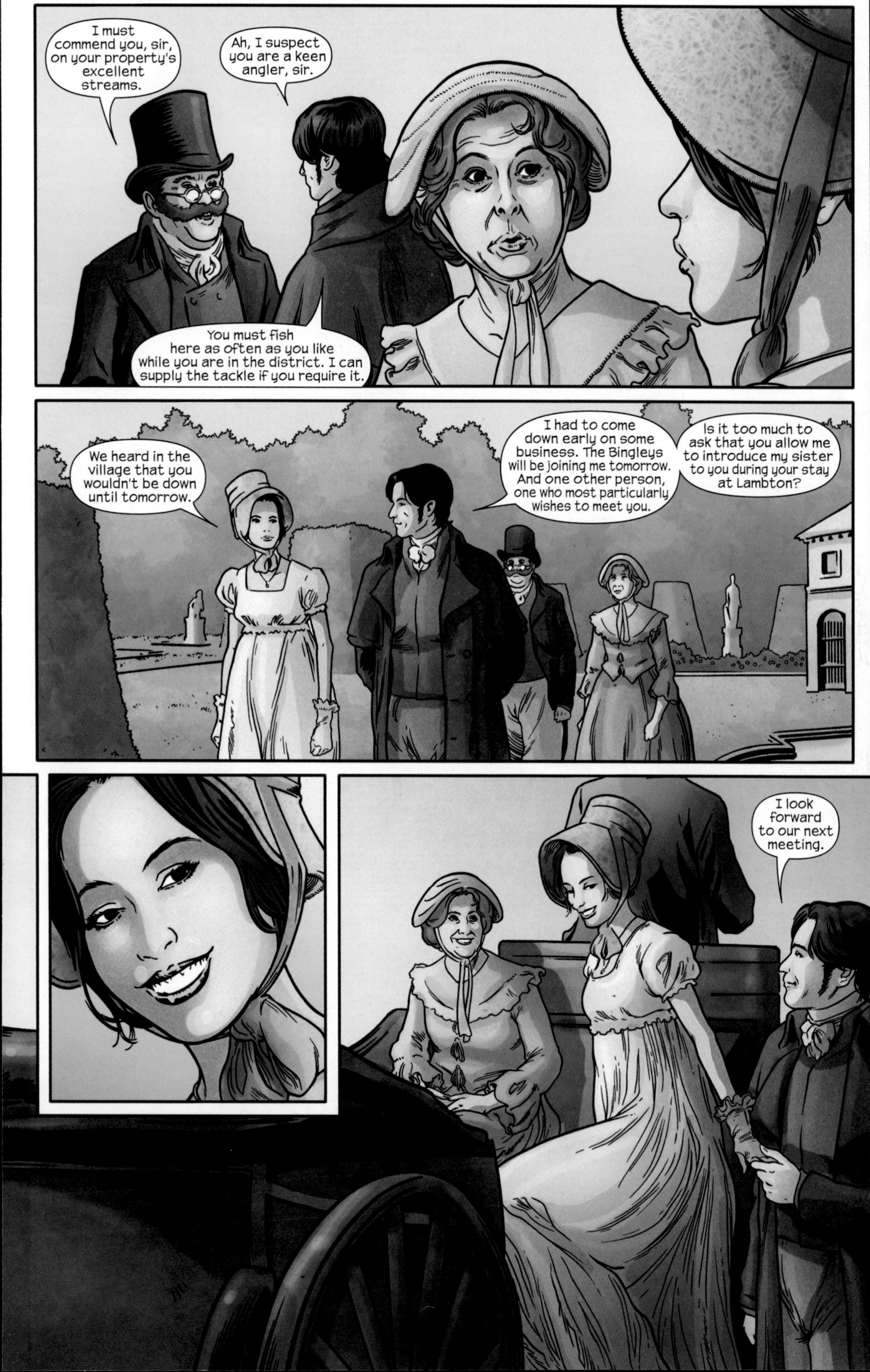
I must commend you, sir, on your property's excellent streams.
Ah, I suspect you are a keen angler, sir.
You must fish here as often as you like while you are in the district. I can supply the tackle if you require it.
We heard in the village that you wouldn't be down until tomorrow.
I had to come down early on some business. The Bingleys will be joining me tomorrow. And one other person, one who most particularly wishes to meet you.
Is it too much to ask that you allow me to introduce my sister to you during your stay at Lambton?
I look forward to our next meeting.

I admit Mr. Darcy seems a little reserved, but I cannot see the proudness others have faulted him for.

Yet you complained he was so disagreeable, Lizzy.

I liked him better when we met in Kent.

And I have never seen him so pleasant as this morning.

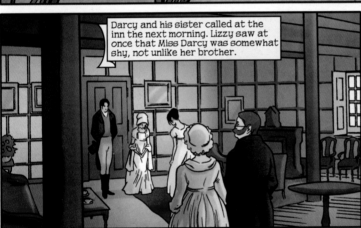

Darcy and his sister called at the inn the next morning. Lizzy saw at once that Miss Darcy was somewhat shy, not unlike her brother.

Miss Bennet, at last we meet...

Bingley also soon arrived with a fond hello to Lizzy.

So, are all your sisters still at Longbourn?

All but Lydia, who is gone to Brighton with the Forsters.

Lizzy watched while Mr. Bingley spoke to Miss Darcy and detected no spark of attraction between them.

Miss Bennet, you must come and dine with us before you leave Lambton.

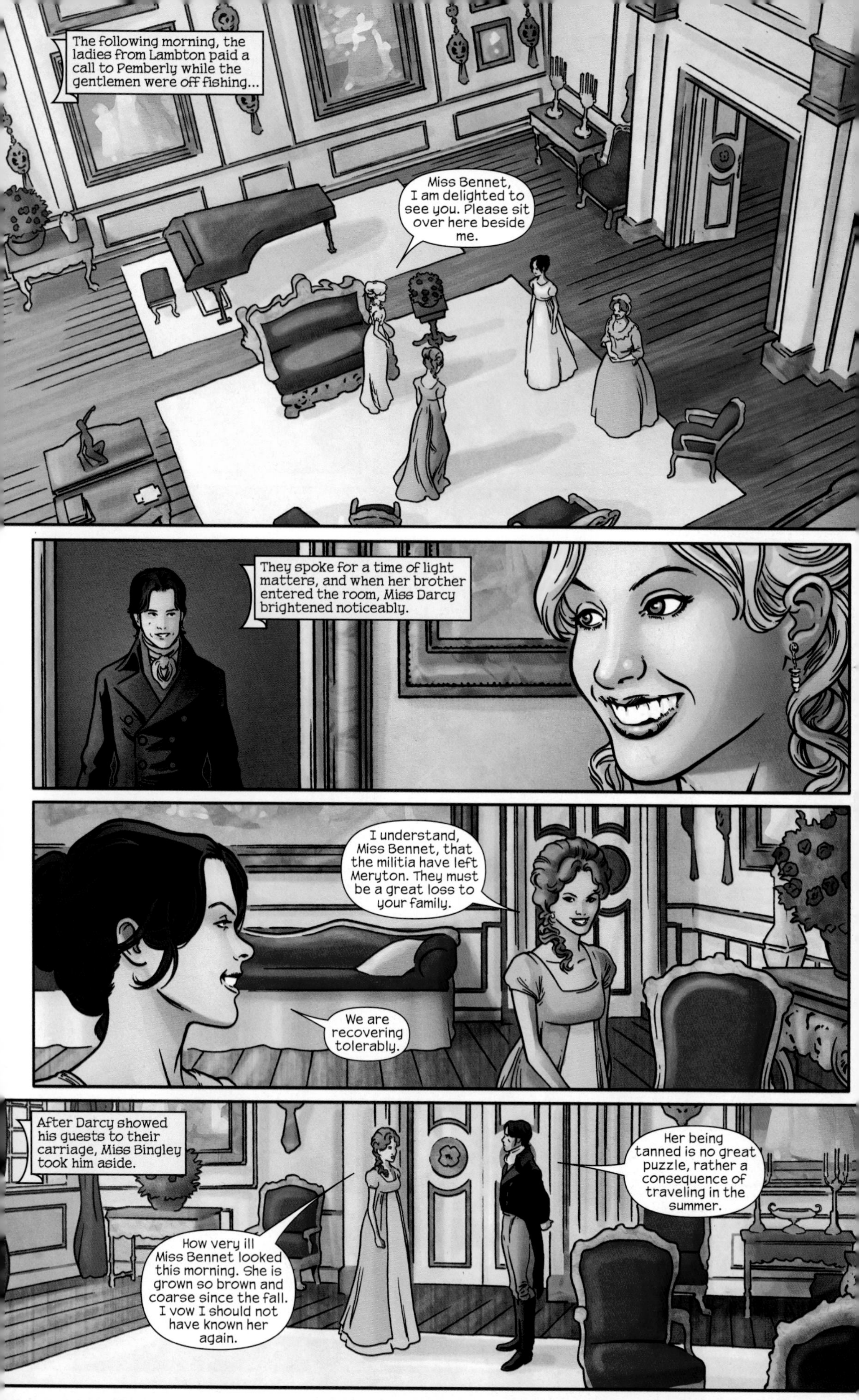
The following morning, the ladies from Lambton paid a call to Pemberly while the gentlemen were off fishing...
Miss Bennet, I am delighted to see you. Please sit over here beside me.
They spoke for a time of light matters, and when her brother entered the room, Miss Darcy brightened noticeably.
I understand, Miss Bennet, that the militia have left Meryton. They must be a great loss to your family.
We are recovering tolerably.
After Darcy showed his guests to their carriage, Miss Bingley took him aside.
How very ill Miss Bennet looked this morning. She is grown so brown and coarse since the fall. I vow I should not have known her again.
Her being tanned is no great puzzle, rather a consequence of traveling in the summer.

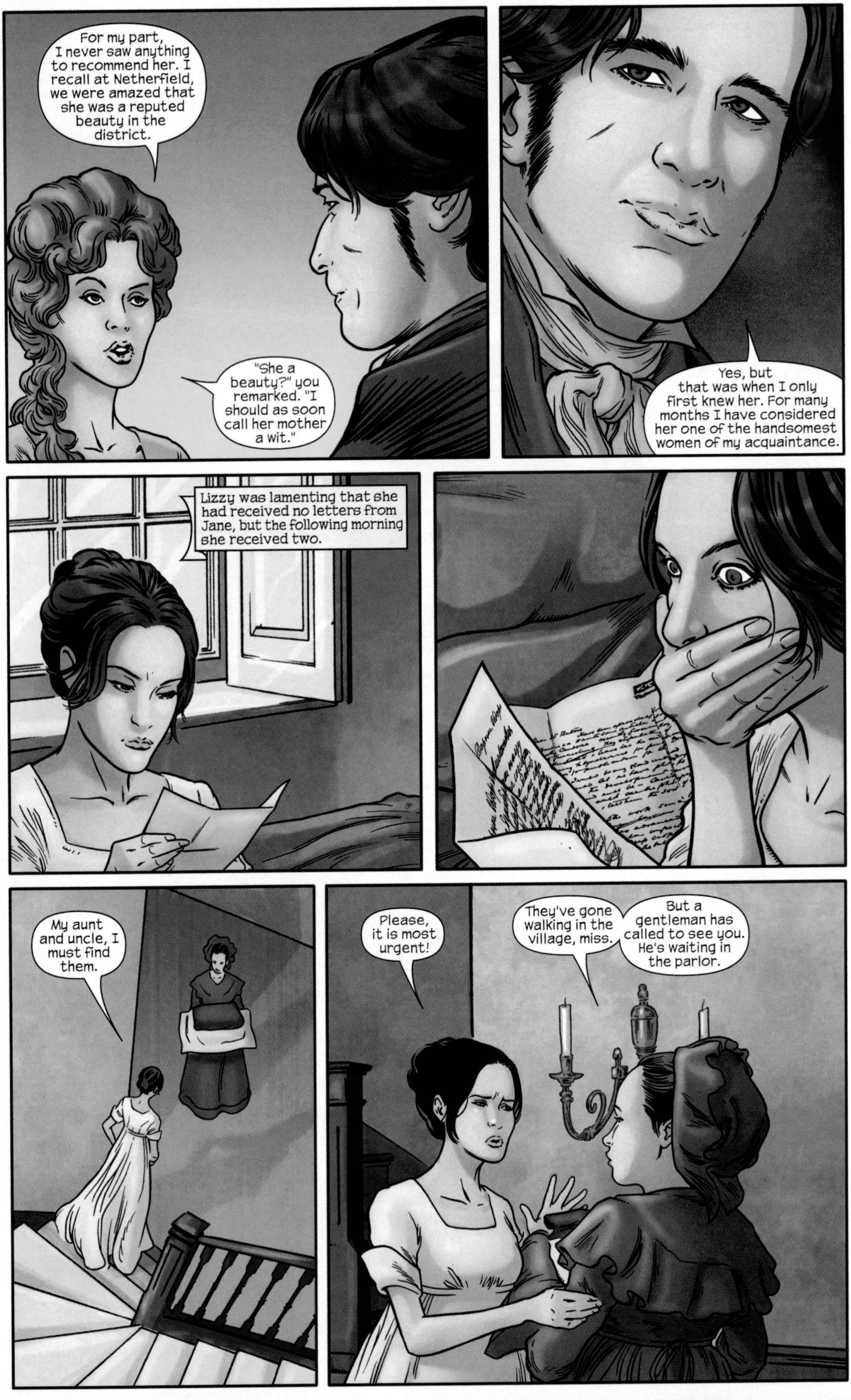
For my part, I never saw anything to recommend her. I recall at Netherfield, we were amazed that she was a reputed beauty in the district.
"She a beauty?" you remarked. "I should as soon call her mother a wit."
Yes, but that was when I only first knew her. For many months I have considered her one of the handsomest women of my acquaintance.
Lizzy was lamenting that she had received no letters from Jane, but the following morning she received two.
My aunt and uncle, I must find them.
Please, it is most urgent!
They've gone walking in the village, miss.
But a gentleman has called to see you. He's waiting in the parlor.

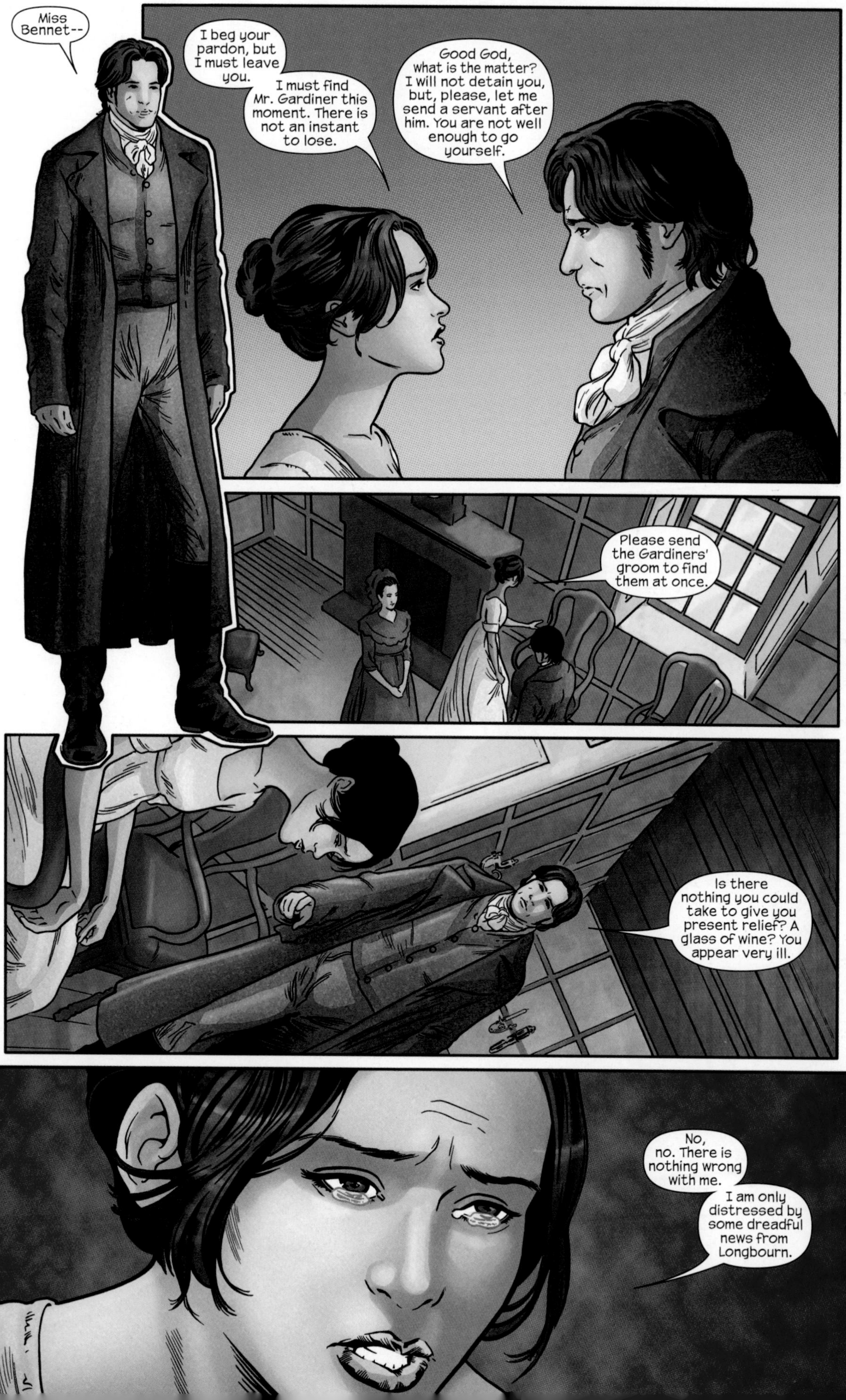
Miss Bennet--
I beg your pardon, but I must leave you.
I must find Mr. Gardiner this moment. There is not an instant to lose.
Good God, what is the matter? I will not detain you, but, please, let me send a servant after him. You are not well enough to go yourself.
Please send the Gardiners' groom to find them at once.
Is there nothing you could take to give you present relief? A glass of wine? You appear very ill.
No, no. There is nothing wrong with me.
I am only distressed by some dreadful news from Longbourn.

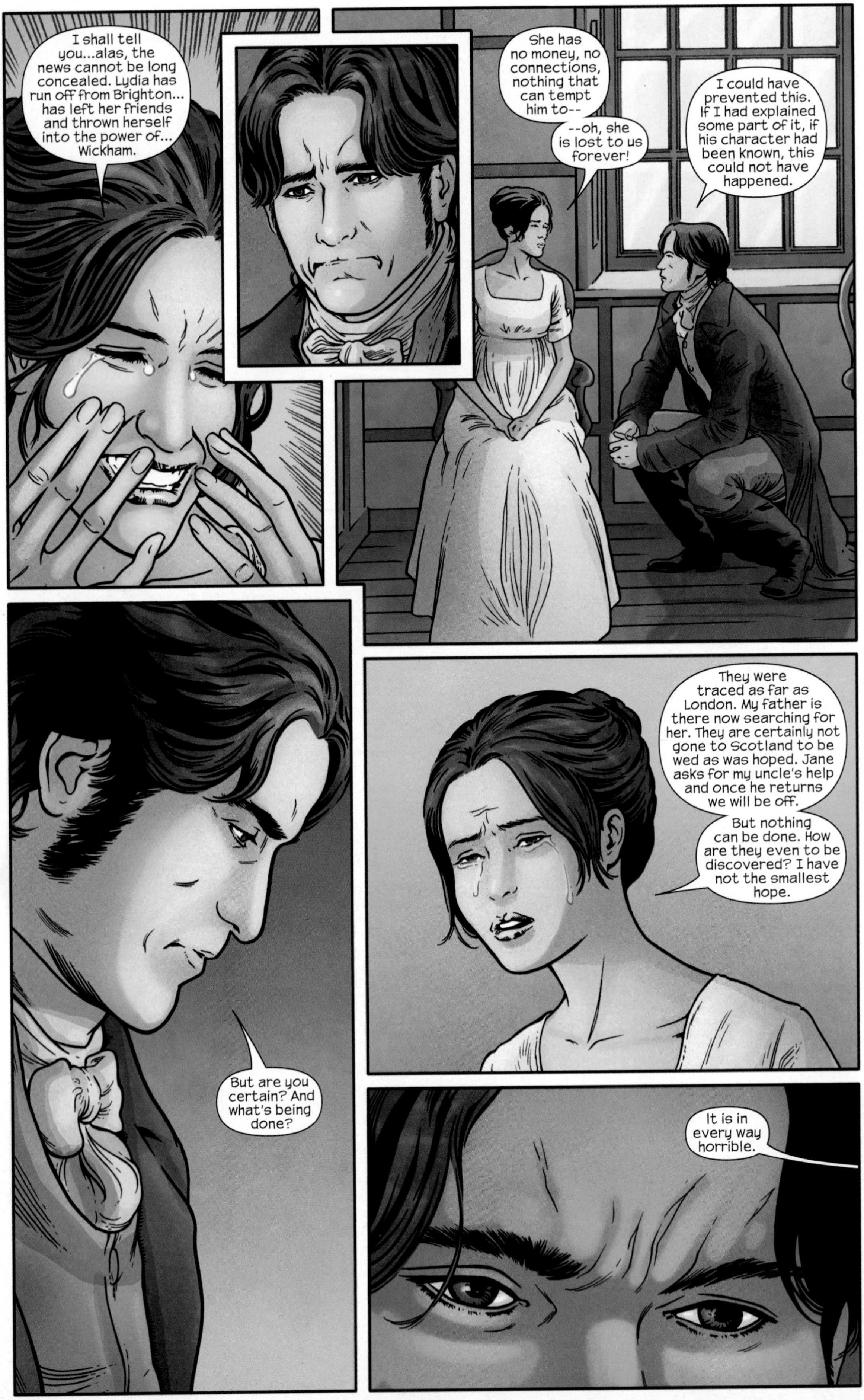

I shall tell you...alas, the news cannot be long concealed. Lydia has run off from Brighton... has left her friends and thrown herself into the power of... Wickham.
She has no money, no connections, nothing that can tempt him to--
--oh, she is lost to us forever!
I could have prevented this. If I had explained some part of it, if his character had been known, this could not have happened.
But are you certain? And what's being done?
They were traced as far as London. My father is there now searching for her. They are certainly not gone to Scotland to be wed as was hoped. Jane asks for my uncle's help and once he returns we will be off.
But nothing can be done. How are they even to be discovered? I have not the smallest hope.
It is in every way horrible.

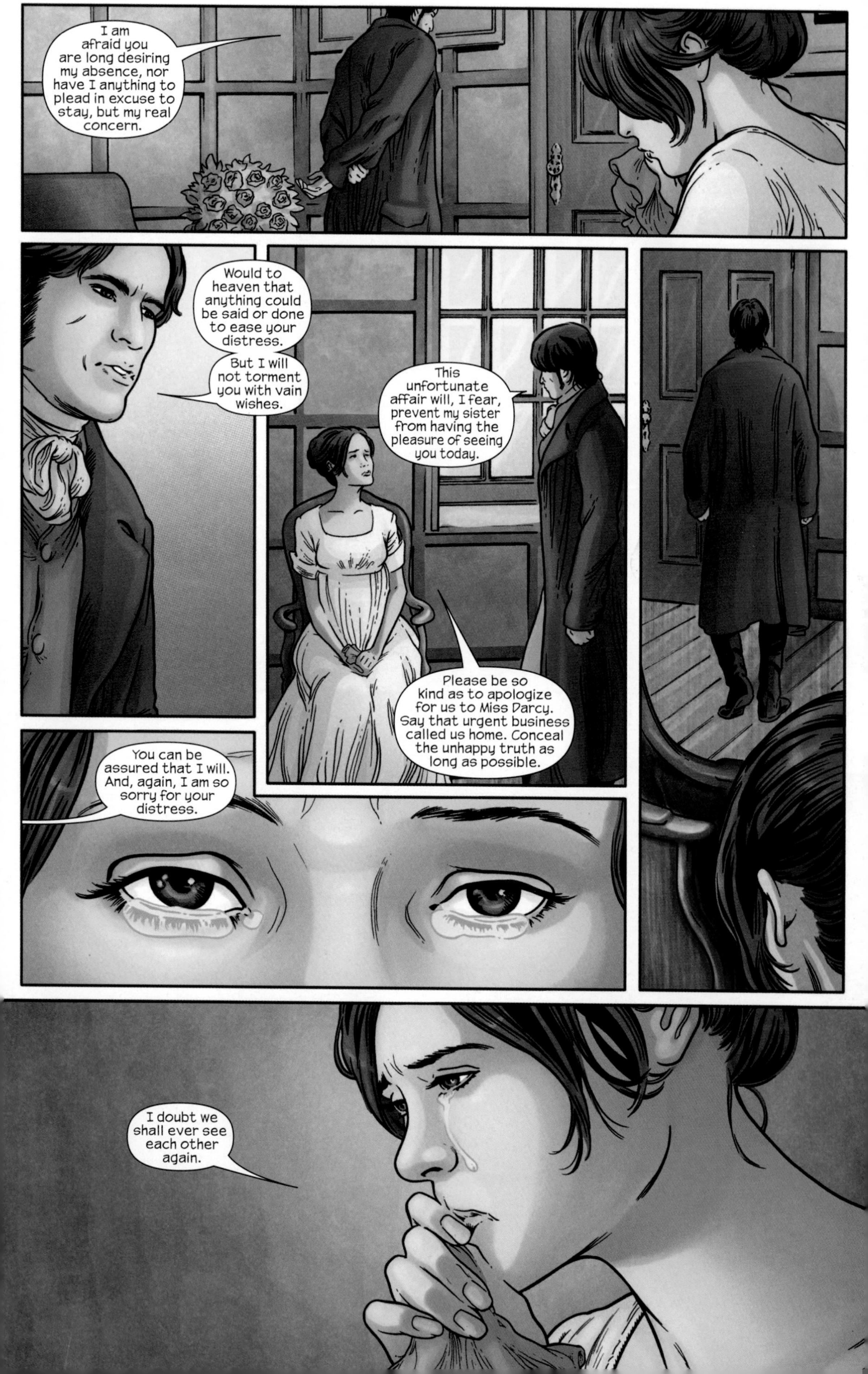
I am afraid you are long desiring my absence, nor have I anything to plead in excuse to stay, but my real concern.
Would to heaven that anything could be said or done to ease your distress.
But I will not torment you with vain wishes.
This unfortunate affair will, I fear, prevent my sister from having the pleasure of seeing you today.
Please be so kind as to apologize for us to Miss Darcy. Say that urgent business called us home. Conceal the unhappy truth as long as possible.
You can be assured that I will. And, again, I am so sorry for your distress.
I doubt we shall ever see each other again.

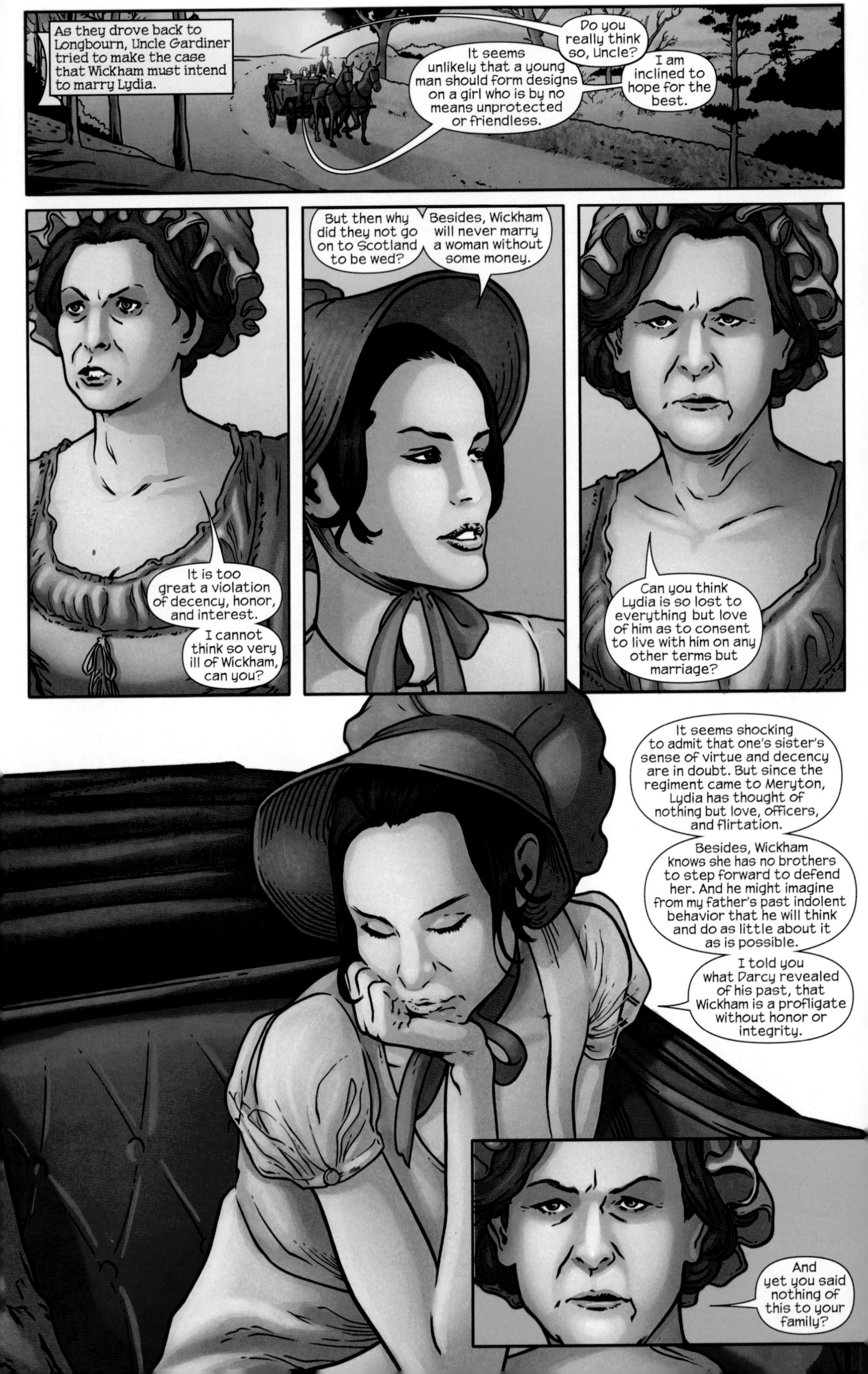
As they drove back to Longbourn, Uncle Gardiner tried to make the case that Wickham must intend to marry Lydia.
It seems unlikely that a young man should form designs on a girl who is by no means unprotected or friendless.
Do you really think so, Uncle?
I am inclined to hope for the best.
It is too great a violation of decency, honor, and interest.
I cannot think so very ill of Wickham, can you?
But then why did they not go on to Scotland to be wed?
Besides, Wickham will never marry a woman without some money.
Can you think Lydia is so lost to everything but love of him as to consent to live with him on any other terms but marriage?
It seems shocking to admit that one's sister's sense of virtue and decency are in doubt. But since the regiment came to Meryton, Lydia has thought of nothing but love, officers, and flirtation.
Besides, Wickham knows she has no brothers to step forward to defend her. And he might imagine from my father's past indolent behavior that he will think and do as little about it as is possible.
I told you what Darcy revealed of his past, that Wickham is a profligate without honor or integrity.
And yet you said nothing of this to your family?

Only Jane knew about Wickham's past. And when I learned the regiment would be leaving Meryton, there was no longer the necessity of revealing his character to the neighborhood.

But weren't you worried about Lydia going off to Brighton?

Not over Wickham. That she could be in danger from him never entered my head.

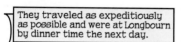

They traveled as expeditiously as possible and were at Longbourn by dinner time the next day.

Oh, Lizzy, I am so relieved to see you.

Dearest Jane. Tell me at once-- has there been any news of the fugitives?

Not yet. But now that my dear uncle is come, I hope everything will be well. Father went to London the day I wrote you and said he will not contact us until he has news.

And our mother--how is she? How are you all?

Her spirits are greatly shaken and she remains upstairs. Seeing you all will give her some satisfaction. Mary and Kitty are quite well.

And you? You look pale. How much you must have gone through.

I assure you, I am perfectly well.

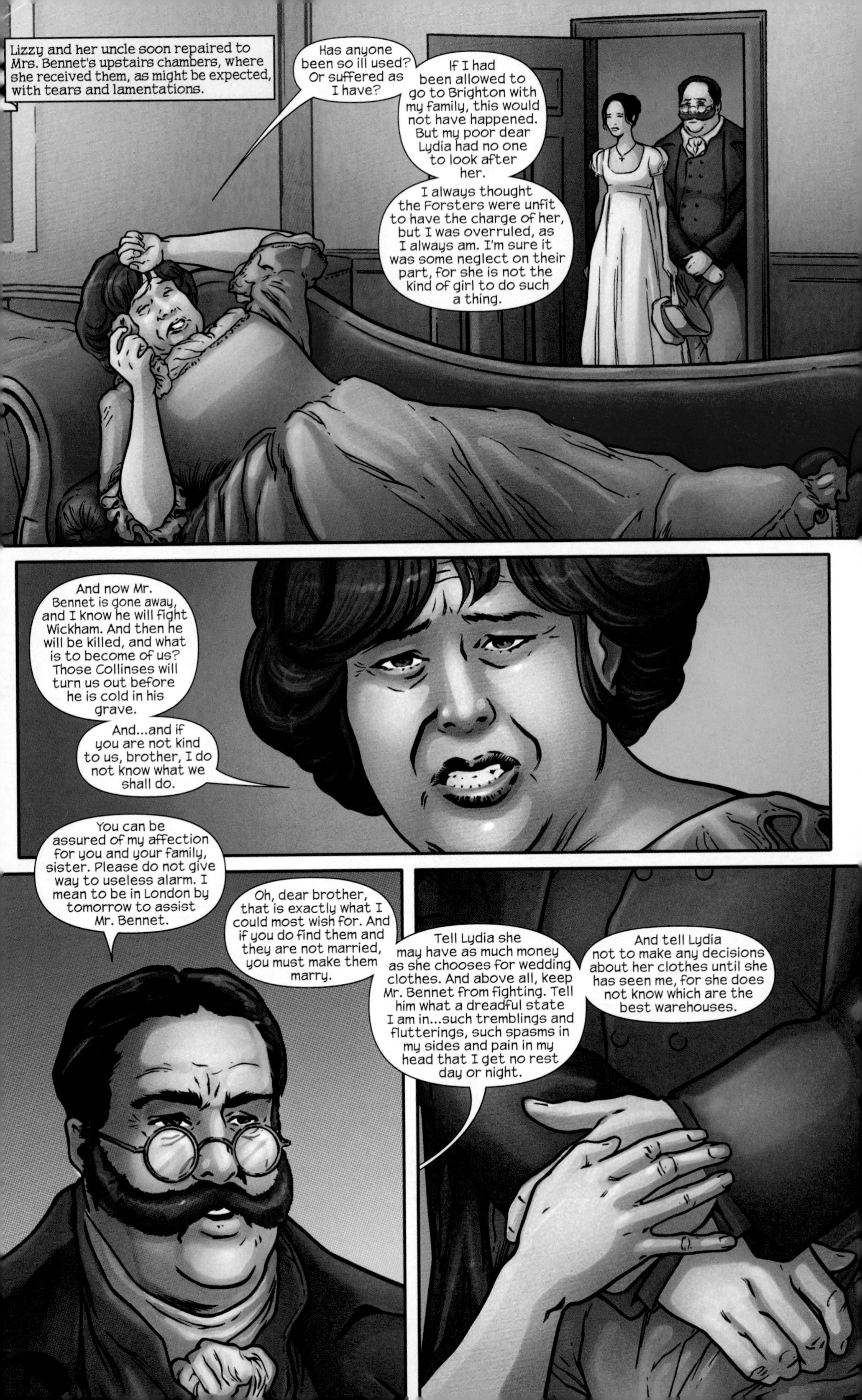
Lizzy and her uncle soon repaired to Mrs. Bennet's upstairs chambers, where she received them, as might be expected, with tears and lamentations.
Has anyone been so ill used? Or suffered as I have?
If I had been allowed to go to Brighton with my family, this would not have happened. But my poor dear Lydia had no one to look after her.
I always thought the Forsters were unfit to have the charge of her, but I was overruled, as I always am. I'm sure it was some neglect on their part, for she is not the kind of girl to do such a thing.
And now Mr. Bennet is gone away, and I know he will fight Wickham. And then he will be killed, and what is to become of us? Those Collinses will turn us out before he is cold in his grave.
And...and if you are not kind to us, brother, I do not know what we shall do.
You can be assured of my affection for you and your family, sister. Please do not give way to useless alarm. I mean to be in London by tomorrow to assist Mr. Bennet.
Oh, dear brother, that is exactly what I could most wish for. And if you do find them and they are not married, you must make them marry.
Tell Lydia she may have as much money as she chooses for wedding clothes. And above all, keep Mr. Bennet from fighting. Tell him what a dreadful state I am in...such tremblings and flutterings, such spasms in my sides and pain in my head that I get no rest day or night.
And tell Lydia not to make any decisions about her clothes until she has seen me, for she does not know which are the best warehouses.

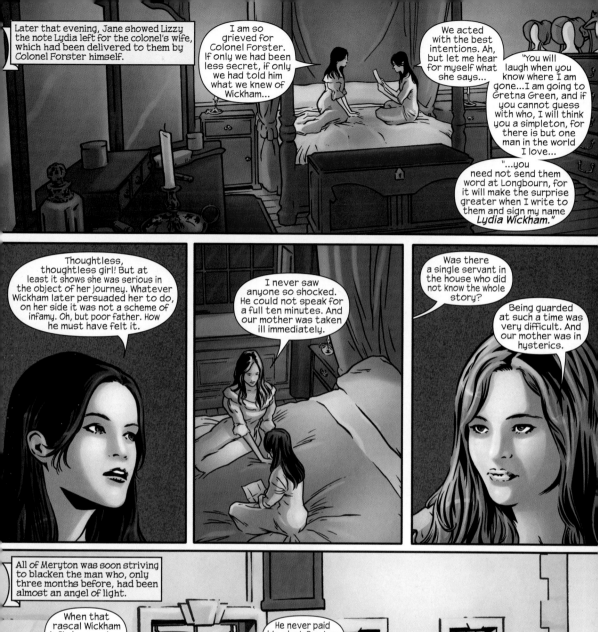

Later that evening, Jane showed Lizzy the note Lydia left for the colonel's wife, which had been delivered to them by Colonel Forster himself.

I am so grieved for Colonel Forster. If only we had been less secret, if only we had told him what we knew of Wickham...

We acted with the best intentions. Ah, but let me hear for myself what she says...

"You will laugh when you know where I am gone...I am going to Gretna Green, and if you cannot guess with who, I will think you a simpleton, for there is but one man in the world I love...

"...you need not send them word at Longbourn, for it will make the surprise greater when I write to them and sign my name Lydia Wickham."

Thoughtless, thoughtless girl! But at least it shows she was serious in the object of her journey. Whatever Wickham later persuaded her to do, on her side it was not a scheme of infamy. Oh, but poor father. How he must have felt it.

I never saw anyone so shocked. He could not speak for a full ten minutes. And our mother was taken ill immediately.

Was there a single servant in the house who did not know the whole story?

Being guarded at such a time was very difficult. And our mother was in hysterics.

All of Meryton was soon striving to blacken the man who, only three months before, had been almost an angel of light.

When that rascal Wickham left, he owed me for three pairs of boots.

He still owes me the ten pounds he lost at dice.

He never paid his shot for two month's worth of dinners.

He promised my girl Bessie a new shawl...in return for what I dare not imagine.

I fear he is the wickedest young man in the world.

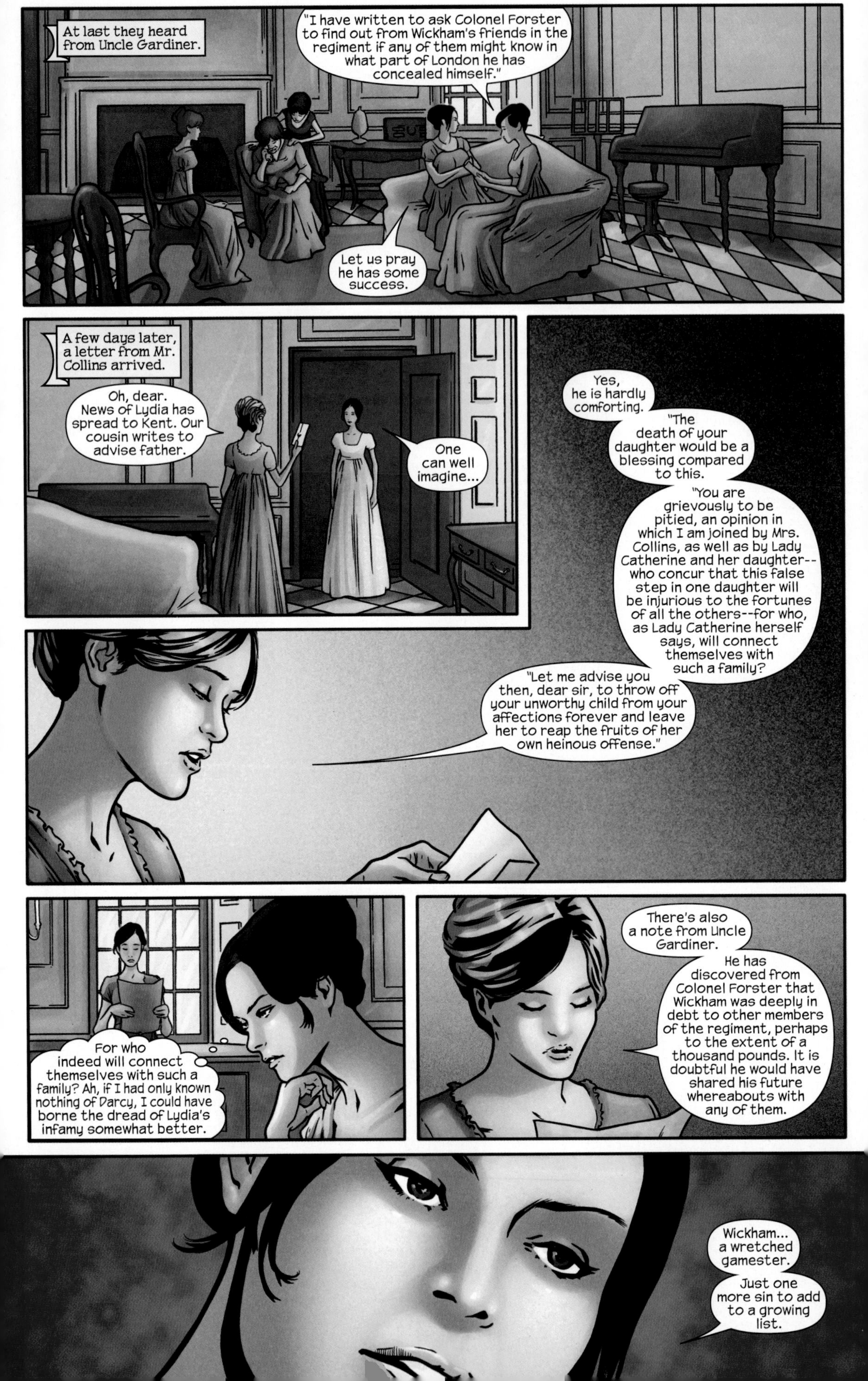
At last they heard from Uncle Gardiner.
"I have written to ask Colonel Forster to find out from Wickham's friends in the regiment if any of them might know in what part of London he has concealed himself."
Let us pray he has some success.
A few days later, a letter from Mr. Collins arrived.
Oh, dear. News of Lydia has spread to Kent. Our cousin writes to advise father.
One can well imagine...
Yes, he is hardly comforting.
"The death of your daughter would be a blessing compared to this.
"You are grievously to be pitied, an opinion in which I am joined by Mrs. Collins, as well as by Lady Catherine and her daughter-- who concur that this false step in one daughter will be injurious to the fortunes of all the others--for who, as Lady Catherine herself says, will connect themselves with such a family?
"Let me advise you then, dear sir, to throw off your unworthy child from your affections forever and leave her to reap the fruits of her own heinous offense."
For who indeed will connect themselves with such a family? Ah, if I had only known nothing of Darcy, I could have borne the dread of Lydia's infamy somewhat better.
There's also a note from Uncle Gardiner.
He has discovered from Colonel Forster that Wickham was deeply in debt to other members of the regiment, perhaps to the extent of a thousand pounds. It is doubtful he would have shared his future whereabouts with any of them.
Wickham... a wretched gamester.
Just one more sin to add to a growing list.

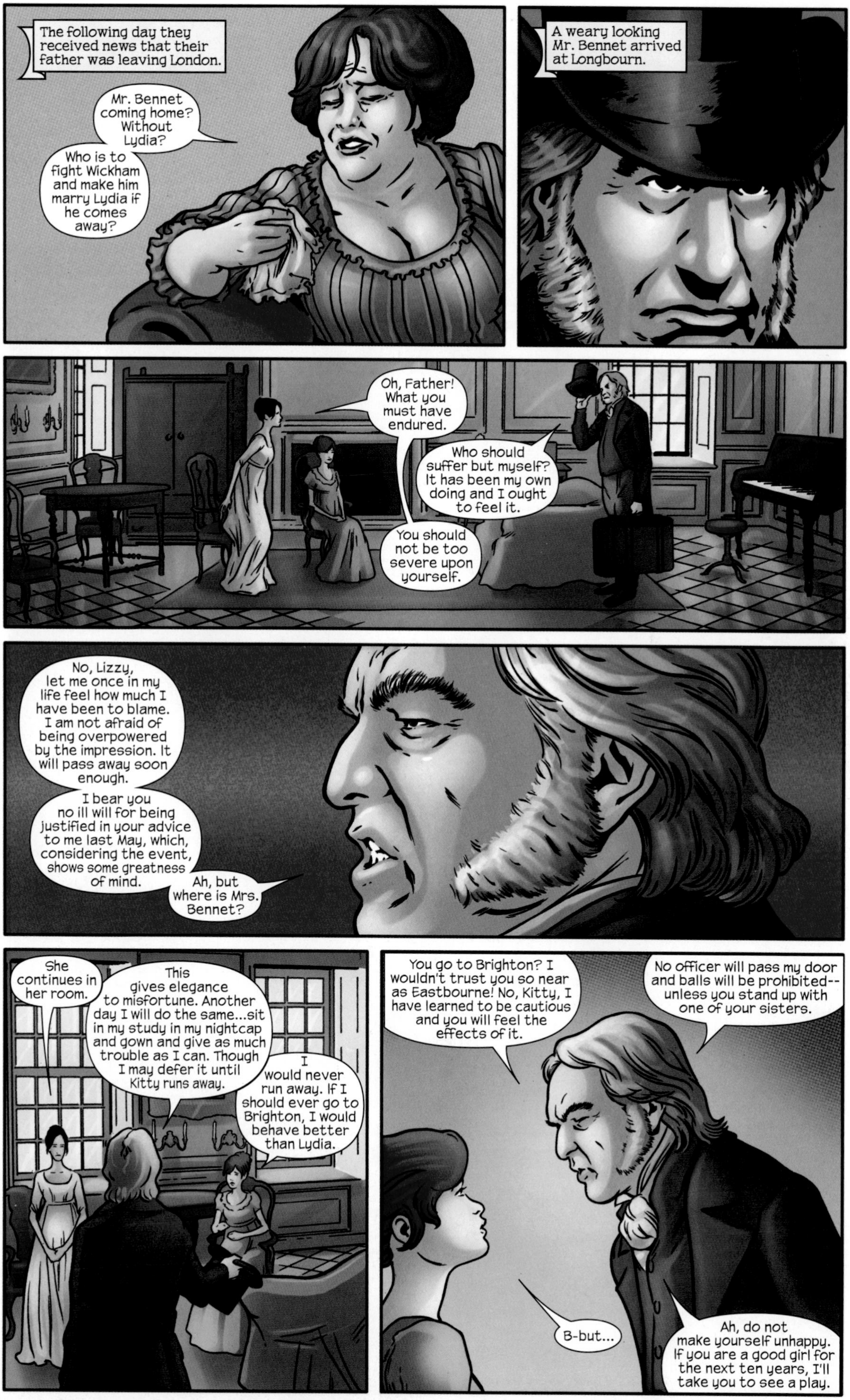

The following day they received news that their father was leaving London.
Mr. Bennet coming home? Without Lydia?
Who is to fight Wickham and make him marry Lydia if he comes away?
A weary looking Mr. Bennet arrived at Longbourn.
Oh, Father! What you must have endured.
Who should suffer but myself? It has been my own doing and I ought to feel it.
You should not be too severe upon yourself.
No, Lizzy, let me once in my life feel how much I have been to blame. I am not afraid of being overpowered by the impression. It will pass away soon enough.
I bear you no ill will for being justified in your advice to me last May, which, considering the event, shows some greatness of mind.
Ah, but where is Mrs. Bennet?
She continues in her room.
This gives elegance to misfortune. Another day I will do the same...sit in my study in my nightcap and gown and give as much trouble as I can. Though I may defer it until Kitty runs away.
I would never run away. If I should ever go to Brighton, I would behave better than Lydia.
You go to Brighton? I wouldn't trust you so near as Eastbourne! No, Kitty, I have learned to be cautious and you will feel the effects of it.
No officer will pass my door and balls will be prohibited-- unless you stand up with one of your sisters.
B-but...
Ah, do not make yourself unhappy. If you are a good girl for the next ten years, I'll take you to see a play.

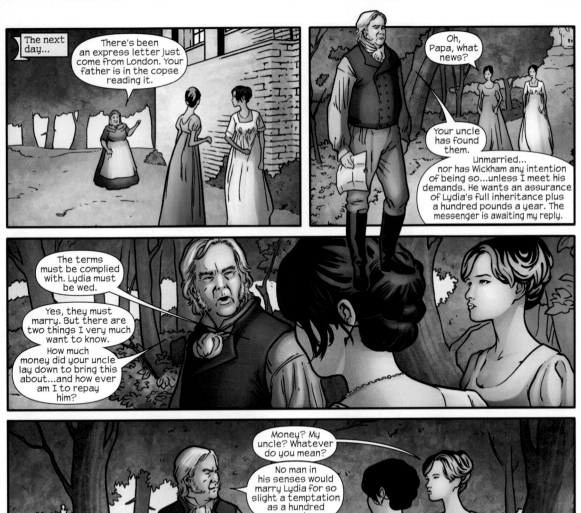

The next day... There's been an express letter just come from London. Your father is in the copse reading it.

Oh, Papa, what news?

Your uncle has found them. Unmarried... nor has Wickham any intention of being so...unless I meet his demands. He wants an assurance of Lydia's full inheritance plus a hundred pounds a year. The messenger is awaiting my reply.

The terms must be complied with. Lydia must be wed.

Yes, they must marry. But there are two things I very much want to know.

How much money did your uncle lay down to bring this about...and how ever am I to repay him?

Money? My uncle? Whatever do you mean?

No man in his senses would marry Lydia for so slight a temptation as a hundred pounds.

Your uncle, good man, doubtless paid off the fellow's debts and caused himself even further distress, since a small sum could not do all this.

Wickham's a fool to take her for a farthing less than ten thousand pounds.

But how is such a sum to be repaid?

Precisely.

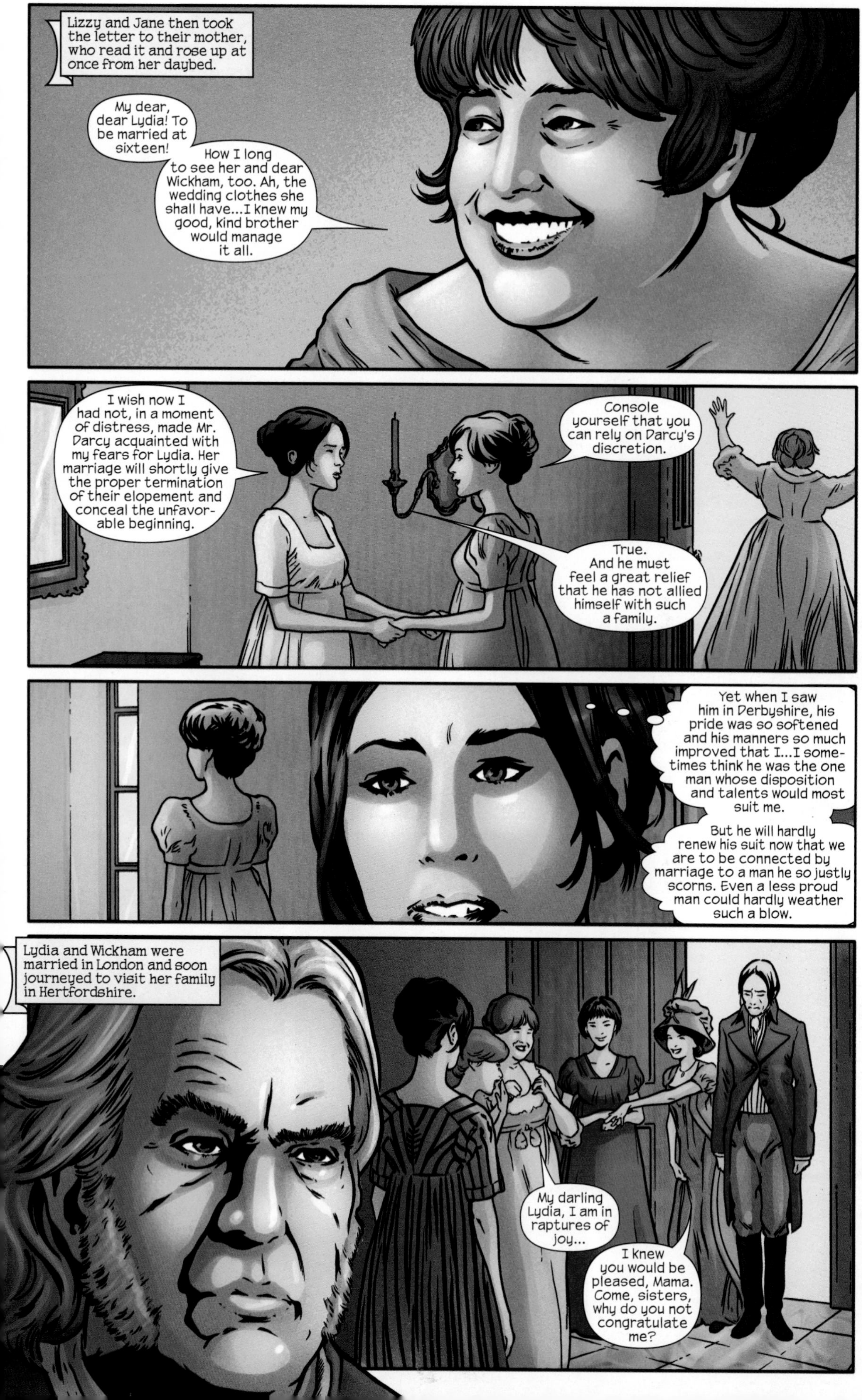
Lizzy and Jane then took the letter to their mother, who read it and rose up at once from her daybed.
My dear, dear Lydia! To be married at sixteen!
How I long to see her and dear Wickham, too. Ah, the wedding clothes she shall have...I knew my good, kind brother would manage it all.
I wish now I had not, in a moment of distress, made Mr. Darcy acquainted with my fears for Lydia. Her marriage will shortly give the proper termination of their elopement and conceal the unfavor-able beginning.
Console yourself that you can rely on Darcy's discretion.
True. And he must feel a great relief that he has not allied himself with such a family.
Yet when I saw him in Derbyshire, his pride was so softened and his manners so much improved that I...I some-times think he was the one man whose disposition and talents would most suit me.
But he will hardly renew his suit now that we are to be connected by marriage to a man he so justly scorns. Even a less proud man could hardly weather such a blow.
Lydia and Wickham were married in London and soon journeyed to visit her family in Hertfordshire.
My darling Lydia, I am in raptures of joy...
I knew you would be pleased, Mama. Come, sisters, why do you not congratulate me?

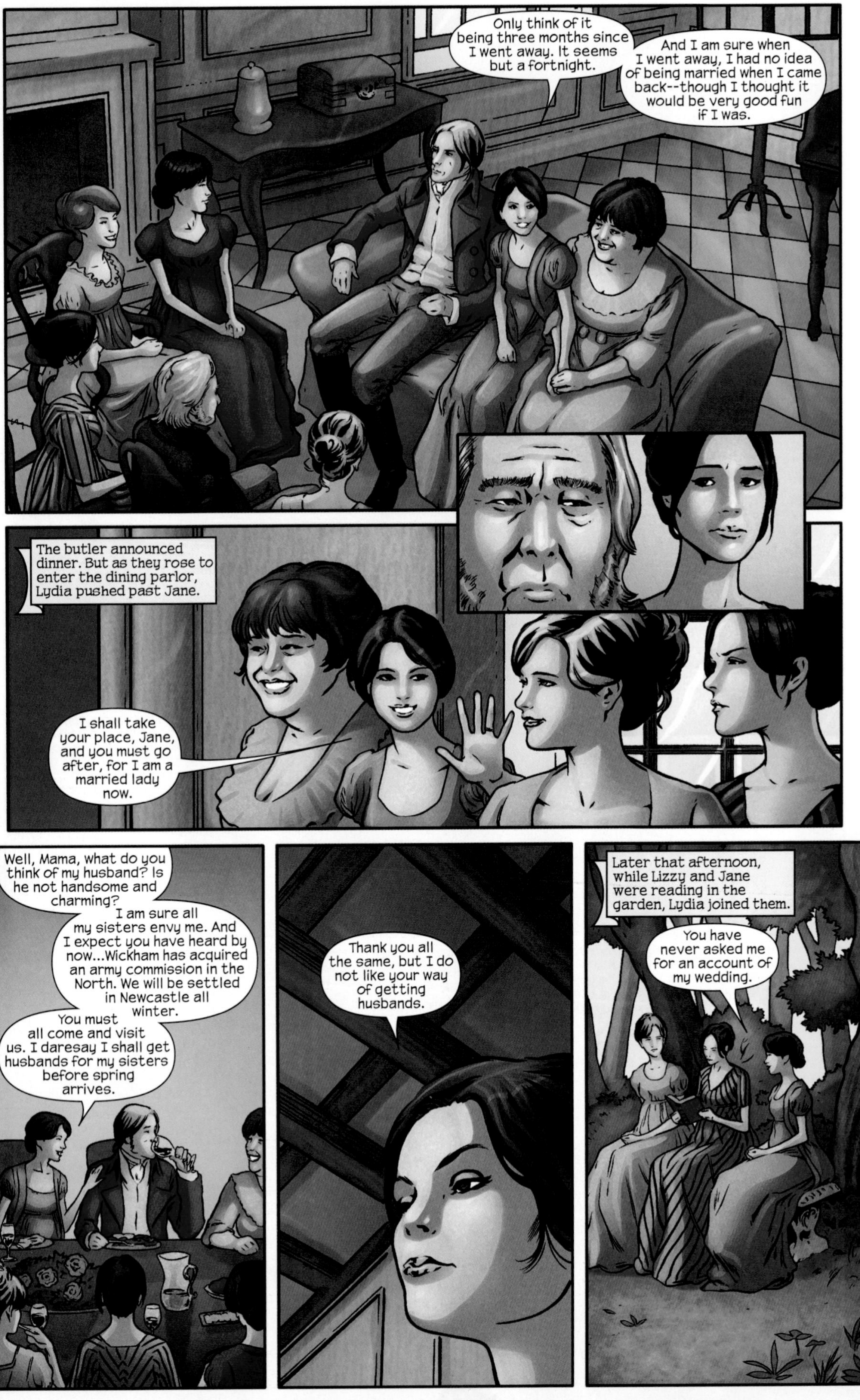
Only think of it being three months since I went away. It seems but a fortnight.
And I am sure when I went away, I had no idea of being married when I came back--though I thought it would be very good fun if I was.
The butler announced dinner. But as they rose to enter the dining parlor, Lydia pushed past Jane.
I shall take your place, Jane, and you must go after, for I am a married lady now.
Well, Mama, what do you think of my husband? Is he not handsome and charming?
I am sure all my sisters envy me. And I expect you have heard by now...Wickham has acquired an army commission in the North. We will be settled in Newcastle all winter.
You must all come and visit us. I daresay I shall get husbands for my sisters before spring arrives.
Thank you all the same, but I do not like your way of getting husbands.
Later that afternoon, while Lizzy and Jane were reading in the garden, Lydia joined them.
You have never asked me for an account of my wedding.

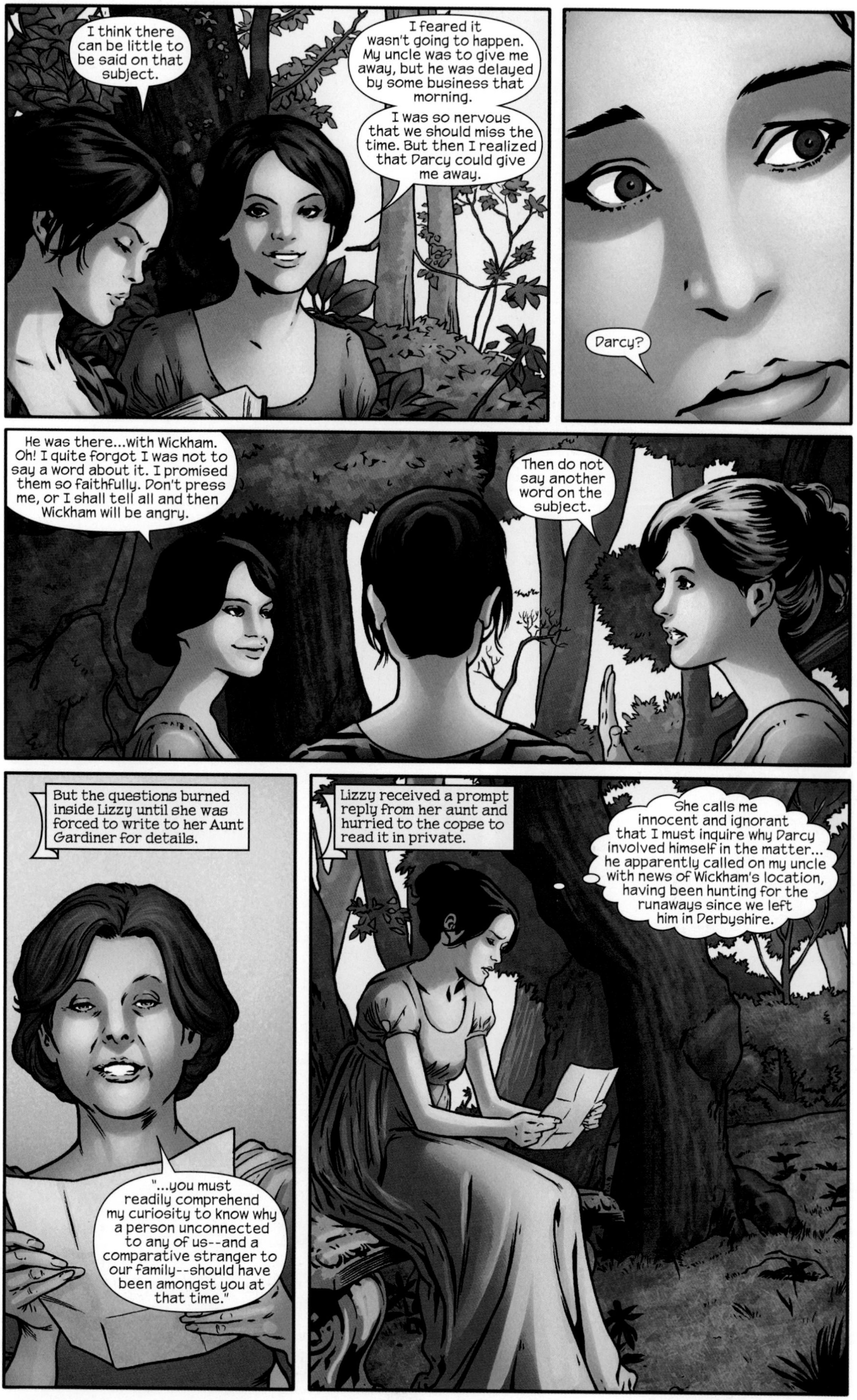
I think there can be little to be said on that subject.
I feared it wasn't going to happen. My uncle was to give me away, but he was delayed by some business that morning.
I was so nervous that we should miss the time. But then I realized that Darcy could give me away.
Darcy?
He was there...with Wickham. Oh! I quite forgot I was not to say a word about it. I promised them so faithfully. Don't press me, or I shall tell all and then Wickham will be angry.
Then do not say another word on the subject.
But the questions burned inside Lizzy until she was forced to write to her Aunt Gardiner for details.
"...you must readily comprehend my curiosity to know why a person unconnected to any of us--and a comparative stranger to our family--should have been amongst you at that time."
Lizzy received a prompt reply from her aunt and hurried to the copse to read it in private.
She calls me innocent and ignorant that I must inquire why Darcy involved himself in the matter... he apparently called on my uncle with news of Wickham's location, having been hunting for the runaways since we left him in Derbyshire.

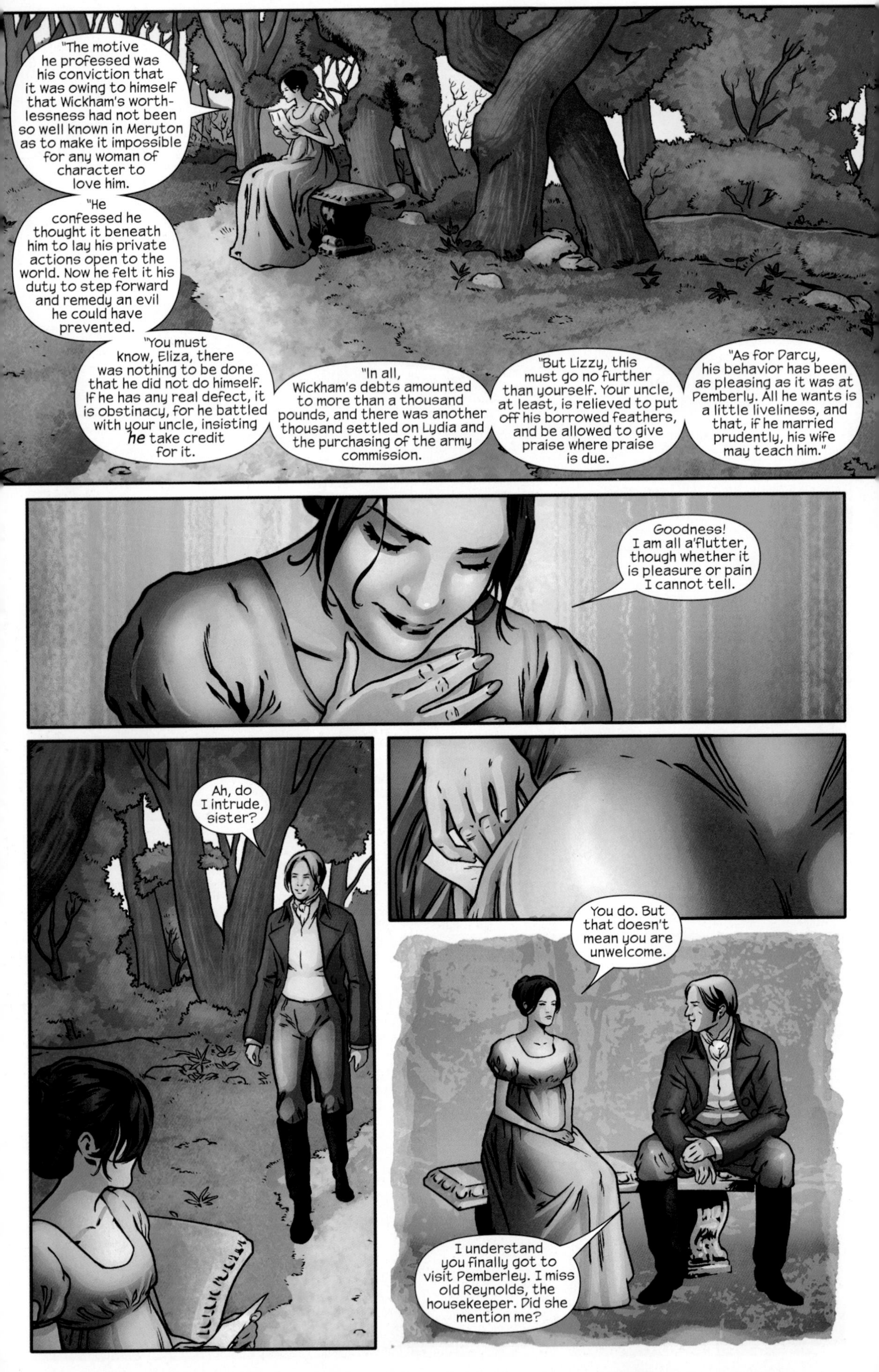
"The motive he professed was his conviction that it was owing to himself that Wickham's worthlessness had not been so well known in Meryton as to make it impossible for any woman of character to love him.
"He confessed he thought it beneath him to lay his private actions open to the world. Now he felt it his duty to step forward and remedy an evil he could have prevented.
"You must know, Eliza, there was nothing to be done that he did not do himself. If he has any real defect, it is obstinacy, for he battled with your uncle, insisting *he* take credit for it.
"In all, Wickham's debts amounted to more than a thousand pounds, and there was another thousand settled on Lydia and the purchasing of the army commission.
"But Lizzy, this must go no further than yourself. Your uncle, at least, is relieved to put off his borrowed feathers, and be allowed to give praise where praise is due.
"As for Darcy, his behavior has been as pleasing as it was at Pemberly. All he wants is a little liveliness, and that, if he married prudently, his wife may teach him."
Goodness! I am all a'flutter, though whether it is pleasure or pain I cannot tell.
Ah, do I intrude, sister?
You do. But that doesn't mean you are unwelcome.
I understand you finally got to visit Pemberley. I miss old Reynolds, the housekeeper. Did she mention me?

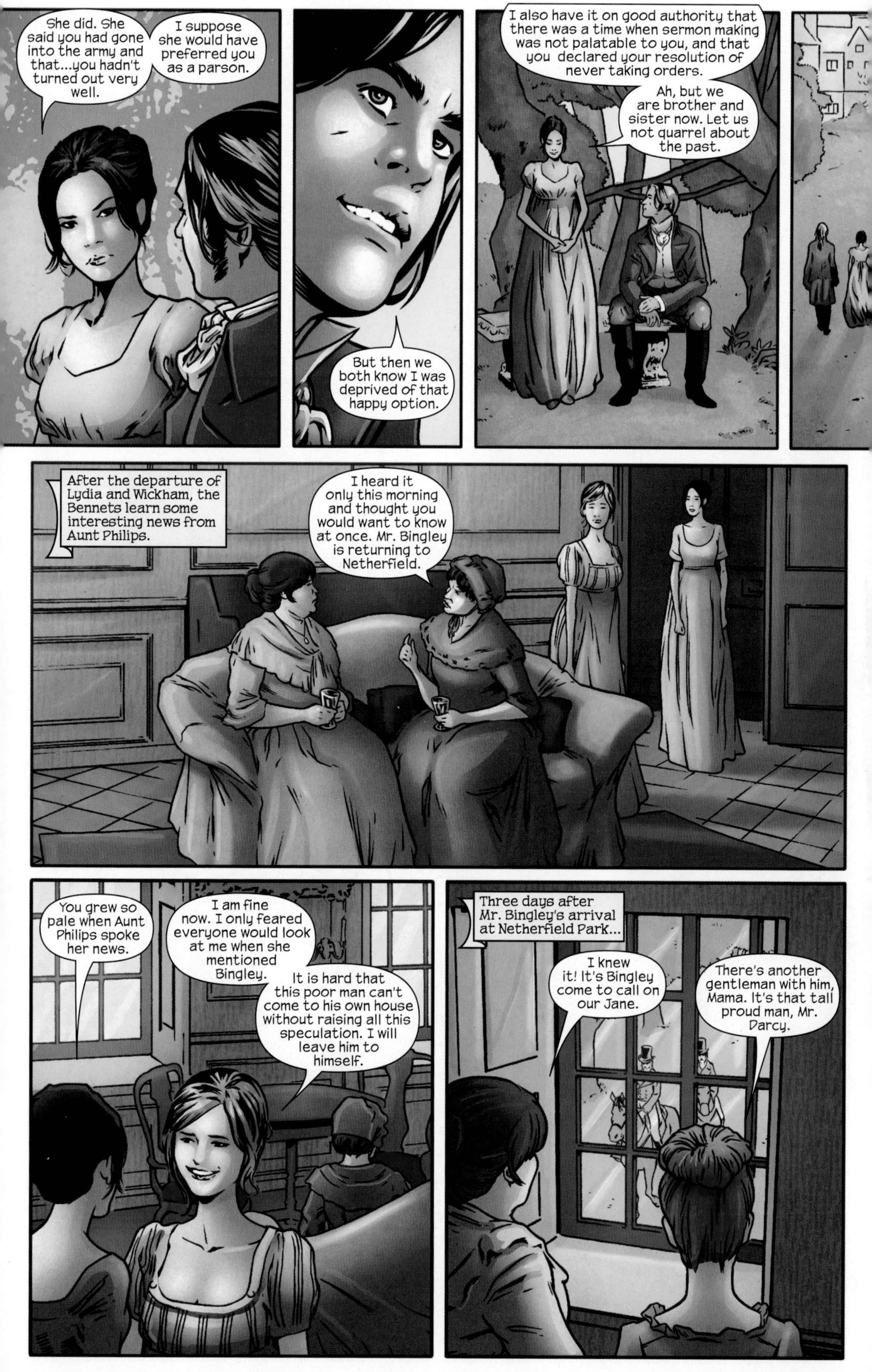
She did. She said you had gone into the army and that...you hadn't turned out very well.
I suppose she would have preferred you as a parson.
But then we both know I was deprived of that happy option.
I also have it on good authority that there was a time when sermon making was not palatable to you, and that you declared your resolution of never taking orders.
Ah, but we are brother and sister now. Let us not quarrel about the past.
After the departure of Lydia and Wickham, the Bennets learn some interesting news from Aunt Philips.
I heard it only this morning and thought you would want to know at once. Mr. Bingley is returning to Netherfield.
You grew so pale when Aunt Philips spoke her news.
I am fine now. I only feared everyone would look at me when she mentioned Bingley.
It is hard that this poor man can't come to his own house without raising all this speculation. I will leave him to himself.
Three days after Mr. Bingley's arrival at Netherfield Park...
I knew it! It's Bingley come to call on our Jane.
There's another gentleman with him, Mama. It's that tall proud man, Mr. Darcy.

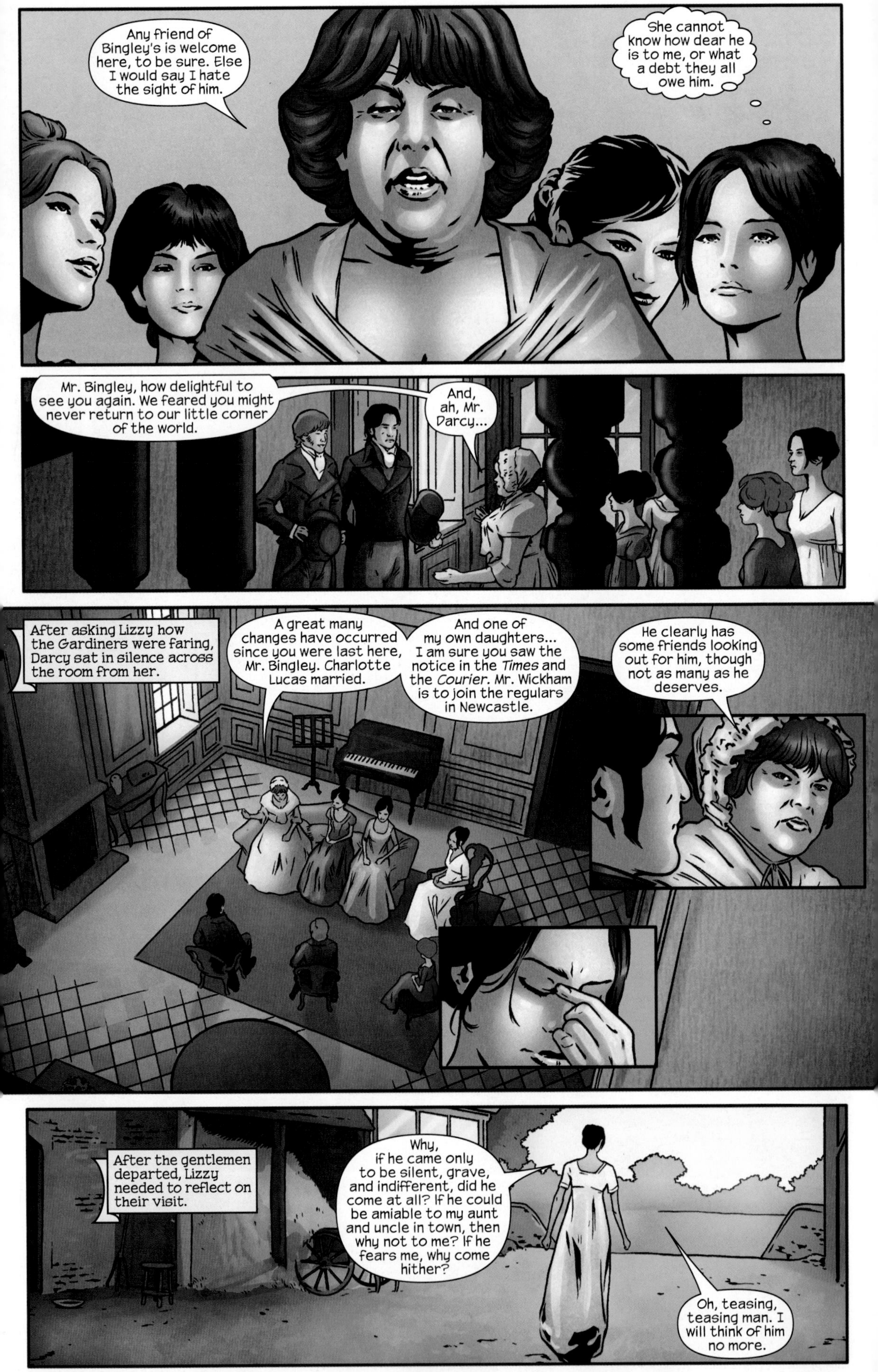
Any friend of Bingley's is welcome here, to be sure. Else I would say I hate the sight of him.
She cannot know how dear he is to me, or what a debt they all owe him.
Mr. Bingley, how delightful to see you again. We feared you might never return to our little corner of the world.
And, ah, Mr. Darcy...
After asking Lizzy how the Gardiners were faring, Darcy sat in silence across the room from her.
A great many changes have occurred since you were last here, Mr. Bingley. Charlotte Lucas married.
And one of my own daughters... I am sure you saw the notice in the *Times* and the *Courier*. Mr. Wickham is to join the regulars in Newcastle.
He clearly has some friends looking out for him, though not as many as he deserves.
After the gentlemen departed, Lizzy needed to reflect on their visit.
Why, if he came only to be silent, grave, and indifferent, did he come at all? If he could be amiable to my aunt and uncle in town, then why not to me? If he fears me, why come hither?
Oh, teasing, teasing man. I will think of him no more.

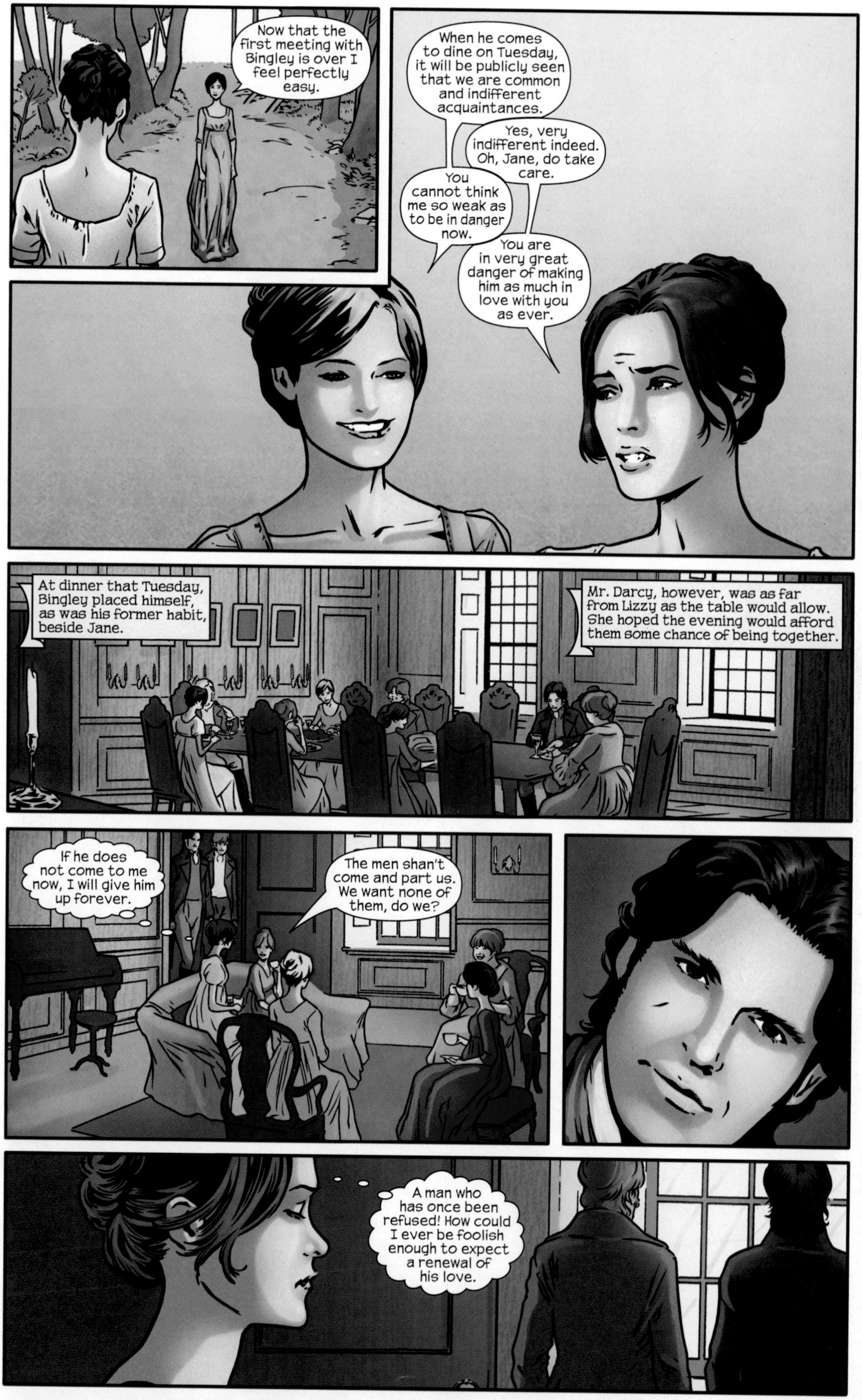
Now that the first meeting with Bingley is over I feel perfectly easy.
When he comes to dine on Tuesday, it will be publicly seen that we are common and indifferent acquaintances.
Yes, very indifferent indeed. Oh, Jane, do take care.
You cannot think me so weak as to be in danger now.
You are in very great danger of making him as much in love with you as ever.
At dinner that Tuesday, Bingley placed himself, as was his former habit, beside Jane.
Mr. Darcy, however, was as far from Lizzy as the table would allow. She hoped the evening would afford them some chance of being together.
If he does not come to me now, I will give him up forever.
The men shan't come and part us. We want none of them, do we?
A man who has once been refused! How could I ever be foolish enough to expect a renewal of his love.

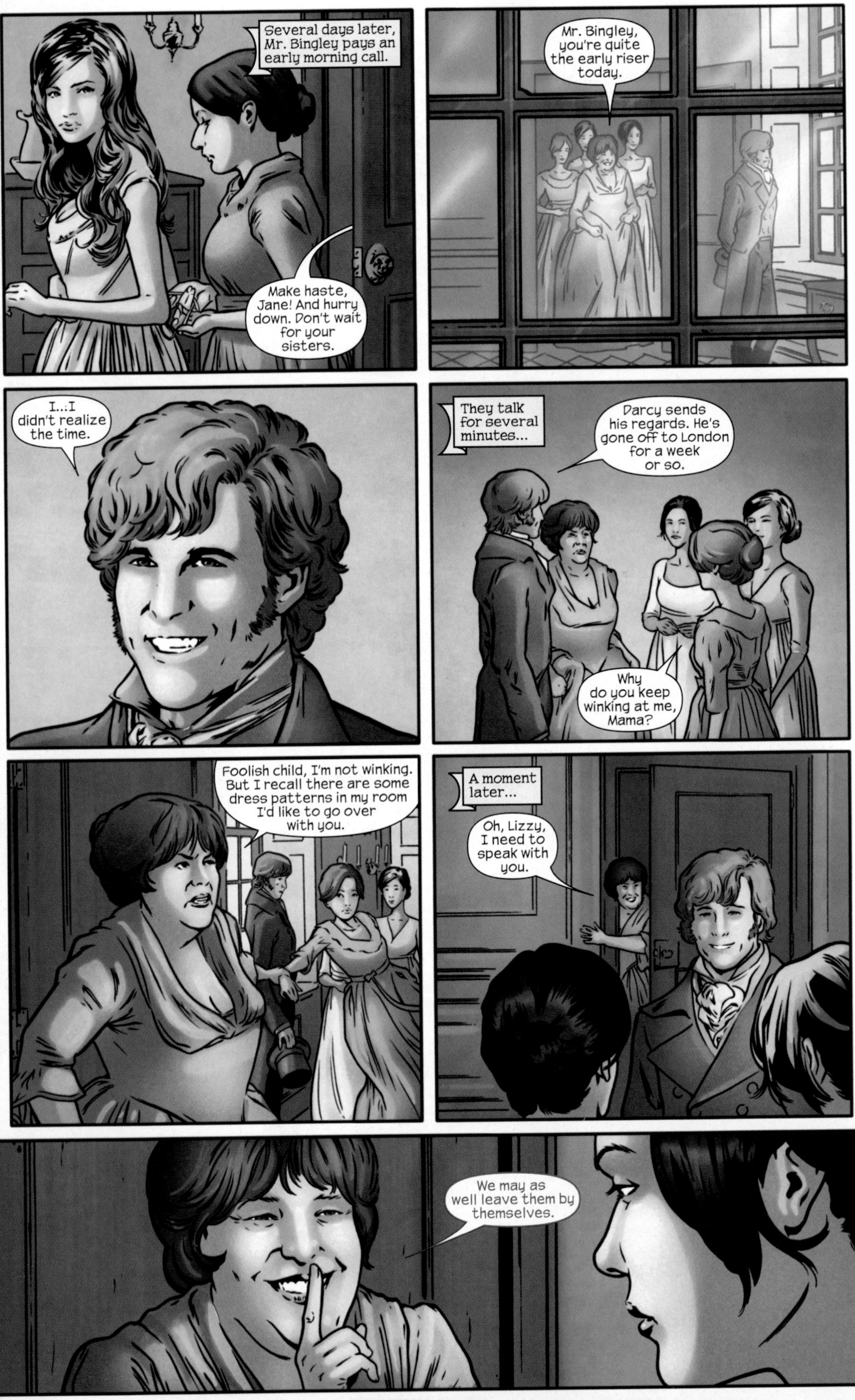
Several days later, Mr. Bingley pays an early morning call.
Make haste, Jane! And hurry down. Don't wait for your sisters.
Mr. Bingley, you're quite the early riser today.
I...I didn't realize the time.
They talk for several minutes...
Darcy sends his regards. He's gone off to London for a week or so.
Why do you keep winking at me, Mama?
Foolish child, I'm not winking. But I recall there are some dress patterns in my room I'd like to go over with you.
A moment later...
Oh, Lizzy, I need to speak with you.
We may as well leave them by themselves.

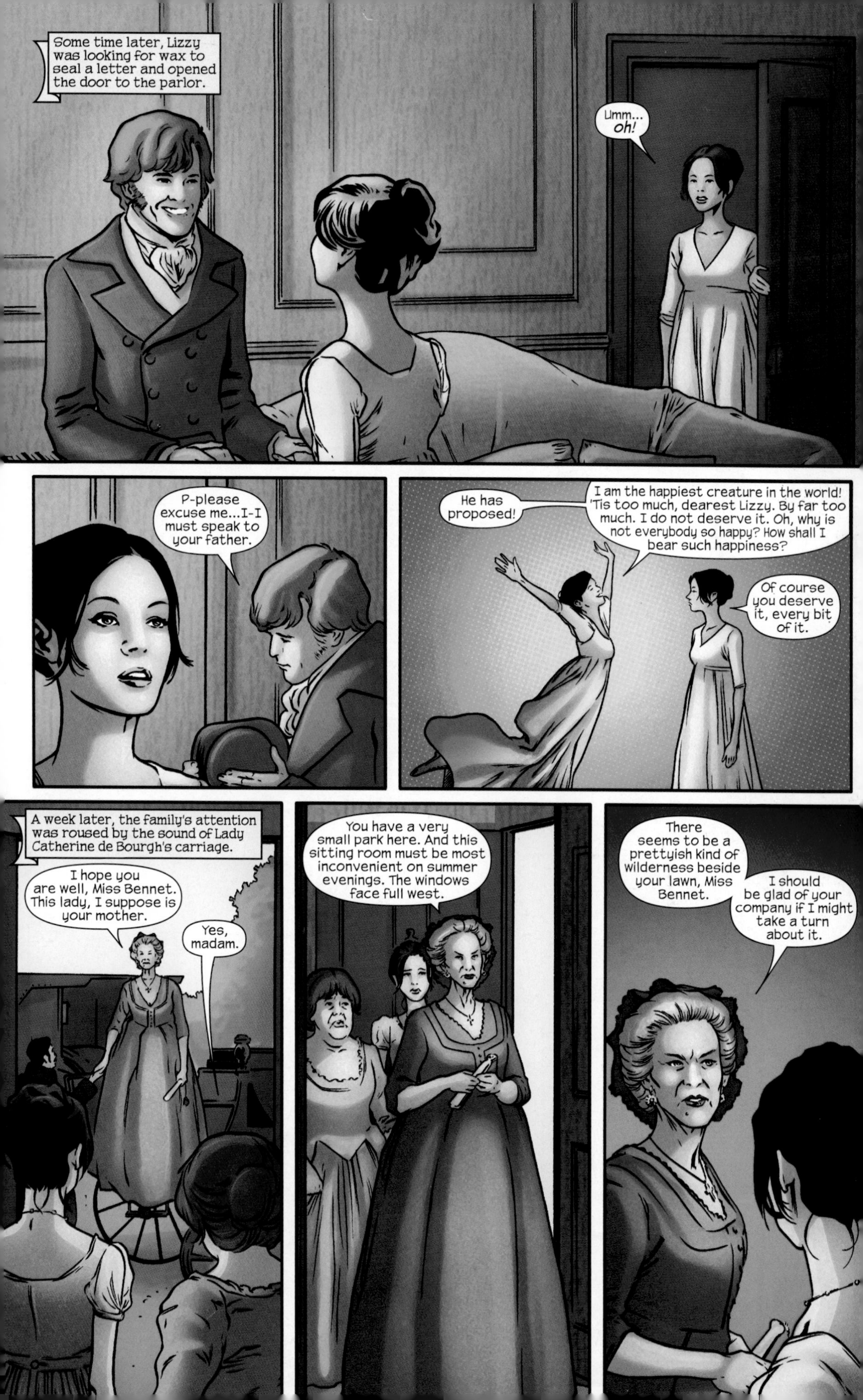
Some time later, Lizzy was looking for wax to seal a letter and opened the door to the parlor.
Umm... oh!
P-please excuse me...I-I must speak to your father.
He has proposed!
I am the happiest creature in the world! 'Tis too much, dearest Lizzy. By far too much. I do not deserve it. Oh, why is not everybody so happy? How shall I bear such happiness?
Of course you deserve it, every bit of it.
A week later, the family's attention was roused by the sound of Lady Catherine de Bourgh's carriage.
I hope you are well, Miss Bennet. This lady, I suppose is your mother.
Yes, madam.
You have a very small park here. And this sitting room must be most inconvenient on summer evenings. The windows face full west.
There seems to be a prettyish kind of wilderness beside your lawn, Miss Bennet.
I should be glad of your company if I might take a turn about it.

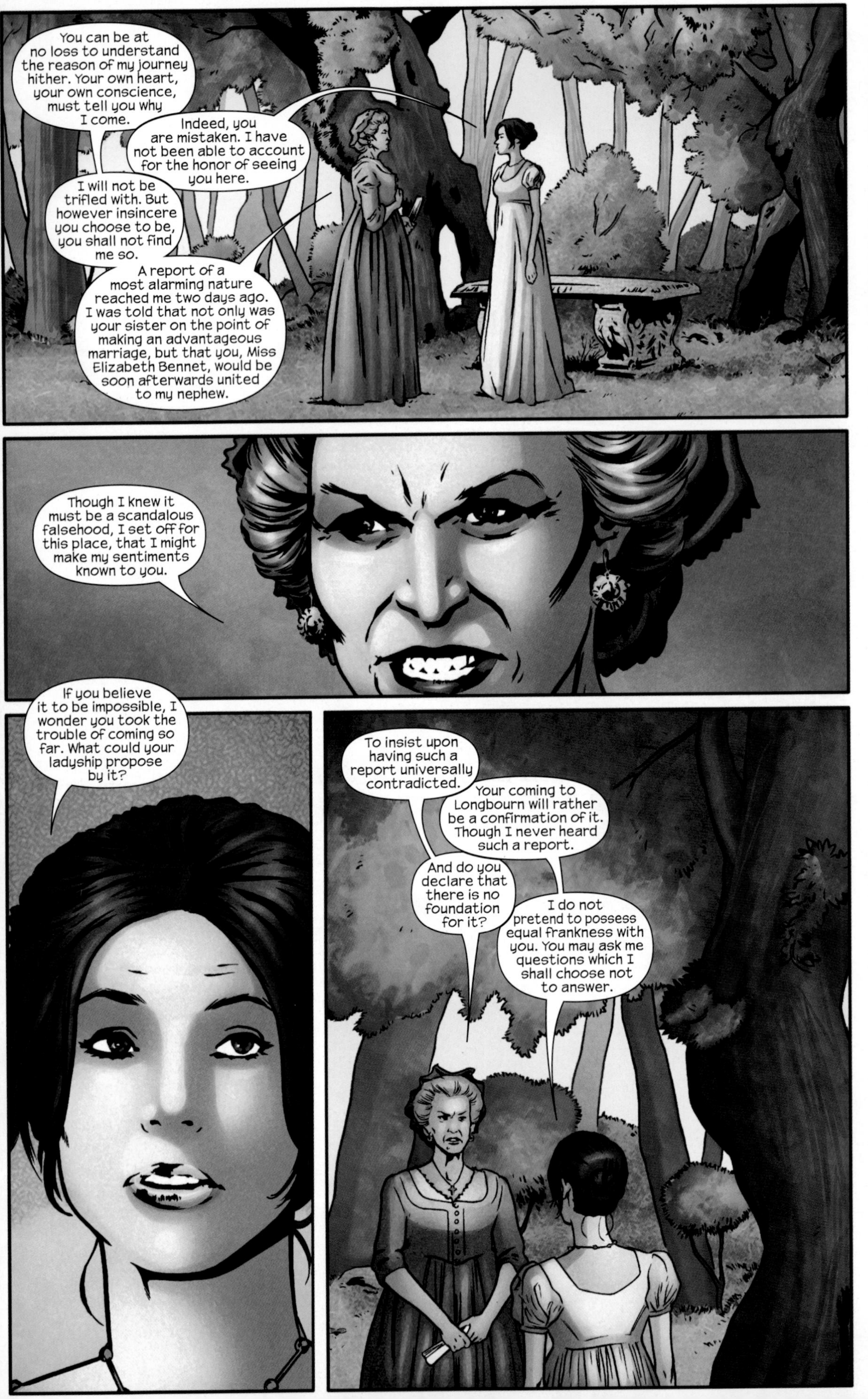
You can be at no loss to understand the reason of my journey hither. Your own heart, your own conscience, must tell you why I come.
Indeed, you are mistaken. I have not been able to account for the honor of seeing you here.
I will not be trifled with. But however insincere you choose to be, you shall not find me so.
A report of a most alarming nature reached me two days ago. I was told that not only was your sister on the point of making an advantageous marriage, but that you, Miss Elizabeth Bennet, would be soon afterwards united to my nephew.
Though I knew it must be a scandalous falsehood, I set off for this place, that I might make my sentiments known to you.
If you believe it to be impossible, I wonder you took the trouble of coming so far. What could your ladyship propose by it?
To insist upon having such a report universally contradicted.
Your coming to Longbourn will rather be a confirmation of it. Though I never heard such a report.
And do you declare that there is no foundation for it?
I do not pretend to possess equal frankness with you. You may ask me questions which I shall choose not to answer.

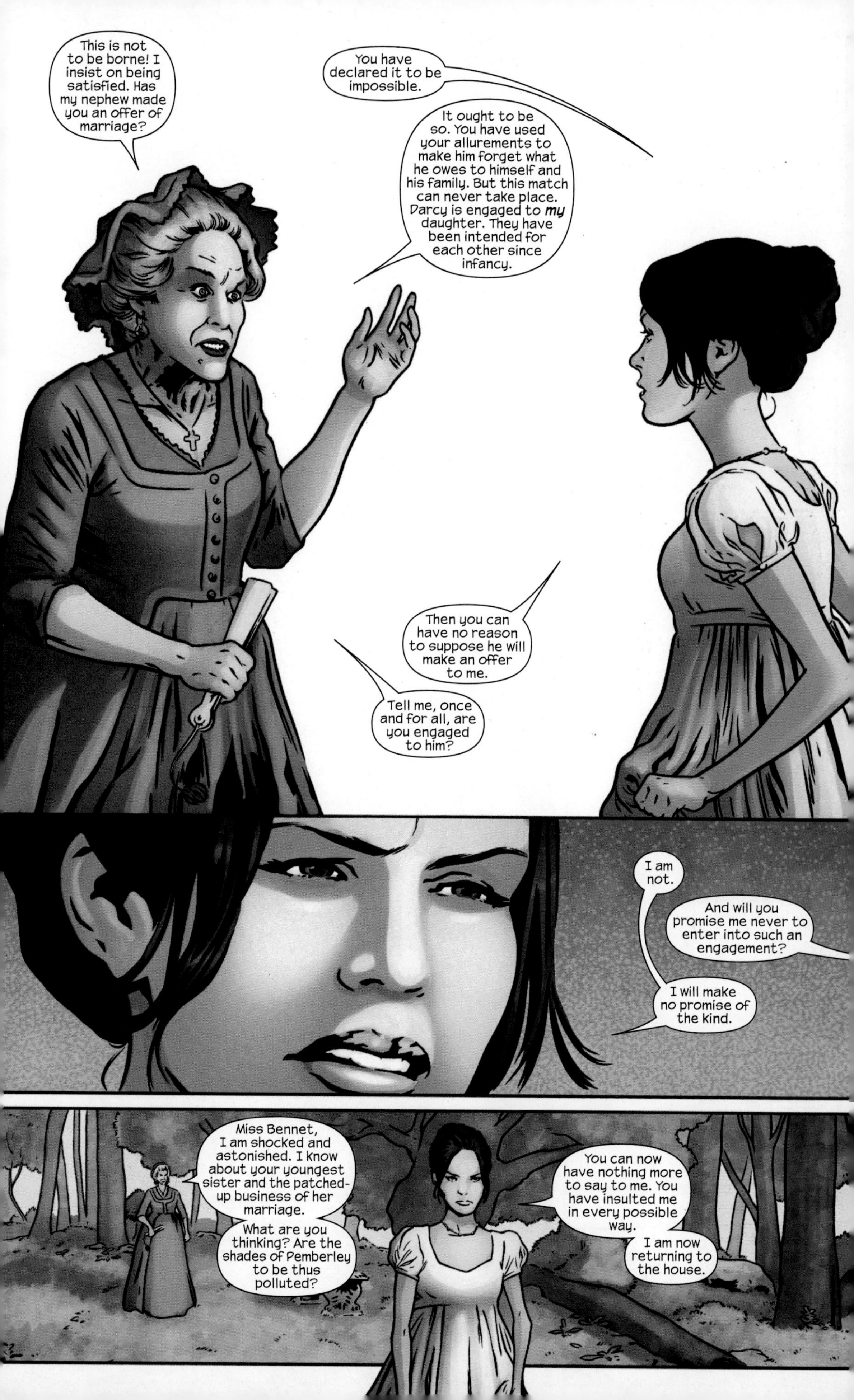
This is not to be borne! I insist on being satisfied. Has my nephew made you an offer of marriage?
You have declared it to be impossible.
It ought to be so. You have used your allurements to make him forget what he owes to himself and his family. But this match can never take place. Darcy is engaged to *my* daughter. They have been intended for each other since infancy.
Then you can have no reason to suppose he will make an offer to me.
Tell me, once and for all, are you engaged to him?
I am not.
And will you promise me never to enter into such an engagement?
I will make no promise of the kind.
Miss Bennet, I am shocked and astonished. I know about your youngest sister and the patched-up business of her marriage.
What are you thinking? Are the shades of Pemberley to be thus polluted?
You can now have nothing more to say to me. You have insulted me in every possible way.
I am now returning to the house.

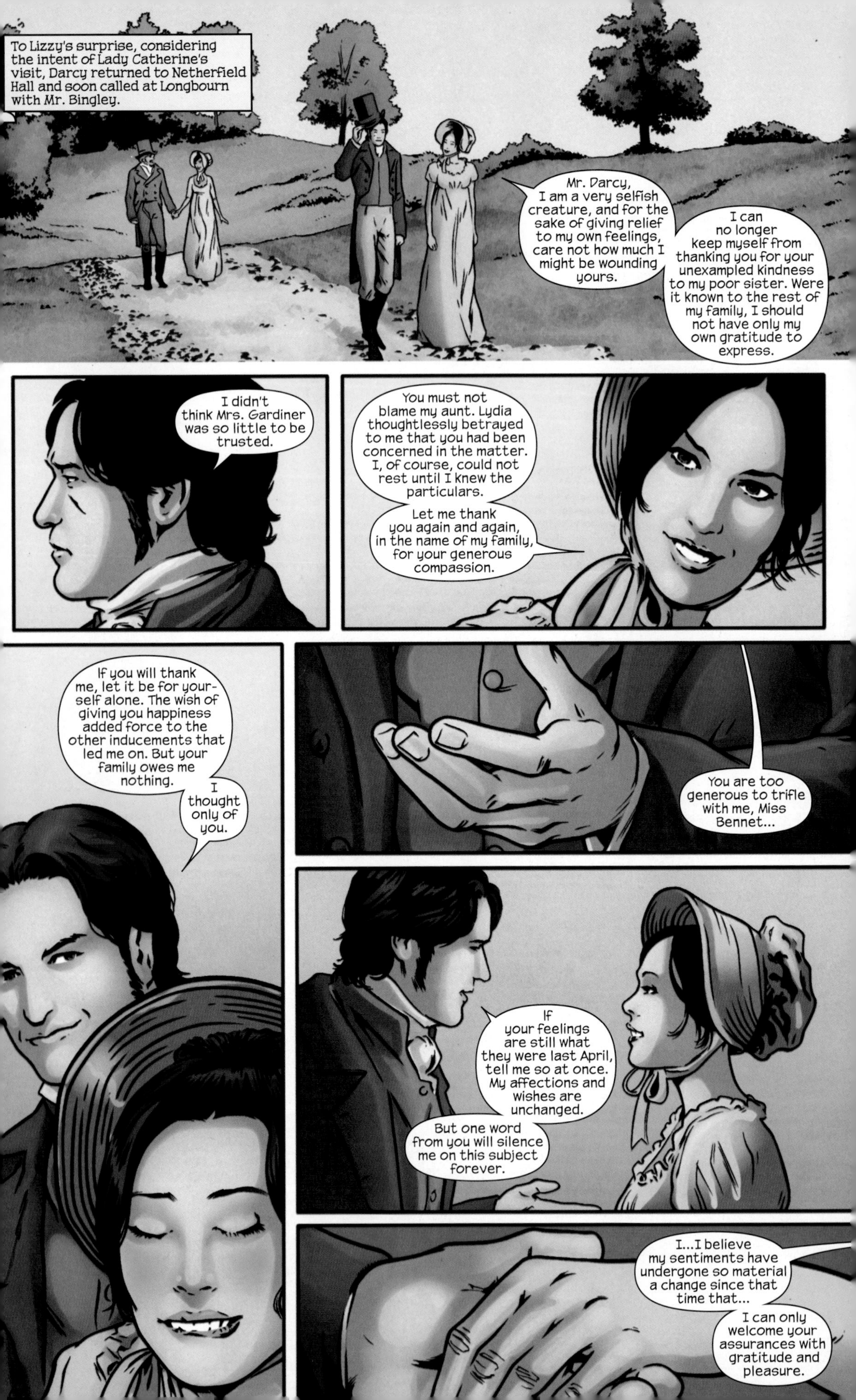

To Lizzy's surprise, considering the intent of Lady Catherine's visit, Darcy returned to Netherfield Hall and soon called at Longbourn with Mr. Bingley.
Mr. Darcy, I am a very selfish creature, and for the sake of giving relief to my own feelings, care not how much I might be wounding yours.
I can no longer keep myself from thanking you for your unexampled kindness to my poor sister. Were it known to the rest of my family, I should not have only my own gratitude to express.
I didn't think Mrs. Gardiner was so little to be trusted.
You must not blame my aunt. Lydia thoughtlessly betrayed to me that you had been concerned in the matter. I, of course, could not rest until I knew the particulars.
Let me thank you again and again, in the name of my family, for your generous compassion.
If you will thank me, let it be for your-self alone. The wish of giving you happiness added force to the other inducements that led me on. But your family owes me nothing.
I thought only of you.
You are too generous to trifle with me, Miss Bennet...
If your feelings are still what they were last April, tell me so at once. My affections and wishes are unchanged.
But one word from you will silence me on this subject forever.
I...I believe my sentiments have undergone so material a change since that time that...
I can only welcome your assurances with gratitude and pleasure.

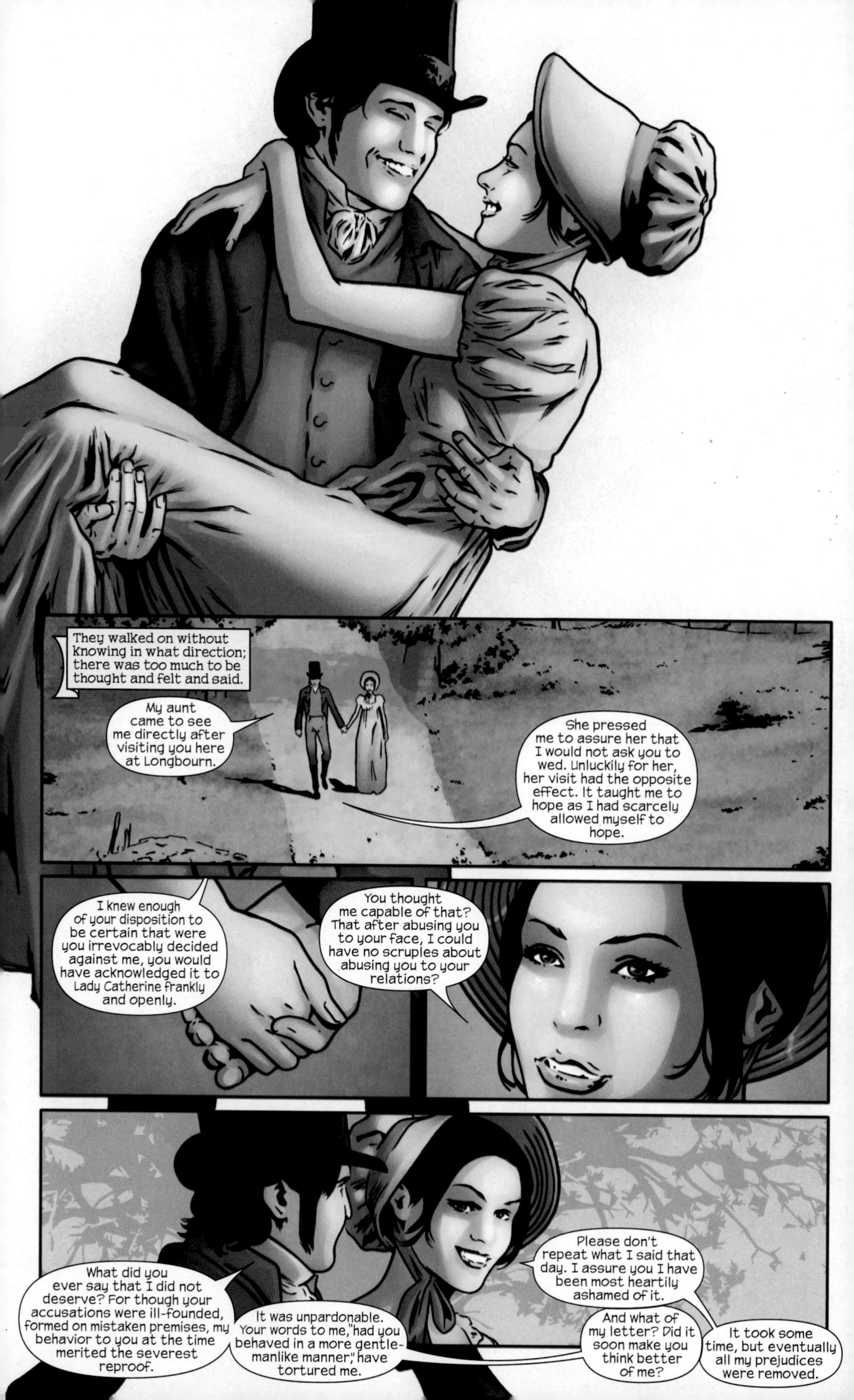
They walked on without knowing in what direction; there was too much to be thought and felt and said.
My aunt came to see me directly after visiting you here at Longbourn.
She pressed me to assure her that I would not ask you to wed. Unluckily for her, her visit had the opposite effect. It taught me to hope as I had scarcely allowed myself to hope.
I knew enough of your disposition to be certain that were you irrevocably decided against me, you would have acknowledged it to Lady Catherine frankly and openly.
You thought me capable of that? That after abusing you to your face, I could have no scruples about abusing you to your relations?
What did you ever say that I did not deserve? For though your accusations were ill-founded, formed on mistaken premises, my behavior to you at the time merited the severest reproof.
Please don't repeat what I said that day. I assure you I have been most heartily ashamed of it.
It was unpardonable. Your words to me, "had you behaved in a more gentle-manlike manner," have tortured me.
And what of my letter? Did it soon make you think better of me?
It took some time, but eventually all my prejudices were removed.

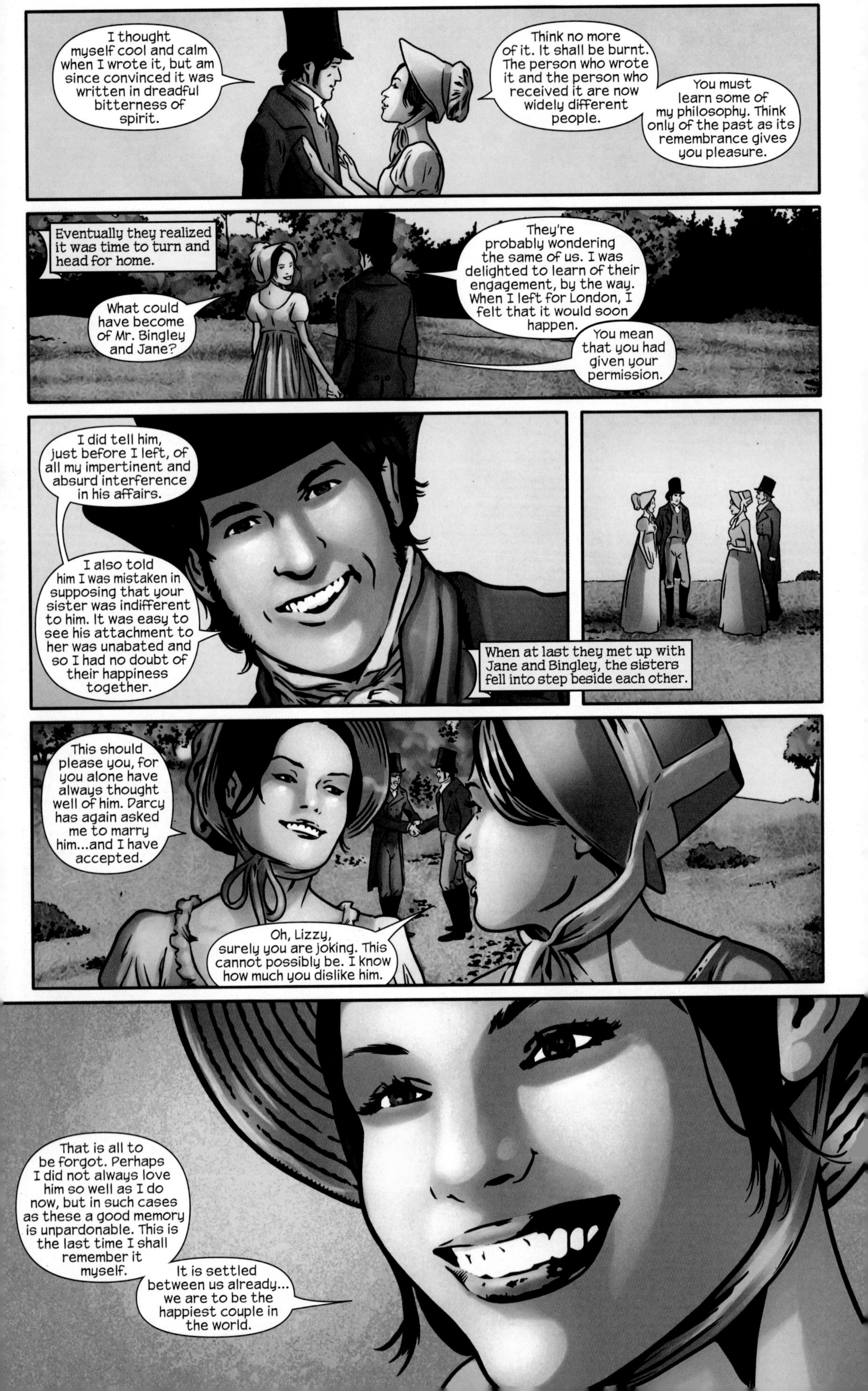
I thought myself cool and calm when I wrote it, but am since convinced it was written in dreadful bitterness of spirit.
Think no more of it. It shall be burnt. The person who wrote it and the person who received it are now widely different people.
You must learn some of my philosophy. Think only of the past as its remembrance gives you pleasure.
Eventually they realized it was time to turn and head for home.
What could have become of Mr. Bingley and Jane?
They're probably wondering the same of us. I was delighted to learn of their engagement, by the way. When I left for London, I felt that it would soon happen.
You mean that you had given your permission.
I did tell him, just before I left, of all my impertinent and absurd interference in his affairs.
I also told him I was mistaken in supposing that your sister was indifferent to him. It was easy to see his attachment to her was unabated and so I had no doubt of their happiness together.
When at last they met up with Jane and Bingley, the sisters fell into step beside each other.
This should please you, for you alone have always thought well of him. Darcy has again asked me to marry him...and I have accepted.
Oh, Lizzy, surely you are joking. This cannot possibly be. I know how much you dislike him.
That is all to be forgot. Perhaps I did not always love him so well as I do now, but in such cases as these a good memory is unpardonable. This is the last time I shall remember it myself.
It is settled between us already... we are to be the happiest couple in the world.

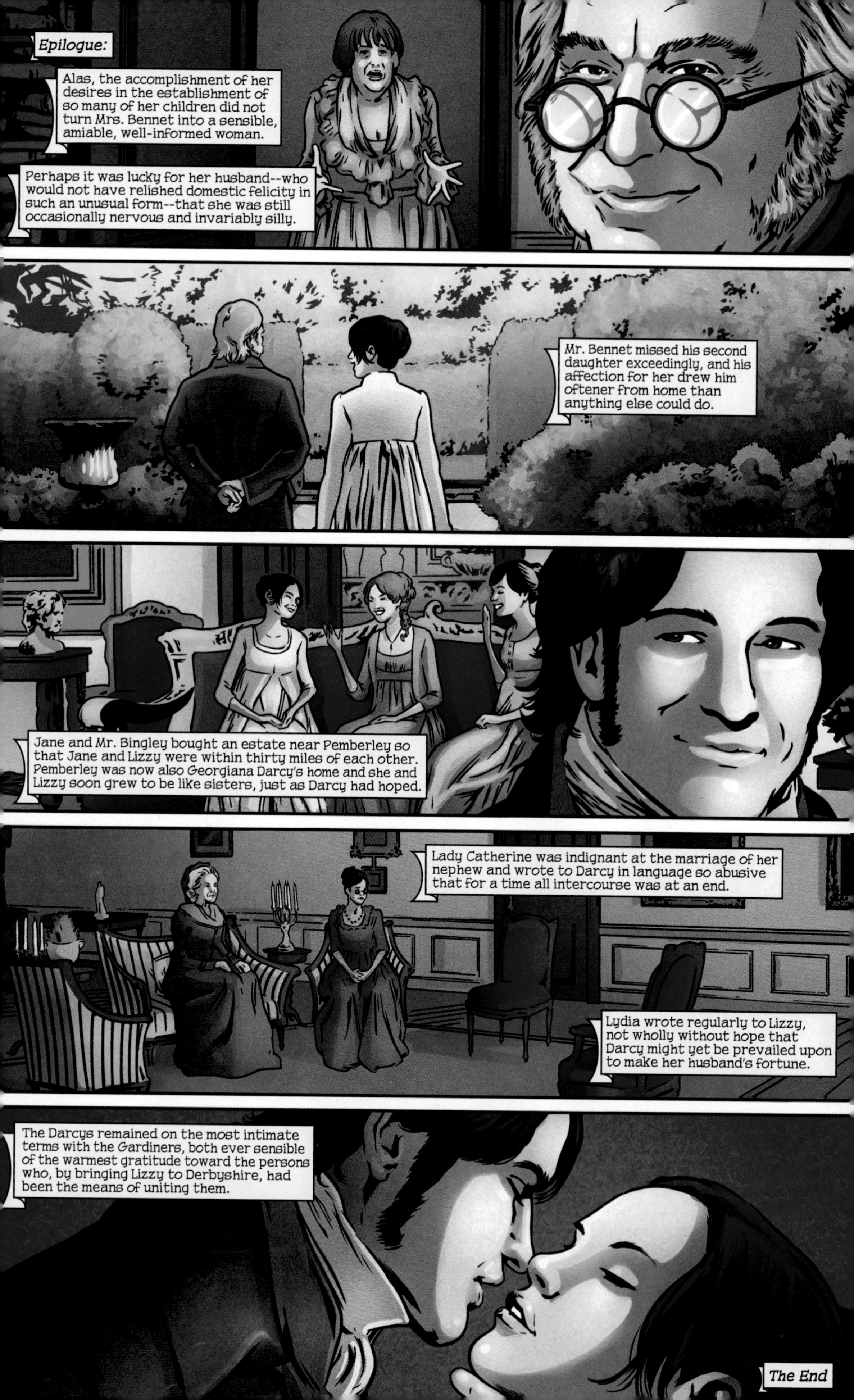
Epilogue:
Alas, the accomplishment of her desires in the establishment of so many of her children did not turn Mrs. Bennet into a sensible, amiable, well-informed woman.
Perhaps it was lucky for her husband--who would not have relished domestic felicity in such an unusual form--that she was still occasionally nervous and invariably silly.
Mr. Bennet missed his second daughter exceedingly, and his affection for her drew him oftener from home than anything else could do.
Jane and Mr. Bingley bought an estate near Pemberley so that Jane and Lizzy were within thirty miles of each other. Pemberley was now also Georgiana Darcy's home and she and Lizzy soon grew to be like sisters, just as Darcy had hoped.
Lady Catherine was indignant at the marriage of her nephew and wrote to Darcy in language so abusive that for a time all intercourse was at an end.
Lydia wrote regularly to Lizzy, not wholly without hope that Darcy might yet be prevailed upon to make her husband's fortune.
The Darcys remained on the most intimate terms with the Gardiners, both ever sensible of the warmest gratitude toward the persons who, by bringing Lizzy to Derbyshire, had been the means of uniting them.
The End

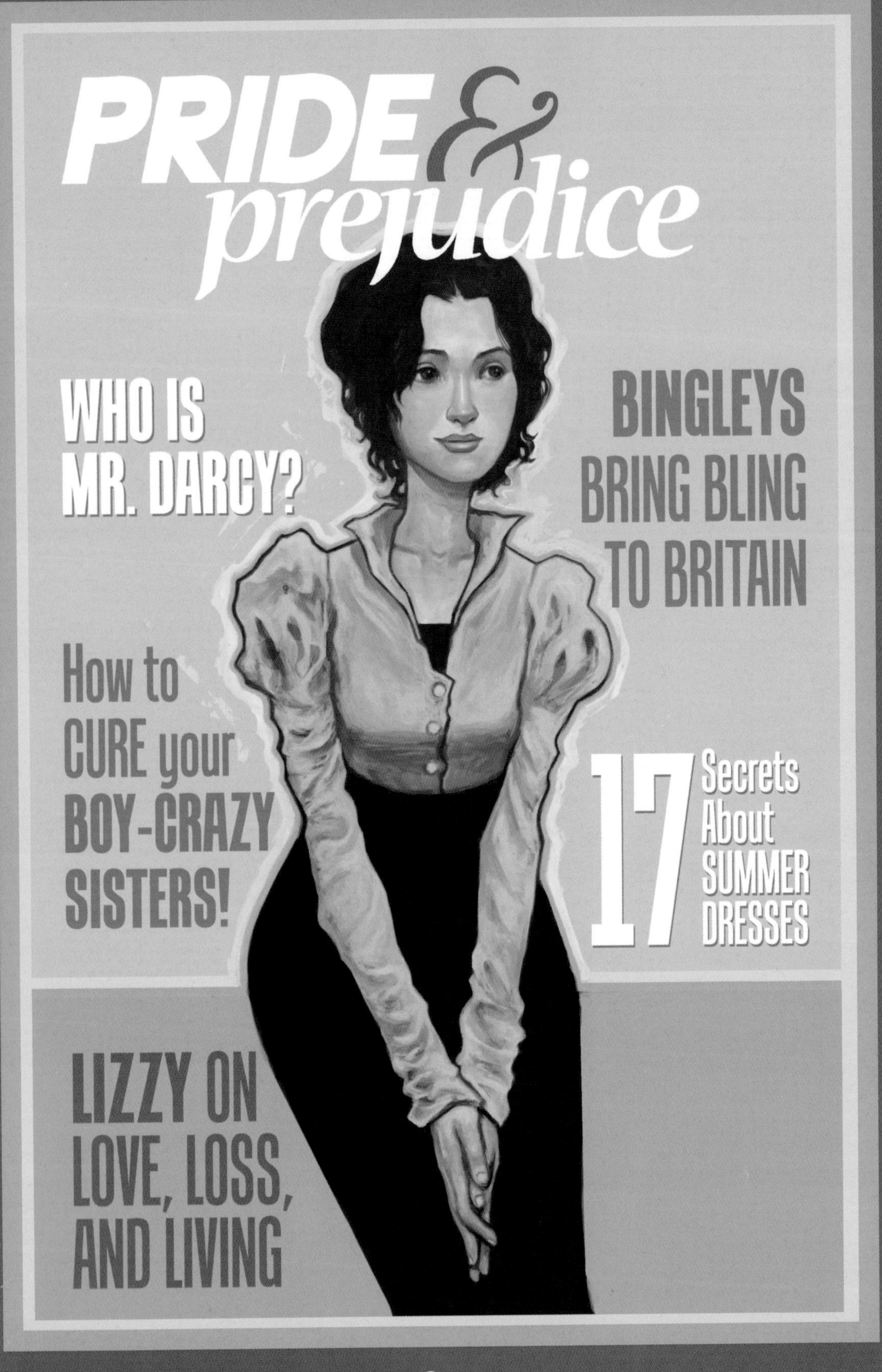
PRIDE & prejudice
WHO IS MR. DARCY?
BINGLEYS BRING BLING TO BRITAIN
How to CURE your BOY-CRAZY SISTERS!
17 Secrets About SUMMER DRESSES
LIZZY ON LOVE, LOSS, AND LIVING

*One*

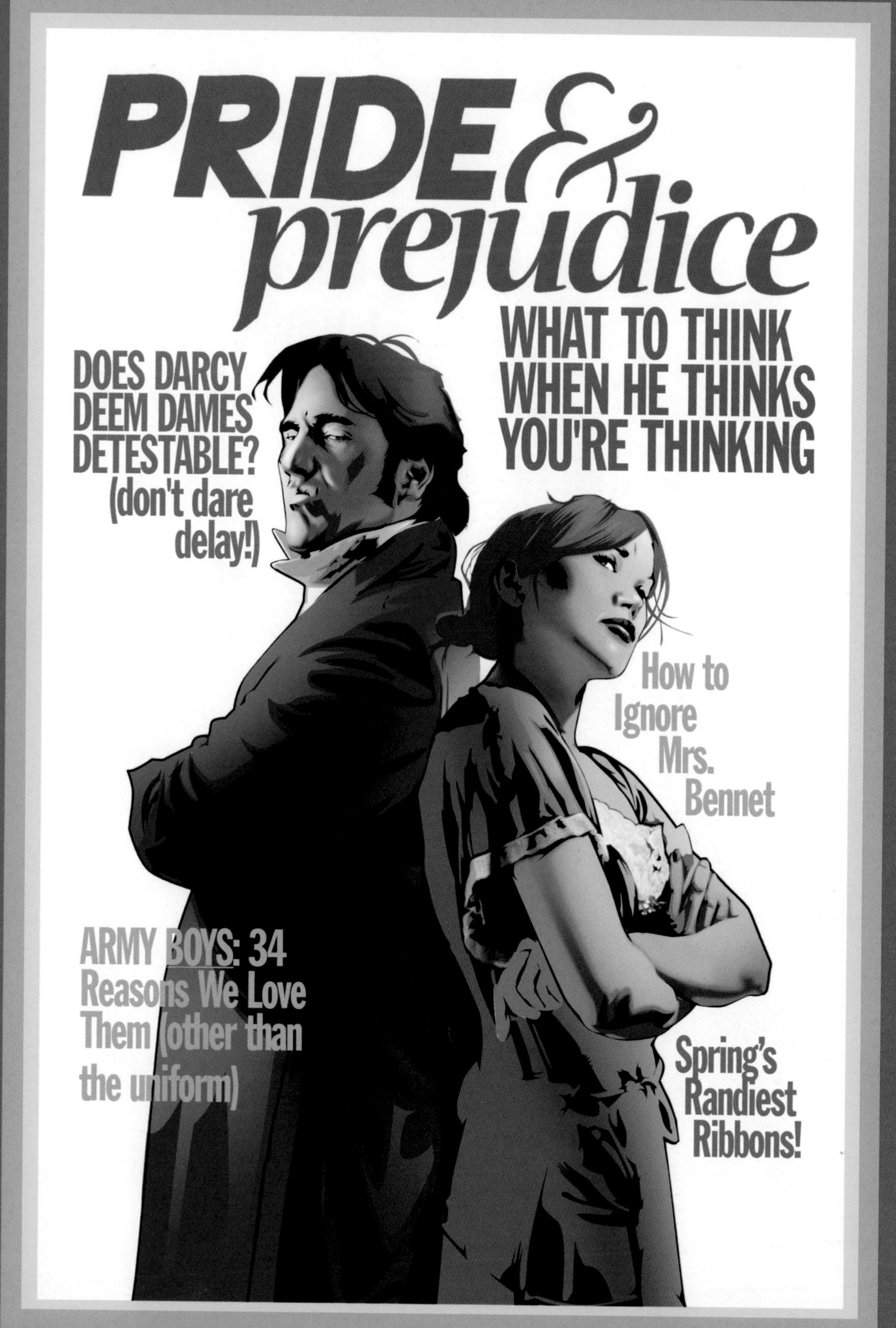
PRIDE & prejudice
DOES DARCY DEEM DAMES DETESTABLE? (don't dare delay!)
WHAT TO THINK WHEN HE THINKS YOU'RE THINKING
How to Ignore Mrs. Bennet
ARMY BOYS: 34 Reasons We Love Them (other than the uniform)
Spring's Randiest Ribbons!

*Two*

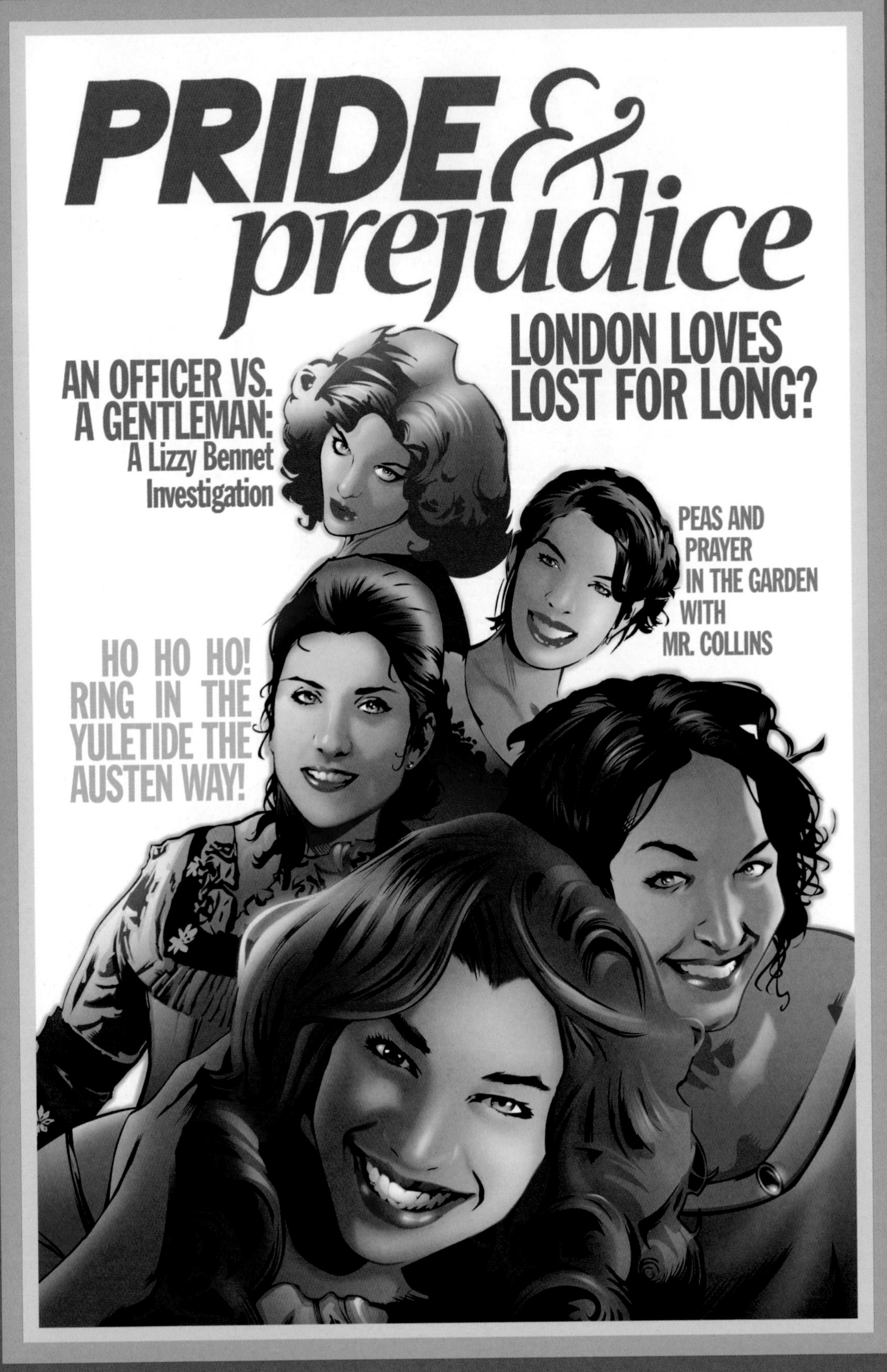

PRIDE & prejudice
AN OFFICER VS. A GENTLEMAN: A Lizzy Bennet Investigation
LONDON LOVES LOST FOR LONG?
PEAS AND PRAYER IN THE GARDEN WITH MR. COLLINS
HO HO HO! RING IN THE YULETIDE THE AUSTEN WAY!


Three

# PRIDE &
# *prejudice*

## Lizzy in full?

*Four*

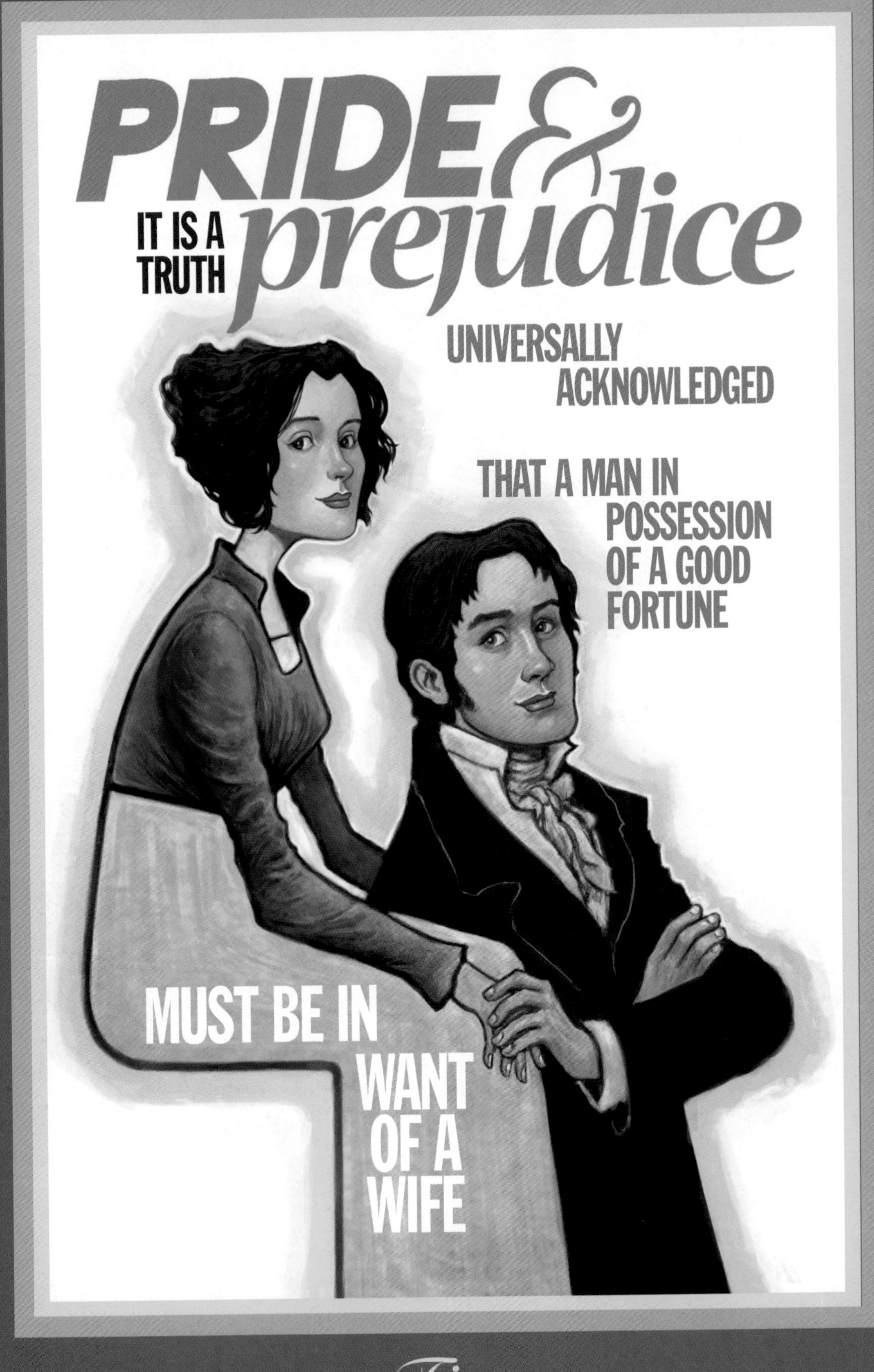
PRIDE & prejudice
IT IS A TRUTH
UNIVERSALLY ACKNOWLEDGED
THAT A MAN IN POSSESSION OF A GOOD FORTUNE
MUST BE IN
WANT OF A WIFE

Five